ADVANCE PRAISE FOR
ATTITUDE RECONSTRUCTION

"Jude Bijou shows us how we can transform feelings of sadness, anger, and fear into joy, love, and peace. Attitude Reconstruction really works."

— John Gray, Ph.D., author of *Men Are from Mars, Women Are from Venus* and many other bestselling books

"Jude Bijou has given the most practical direction to deal with our emotions in her book, *Attitude Reconstruction*. Her teaching beautifully integrates eastern Vedic thoughts and the western approaches in order to heal the emotions in our daily life. Jude Bijou gives direct, applied ways to transform emotions into right understanding and love, in order to bring self-healing."

— Dr. Vasant Lad, B.A.M.S., M.A.Sc., Ayurvedic physician, scholar, founder and director of the Ayurvedic Institute, Albuquerque, New Mexico, and author of *Ayurveda: The Science of Self Healing* and *Textbook of Ayurveda*

"Jude Bijou's wonderful book is a beautifully written guide to transforming your life from the inside out. Her playful spirit makes the journey exciting, thought provoking, and, most of all, highly useful and effective."

— Robert Maurer, Ph.D., faculty, UCLA School of Medicine, and author of *One Small Step C*

"Bijou has put together a c[ ]al tips, and examples for dealing with th[ ]

— Library Journal, Sept. 1

"To all parents who find themselves repeating the same dysfunctional, emotional tirades over and over again: read this book. *Attitude Reconstruction* is a guidebook to getting out of the swamp of toxic emotions. Jude Bijou offers readers a way to interact clearly and effectively, and respond to daily challenges with a calm and happy heart."

> — Dr. Sharon Maxwell, clinical psychologist, and author of
> *What Your Kids Need to Hear from You about Sex*

"*Attitude Reconstruction* is a practical book filled with powerful methods that can help you through any problem or emotional upset. Jude is a rare psychotherapist who is both highly caring and clear in presenting what really works and why. I have found her guidance helpful in my therapy practice as well as with handling issues in my own life."

> — Jonathan Robinson, M.F.T., author of several bestsellers,
> including *Communication Miracles for Couples* and *The Complete Idiot's Guide to Awakening Your Spirituality*

"This work should be required reading for everyone, whether professional or personal. If we all knew how to manage ourselves using *Attitude Reconstruction*, we would live in a peaceful world free from judgment.

Both medicine and psychology would be greatly enhanced by taking another look at what people really want, which is not to be labeled, but guided toward self-help and insight, resulting in a life with more meaning and wholeness. Therein is the contribution which Jude Bijou has made with the stroke of her pen and twenty years of inquiry."

> — Linda W. Peterson, Ph.D., professor emerita, University
> of Nevada Medical School, marriage and family therapist,
> diplomat in forensic counseling

"Applying Jude Bijou's proven techniques, we can all reconstruct our attitudes so that we consistently behave as the people we most desire to be — joyful, peaceful, and full of love. This is *the* guidebook for ensuring a happy life."

> — Jan C. Hill, international leadership and teamwork consultant to Fortune 500 companies, certified coach, and coauthor
> with Vanessa Weaver of *Smart Women, Smart Moves*

ATTITUDE
RECONSTRUCTION

A Blueprint for Building a Better Life

Jude Bijou, M.A., M.F.T.

Attitude Reconstruction: A Blueprint for Building a Better Life
Riviera Press
133 East De la Guerra #25
Santa Barbara, CA 93101

The information contained in this book is not intended as a substitute for consultation with a licensed health care professional.

Bijou, Jude.
Attitude reconstruction : a blueprint for building a
better life / Jude Bijou.
p. cm.
Includes bibliographical references and index.
Library of Congress Control Number: 2011906536
ISBN-13: 978-0-9835287-7-7
ISBN-10: 0983528772
1. Change (Psychology) 2. Attitude (Psychology)
I. Title.

BF637.C4B55 2011   158.1
    QBI10-600044

10 9 8 7 6 5 4 3 2 1

Cover design by the Book Designers
Author photo by Stephanie Baker

Printed in the United States of America

I gave it my best shot and now I offer this book to you
with appreciation and admiration.

CONTENTS

INTRODUCTION

You picked this guide up for a reason. Maybe you're tired of feeling empty and unhappy, or you're addicted to screaming at the kids. Perhaps you're single and alone again or clueless what to do now that you just got laid off. Life's accelerator has hit the floor, and you're doing all you can just to keep hold of the wheel and not veer out of control. Having a map to navigate around the emotional roadblocks and avoid some of the dangerous potholes that keep puncturing your tires would be great about now.

Attitude Reconstruction is somewhat of a GPS for your internal navigational system, and will be an inside guide you can refer to the rest of your life. You could say that my desire to write this may have been coded in my DNA, inherited from my father, pioneer child behavioral psychologist, Sidney W. Bijou. I had a strong foundation to cull from, but something was missing. An insatiable curiosity drew me east, to the expansive silence of meditation, the contemplative studies of ancient texts, and ways of existence quite unfamiliar to my western conditioning. My understanding took quantum leaps. Just as the soil needs the honeybee to draw its flower into blossom, so the west needs the east to find its fullness. I merged these two worlds in my heart, in teaching communication, and in my practice for the last three decades as a marriage and family counselor. And the fruits of my journey culminate on these pages.

If the title, Attitude Reconstruction suggests you're going to have to shift your perspective, you're reading it correctly. Everything you need is within you. The original design of **YOU** is perfect. The margins just got a little blurry along the way. I'm offering what's been missing — your blueprint, the very foundation of your inner wiring, so that you can remodel your life with joy, love and peace.

If that sounds a bit like pie-in-the-sky, new age hype, my clients and students would disagree. Using these same tools I'm about to offer you, they've created the emotional dream lives they deserve, full of satisfying relationships, authentic expression, and inner serenity.

Moving from Sadness, Anger, and Fear to Joy, Love, and Peace

The technical way to look at Attitude Reconstruction is that it's a holistic theory of human behavior. It's an approach that suggests only one thing unlocks the door to happiness — our emotions. Our poor attitudes and rocky relationships are caused by *unexpressed* anger and fear. But this is a lot more than just a theory. I've put together an accessible, step-by-step handbook to get you in touch with what you're *really* feeling so you can take appropriate action and get the results you want: more joy, love, and peace. Think of it as a map when you're about to take a detour you know ends up in an emotional ditch.

In these pages, you will learn:

- How to express and release sadness, anger, and fear physically and constructively so you can create the life you want

- How to replace habitual negative thinking with thoughts that befriend your mind

- How to access and follow your natural intuition (yes, we all have it!) in ways that honor yourself and respect others

- How to use the Four Rules of Communication to talk effectively and resolve differences smoothly

- How to take constructive action to handle seemingly "stuck" situations, achieve any goal, and banish unhealthy attitudes and addictions

About This Inside Guide

Personally, I'm a browser and don't tend to read books in order. For that reason I've organized Attitude Reconstruction to be an inside guide you can read cover to cover or begin wherever it resonates with you most. Check out the tabs or go straight to the Quick Charts.

Here is what you'll find in these pages:

❀ Step-by-step approach to move from the emotions of sadness, anger, and fear to joy, love, and peace in less than five minutes

❀ Overview of the entire Attitude Reconstruction model and blueprint of the mind for easy reference

❀ Breakdown of the ultimate attitudes joy, love, and peace inspire – honor yourself, accept other people and situations, and stay present and specific

❀ Five tools you were born with that create lasting change

❀ Communications strategy to talk to anyone, about any topic in an effective and kind way

❀ Quick charts to transform 33 destructive attitudes instantly: overcome everything from feeling unworthy or passive, to judgmental or selfish, to anxious or overwhelmed

This book is about you. As every commercial airline flight reminds us, we need to affix our own oxygen masks before offering assistance to others. Likewise, giving the gift of living in joy, love, and peace to ourselves allows us to truly contribute to our families, friends, and planet.

Finishing Touches

Attitude Reconstruction will get your emotional body into tip-top shape. You'll be able to handle whatever is thrown your way, while maintaining flexibility and balance.

And don't be surprised by the "divine shifts," or "aha!" moments that spontaneously occur through this process. It's in these moments when you're connected to your truest self, you know irrefutably that something is true, and that what you're doing is right. Transformation happens on a fundamental level, as if your neural pathways clear and the vital energy flows freely. You may stop calling yourself names, cease feeling intimidated, ease into relaxing, or start realizing your dreams. Each time you choose constructive action, the effects are cumulative. You'll find yourself "in the flow". Whether you call it nature, God's plan, the tao, or something else, you will know you are safe, whole, and connected.

Get ready to engage with the world in ways that naturally promote your own happiness, create goodwill with others, and actualize your true potential.

May this book be a trustworthy companion and an unfailing guide.

PART I
An Overview

1

Emotions are the Key

Think of your child throwing himself on the floor, wailing in unabashed fury, pounding his hands and feet in revolt because you said 'no' to the candy before dinner. While his generous range of high-pitched demands may embarrass the heck out of you, your child is a model of good behavior.

I'm not saying it's fun when customers confuse your child with a Smurf as his face turns blue from screaming. What I'm getting at is this: emotions color virtually everything we feel, think, say, and do. And expressing them and releasing them physically is as natural and as important as brushing our teeth.

Big statement? Let me take you back to when we were babies. Innocent and pure, we delighted in the world around us and marveled at being alive. We dealt with upsets by spontaneously expressing them, in the moment — crying, sobbing, screaming, shivering, wailing, jumping up and down, moaning, pounding — and then swiftly returning to our trusting, playful selves.

So if our fundamental nature is to show what we're feeling, what happened? As we grew, our parents, schools, peers, and religions all got their two cents in for teaching us the 'appropriate' way to be. Express your emotions and you no longer 'fit in.' Read: keep your emotions under wraps.

Our families and societies had their own time and place constraints, and as adults around us struggled with unexpressed emotions themselves, discouraged from showing what was truly going on inside. We saw no other option than to model ourselves on those around us. Instead of expressing our emotions, we developed defenses and counterproductive ways of compensating.

Crying suddenly became taboo. Your childhood tears may have been met with, "Don't be a cry-baby," "Tears equal weakness," "Don't wear your heart on your sleeve," "Stop crying or I'll give you something to cry about." Expressing healthy anger was also forbidden. Maybe your childhood anger prompted reprimands such as, "Put a lid on it," "Girls aren't pretty when they're angry," "We don't yell in this family," "You're upsetting me," or "You're acting crazy again." Or maybe expressing fear was summarily squashed with messages, "Don't be a scaredy-cat," "You chicken," "There's nothing to be afraid of," or "Snap out of it!"

And it's not just the 'negative' or 'unpleasant' emotions we stifle. We've learned to downplay the emotions , too. As children, our unbridled laughter was often disruptive to the busy routines of adults. When we squealed in sheer delight, our parents' usually firmly told us to tone it down. And when we were peaceful and content to lie on the grass, making elephants and angels out of the clouds, many of us heard, "Don't just sit there" or "Can't you find something better to do?" Bust our bubble? Good moments immediately turned flat — and the cycle continues.

Recently, I saw a youngster's utter joy at being served a huge plate of pancakes extinguished by swift reprimands to "behave" from both parents. Overt messages like these, plus observations of people around us, have cemented the notion we have to camouflage rather than express what's true inside of us.

Because you're a living, breathing human being, you're guaranteed to experience countless emotionally charged events on a daily basis. However, it doesn't even occur to us that we *could* express the emotions we're feeling. I'm not saying we resist laughing at something funny, hugging our children, or experiencing a moment of peace while hiking in nature. But we still put on our running shoes when we need to cry, express anger, or show fear. Expressing our emotions has become a bit foreign, and with understandable reason.

Suppressing emotions is tricky business. I agree with ancient religious traditions and philosophies worldwide that joy, love, and peace are fundamental aspects of our spiritual nature. But sadness, anger, and fear are also part of the human condition, and in the process of denying these three emotions, trying to get around them, and attempting to suppress them, we become our own worst enemies.

What We Do Instead of Expressing Our Emotions

There's a thick wad of gunk inside of each of us, jamming up our ability to process experiences. That 'stuck' emotional energy clogs up our vital life force, making us feel numb or as if we're on autopilot. Old, destructive thought patterns are 'driving the bus,' so to speak. Most of us are experiencing major burnout as overload causes us to fly off the handle, rapid firing words as ammunition. Our actions destroy, and our environments become deadly wastelands from unspoken truths.

We get really creative in masking or diverting our emotions. I'm sure you can think of a few winners, but here's a fairly common case scenario: In the middle of his 70-hour work week, a man comes home after choking down his anger all day, mumbles something about the "idiots" he's forced to take orders from and after a drink or two, lashes out at his wife and kids. Ignoring his high blood pressure and diabetes, he shovels down dinner along with two helpings of cream pie before mindlessly numbing out in front of TV to fall asleep. Tomorrow he'll get up and do it all again.

These scenarios stockpile and create a society sitting on a volcano of pent-up emotions. You see the fall-out spewed over the airwaves: suicide, domestic violence, gang warfare, road rage, juvenile delinquency, addictions, and on and on. But casualties on our personal battlefields are even more devastating: destructive, love-less and sometimes violent relationships. We can't enjoy the good times because we're worrying about what's next. We berate ourselves mercilessly for making mistakes. Stress-related illnesses eat at our bodies and create dependency on pharmaceuticals. And our lives become inauthentic, driven by negative programs that keep our hearts in pain and our experiences vacant of joy.

So now it's time for the good news. As I've said, everything you need is inside of you. You don't need a new heart or mind, thousands of dollars in therapy or to adopt a different family. You are perfect! You just need to shift your attitudes about expressing emotions. Along with bathing and eating your veggies, releasing emotions needs to become part of our daily routines. Just like physical hygiene, "emotional hygiene" is crucial to our health and must become an integral part of our lives.

Having said that, there are precious few situations in our society where it is okay to cry, stomp, or physically show that we are afraid by shivering. But you're about to learn how to do for yourself what no one else can do; unleash your emotions in constructive, physical ways and open the door for limitless joy, love, and peace.

There's one important premise I need you to get a hold of before we move on. All emotions you experience, even if it feels like there are millions of them, break down to just six core emotions. A little hard conceptualize maybe, but I promise it's true. Think for a minute about the brilliant colors in the rainbow; light to dark, all can be made from the primary colors of red, yellow, and blue. Human emotions are just like that. The combinations can be creative but fundamentally the base is the same: sadness, anger, fear and their counters of joy, love and peace.

Each Emotion Feels and Looks Different

One minute you can't look at your emails without missing your ex and the next, you can't stop flirting with the guy at the drive-through espresso bar. Although the issues might be different, every person on the planet experiences the up's and down's of emotions. They come and go, continually shifting like the weather. Sometimes they're fickle; sometimes they're severe.

Across all cultures, human beings share the same emotions. They've been the same throughout the history of *Homo sapiens*. Cave people experienced fear, anger, and sadness as well as joy, love, and peace. The old, the young, and everyone in between experience them all.

Emotions are spontaneous physical reactions to what we experience throughout the day. They are pure sensations in our bodies that have no words. Just look at the word "emotion," and you can see "e-motion," or "energy in motion." These sensations exist in pairs and follow the natural laws of opposites, like yin and yang, east and west, ebony and ivory. Sadness finds it opposite in joy; anger is opposed by love; fear's opposite is peace. Each one of these e-motions sends a unique sensation rippling through our bodies, and they manifest in different physical expressions as well.

Your body is your most reliable clue to finding out what emotion you're feeling. When we're feeling sadness, we feel cold and slow, and it's hard to speak without crying. With joy, we feel exuberant and bouncy. Anger feels hot, tight, ready to strike out and explode. With love, we feel open and warm. Fear will find us cold, shivering all over, and feeling constricted inside. Peace is tranquil and relaxed, yet alert.

The way energy moves in our bodies is different for each emotion, too. Sadness weighs us down while joy's energy moves upward, causing us to feel elated. Anger pushes the energy outward, as we lash out and push people away. With love, the energy pulls inward, and we draw others near. Fear energy is experienced as erratic, and we feel jumpy and wired, or frozen and immobilized. Peace inhabits our bodies as feeling calm, still, and collected. See the chart showing each emotion's bodily sensations on **page 293**

Each emotion is also reflected differently in our faces, posture, movements, tone, and demeanor. Even without hearing words, it's easy to tell the difference between someone bouncing around newly accepted to the university of his choice, and someone running late who can't find important papers for her meeting. The physical expressions of each emotion are distinctive and easy to recognize. Check out the chart on **page 293**

Emotions and Feelings

Although people tend to use the words, 'feelings' and 'emotions' interchangeably, there's a big difference between the two. We use on all kinds of words to describe the same emotions depending on our history and circumstances. Emptiness, helplessness, arrogance, confusion, bliss, contentment, delight; they're all just different labels we attach to the same wordless physical sensation. It doesn't matter whether the source of your fear is a potential diagnosis, meeting your future in-laws for the first time, or giving a presentation in class. And it doesn't matter whether you call what you're feeling anxiety, stress, agitation, or panic — you're talking about fear.

Emotions are physical. Feelings are mental. Feelings are created when we add an interpretation to the emotional physiology we are feeling in our bodies. Here's an example: say you've been under the weather but dread going to the doctor. Your stomach is in knots, and your hands are freezing. You start projecting into the future. "What if I have cancer? I won't be able to work. What will happen to the children?" You might call what you're feeling anxiety, nervousness, or stress, but what you're experiencing on a physical level is the emotion of fear. It's just pure energy.

It's easier to deal with what we're feeling if we identify the underlying emotions. Is it sadness, anger, or fear? Is it joy, love, or peace? Check out the list — Feeling Associated with Each Emotion on **page 293**

Emotions Are Triggered by Specific Events

Everyone experiences all six emotions as normal reactions to specific events. As we go through life, big and little things happen that naturally evoke different emotions. Whether it's a scene in a movie, gossip about a friend, or an upheaval at work, our emotions are continually triggered by events in our lives.

Emotional Triggers

Emotions	Specific Events
Sadness	losses and hurts
Joy	achievements, good news, creative express, beauty
Anger	injustices and violations
Love	kindness, caring, generosity, understanding
Fear	threats to our survival
Peace	safety, comfort, security, serenity

We often experience more than one emotion at a time, and sometimes one emotion masks another. They're like family. They hang out together. Anger is often a cover for sadness and fear. Joy often coexists with feelings of love and peace. You often can't separate them.

Imagine that someone you admire calls you "careless." You feel violated and angry. But it also hurts to be called names, so buried underneath your anger is probably sadness. If the person expresses hostility while blasting you, you probably feel threatened and therefore experience fear as well.

Your Emotional Constitution

Some babies are born mellow, some fussy, and some highly reactive. We each come into this world with an emotional predisposition, that colors how we interpret our experience. Sadness is dominant in some of us. Others of us have a tendency to lead with anger, and others are ruled by fear. Each of us has what I call an "emotional constitution."

You carry that emotional constitution, or leaning towards one emotion over the others, throughout your lifetime, and it affects the way you interpret the world. Visualize this for a moment: your emotional constitution is comprised of three buckets. One bucket holds sadness, another anger, and a third fear. Some people's fear bucket is overflowing, while their other buckets are nearly empty; for others, two may be overflowing; for still others, all three buckets are relatively full. When you look at yourself and others from this perspective, it's easier to understand why people behave the way they do. We're all carrying around heavy bucketfuls of emotions that weigh us down and make life downright difficult!

Another way to get this concept is to look into the eyes of a mother and father. You can usually make a rough guess about what color their child's eyes will be. In the same way, your parents' emotional constitutions have an impact on which emotions are strongest for you. If both of your parents tend to have more sadness than anger or fear, there's a good chance you'll experience a lot of sadness, too. If one parent has an anger constitution and the other a fearful one, you'll get either parent's constitution or a combination of the two.

Though everyone is capable of feeling all six emotions at any moment, some emotions will naturally dominate. Take my mom. Her usual reaction to any event was fear; she constantly worried about my dad, my brother, me, and almost anything, bless her heart. Whenever my father was late getting home from work, she immediately envisioned something horrible had happened to him. She's what I call a "fear gal."

Or how about the shy college student who is turned down by a dozen sororities? It's a hurt or loss, so she feels sadness. If she doesn't allow herself to acknowledge her pain and cry constructively, she will feel rejected and begins to view herself poorly. That unexpressed sadness manifests in feeling unworthy, and shows up in every thought, word, and action. If she doesn't handle her sadness in a healthy way, that low self-esteem can become a chronic condition that colors her every move.

The idea of an emotional constitution has its parallel in Ayurvedic medicine, the ancient system of self-health and healing from India. Ayurveda proposes that all aspects of nature can be viewed in terms of three elements — Kapha, Pitta, and Vata — which correlate with the emotions of sadness, anger, and fear.

Curious about your own emotional constitution? This quiz will give you some insight. If you are going through a particularly stressful time, your results might be slightly skewed, but in general, they'll reflect your basic emotional constitution. Be as honest with yourself as possible.

The Quick Quiz: What's My Emotional Constitution?

Using the scale below, rate yourself from 1 to 5 on each item.

> 1 = almost never
> 2 = occasionally
> 3 = about half the time
> 4 = often
> 5 = almost always

	Score	Set Total
Set A		
1. I feel unworthy.	____	
2. I depend on others for approval.	____	
3. I make negative self-judgments.	____	
4. I am passive.	____	____
Set B		
1. I focus on the outside world.	____	
2. I don't accept people and situations as they are.	____	
3. I make negative judgments of what is.	____	
4. I am selfish.	____	____
Set C		
1. I focus on the future or past.	____	
2. I overgeneralize.	____	
3. I lose sight of what is true or real.	____	
4. I attempt to control.	____	____

Using the same scale, rate how often you feel:

Sadness____   Anger____   Fear____

Joy____   Love____   Peace____

Interpreting Your Results

Add up your numbers for each set of questions. The actual numerical total for each set isn't as important as comparing the three totals to one another. If your highest total is for the first four questions (Set A), your predominant emotion is sadness. If your highest score is in second four questions (Set B), your strongest emotion is anger. If your highest total is for the last four questions (Set C), your ruling emotion is fear.

If your scores are equally high for two sets of questions, you have two dominant emotions. My dear friend Jennifer is a perfect example of a person with a fear-sadness constitution. I've rarely ever seen her angry, she's too busy getting things done, brooding, and putting an inordinate amount of pressure on herself. Some folks have a constitution equally proportioned among the three emotions. They have a sadness-anger-fear constitution and at any moment may lead with any of them.

How did you rate yourself on sadness, anger, and fear at the bottom of the page 9 Do these scores correlate with the three totals above? And how about your scores for joy, love, and peace? If your rating for joy is high, your score for its opposite, sadness, will probably be low. Likewise, if your rating for love is high, your score for its opposite, anger, will probably be low. And if your rating for peace is high, your score for its opposite, fear, is usually low.

Your answers reflect the emotions you feel when dealing with life's twists and turns. When you hear that your partner got in another fender bender, do you feel blue (sadness)? Do you tend to lash out at him about what a reckless driver he is (anger)? Or do you freak out and fret that she'll lose her license (fear)?

Emotions Drive the Mind

Each emotion steers the mind in a certain predictable direction. Your emotions literally determine where you focus your attention and where it stays — on yourself, other people and situations, or time. Your primary focus will be dictated by the emotion you tend to snuggle up with most. That focus will be either destructive or constructive depending on whether you're experiencing sadness, anger, fear, or joy, love, peace.

The first pair of emotions — sadness and joy — turns our attention inward onto ourselves. When we experience sadness but don't express it physically, our minds automatically start to entertain negative thoughts about ourselves. We might regard ourselves as stupid, inadequate, and unlovable. The opposite is true when we experience joy. We naturally feel good about ourselves, happy in our skin and in our lives. We know in every cell of our bodies that we're living this life to its full potential. Remember the ecstasy you felt when finishing your first marathon (or another goal you prepared for)? What did you know about yourself then? You probably felt fabulous about your abilities and knew you could handle whatever would arise.

Anger and love's focus goes in the opposite direction — outward. Our attention is on other people and situations. We direct our unprocessed anger externally, with separating finger-pointing and negative judgments about "them" or "it." Conversely, love's focus is outward as well but we draw others in, with respect and appreciation, while remaining expansive, receptive, and open. We're attuned to what is helpful, compassionate, and kind — and naturally do those things when feeling love, whether volunteering to serve dinner to the homeless on Thanksgiving" or becoming a big sister to a struggling teen.

Fear and peace turn our focus to time. Unexpressed fear propels us out of the present moment and into a dreaded future or dwelled-upon past. If not dealt with, fear distorts our perspective on reality so that we exaggerate dangers and minimize the potential for safety. We overgeneralize, using such words as "always," "never," "everybody," and "no one." Peace brings a welcome opposite because our attention fully resides in the present moment. We think in specifics. When we're not thinking, our minds remain alert yet still. We feel safe, knowing we'll be okay no matter what. Tap into that feeling right now. Visualize an entire day at the spa: soft, wet steam moisturizing every pour of your body; well-oiled hands gently massaging away any traces of strain; bubbling Jacuzzi with soft lavender floating in the air; luscious greens and delicate berries to nourish and sustain you. Time disappears. All your needs are met, and the world wraps you in a blanket of peace.

Core Attitudes

So, let's re-cap. Remember I told you that everything we experience boils down to six emotions — sadness, anger, fear and joy, love, peace? And that each emotion has a focus that directs our perceptions in predictable ways. In addition, each focus has some core attitudes that control our every move. Core attitudes, whether constructive or destructive, are the default settings that define our personalities, actions, and reactions. The original wiring in everyone's house is basically the same, but each of our floor plans is slightly different.

The concept that everyone's wiring is the same was like a lightening bolt. As countless clients and students shared their deepest heartaches, unresolved traumas, and what wasn't working, I realized their entire range of behaviors fell into just a few categories. No matter how outrageous or seemingly benign, the ways their destructive patterns played out could be traced back to 12 core attitudes or mental tendencies.

Unexpressed sadness, for example, always sets its focus on you and what's going on with you, what's wrong with you, what you should do, etc. If your bucket's spilling over with sadness, everything you'll be hyper aware of has to do with you.

Then comes anger, putting its steely focus on other people and situations. No matter the scenario, if your bucket's dragging on the ground with anger, it's always about he/she/it, that's doing it. They are the problem and you're the victim.

And ah, the fear factor. Time is not on your side when fear is spilling over the edges of this too-full bucket. Fear's core attitudes say there's never enough time in the day, in the moment, in your life. You live in the future or the past, but rarely in the present.

It's a good thing that everything in the material world exists in opposites. All our constructive behavior stems back to 12 core attitudes as well. There are four about ourselves associated with giddy joy; four about other people and situations associated with sweet, sweet love; and four about time associated with boundless peace. The Twelve Pairs of Core Attitudes chart can be found on **page 294**

Sadness

Let's take an in-depth look at sadness, first. The core attitudes or defaults associated with sadness boil down to the four ways we don't honor ourselves. Remember when I said it was about you, you, and more you? Core attitude number one is to believe deep down that you're unworthy, incompetent, and empty. You feel bad about yourself regardless of what you look like, have or achieve. This core belief is a big thief, robbing you of feeling whole and complete, no matter what. You confuse your pure, inner self — what remains constant — with accomplishments, qualities, and characteristics.

Emotion	Focus	DESTRUCTIVE CORE ATTITUDES		
Expression	**Attitude**	**FEELINGS**	**WORDS**	**ACTIONS**
S **A** **D** **N** **E** **S** **S** crying sobbing wailing frowning	**YOURSELF** **Don't** **honor** **yourself**	**UNWORTHY**		
		Empty Inadequate Unlovable	• I'm no good. • I'm not enough. • There's something wrong with me.	• Think and talk poorly about yourself • Create false impressions • Feel disconnected from who you are
		DEPEND ON OTHERS FOR APPROVAL		
		Lonely Insecure Needy	• Show me you love me. • I'll do anything to keep you happy. • Tell me I'm okay.	• Please others at own expense • Cling to other people • Seek validation and compliments
		JUDGE SELF NEGATIVELY		
		Self-loathing Stupid Ashamed	• I should have known or done better. • I'm stupid. I'm pathetic. • I hate myself when I make mistakes.	• Set unrealistic expectations for yourself • Put yourself down and beat self up • Demand perfection from yourself
		PASSIVE		
		Helpless Incapable Unassertive	• Poor me. • I can't do anything about this. • I don't know how. It's bigger than me.	• Play the submissive victim • Fail to follow through • Avoid confrontation

That super shaky sense of true self-worth causes an endless search for validation and satisfaction, from anyone or anything that tells you you're okay. This is the second mental tendency — you depend on others for approval. You'll sacrifice your wants, needs, and beliefs just to keep other people happy, usually because you don't want them to react negatively. They have to approve of you, they have to! You can't handle rejection or abandonment, and you'll do almost anything to keep it from happening.

Sadness' third core attitude is to judge yourself negatively and feel bad about what you've done, said, or thought. You're mercilessly hard on yourself, especially when you make a mistake. "I'm a loser." "I'm dumb." Those negative assessments are laced with unrealistic expectations and "shoulds," such as, "I shouldn't have done that" or "What made me say that?"

Lastly, when you fail to express sadness constructively, the person you're staring at in the mirror becomes a passive nobody, and so that's what you become. You feel insignificant and find it hard to speak up and take action. For example, say you've been looking for a new apartment for several months. Several places you thought were perfect were given to other people. You feel more and more like a helpless victim, at the mercy of the big, cruel world. Before you know it, you've quit exercising, started binging on comfort food, and stopped following up on housing leads.

Anger

When anger is your thing but you're not in touch with it, you spray it all over other people, things, and situations in four predictable, negative ways. Your mind is always thinking something or someone "out there" is the cause (of your pain, of your stress, of your 'whatever'). You drown everyone in the blame game and no one wins. When your car breaks down, it's the mechanic's fault. When you have a falling out with your cousin, it's because she's jealous you have a boyfriend.

The second default anger attitude locks onto is refusing to accept people and situations as they are. You hang on to the notion that he, she, it, or they "should" be different. You do a good impression of a Tasmanian devil, raging when your unrealistic expectations aren't met. You think, "They shouldn't have said what they did" or, "It shouldn't be this way."

Unprocessed anger spawns a third mental prison: you negatively judge and label what you don't accept because it doesn't conform to your point of view. "It's not okay," you righteously rage, "It's not fair." You label what you don't like as "bad," "silly," or "wrong".

Emotion	Focus	DESTRUCTIVE CORE ATTITUDES		
Expression	Attitude	FEELINGS	WORDS	ACTIONS
A **N** **G** **E** **R**	PEOPLE AND SITUATIONS	OUTWARD FOCUS		
		Jealous Blaming Alienated	• You make me so mad. • You are the problem. • What do they have? say? think?	• Blame / ridicule / justify • Make "you" statements • Compare yourself to others
		DON'T ACCEPT PEOPLE AND SITUATIONS		
		Intolerant Disappointed Frustrated	• You should be different. • It's not supposed to be like this. • I don't believe it.	• Have unrealistic expectations • Give unsolicited advice / opinions • Reject others and withhold yourself
	Refuse to accept people and situations	MAKE NEGATIVE JUDGMENTS OF WHAT IS		
		Resentful Critical Disgusted	• You are a loser. • Right-Wrong / Fair-Unfair / Good-Bad • It's not enough.	• Expect the worst • Label people and things negatively • Be sarcastic / critical / cynical
hot aggressive hitting stomping shouting pounding		SELFISH		
		Stubborn Rebellious Arrogant	• Me. Me. Me. • My way or I won't play. • I'm special.	• Act as if you are more important • Be vain / pushy / insensitive • Don't listen / opinionated

Anger's final death grip is believing you are entitled to get whatever you want and that you know better than anyone else. (Here is where the ego resides.) You're your own center of the universe, and by the way, why isn't everyone bowing at your feet? You selfishly look out for your own interests at the expense of others. And they had better listen to you — you know what's best for them and their lives!

Just like emotions don't exist in isolation, often you're under the influence of several core attitudes simultaneously. Let's say you've just finished a frustrating telephone conversation with your mother-in-law. You walk into the room where your teenage daughter is sitting. Without even looking at her, you launch into a bitching session of how pathetic her grandmother is (the first core attitude associated with anger: directing your energy outward on to other people and situations).

Your daughter is worried about her test tomorrow, doesn't agree, and responds by whining about her homework. You tell her to shut up (the second core attitude associated with anger: don't accept people and situations), and then call her a "crybaby" (the third mental tendency: make negative judgments). When she pushes back, you say if she'd just listen to you and taken lower level classes, she might actually get above a C and stop costing you so much in tutoring (the fourth core attitude: selfishness). Didn't take long to blow through every one of anger's ugly core attitudes, did it? One conversation in a matter of seconds got it handled.

Fear

Fear is a bit of a time traveler. Maybe you're the leap first, ask questions later type of gal. Or people might say you're the motor-mouth filling up air space so no one else can. Regardless of which fits, being a space case, living in regret or sleeping with your Blackberry, means you're in the la-la land delusion of maxed out fear.

Emotion	Focus	DESTRUCTIVE CORE ATTITUDES		
Expression	Attitude	FEELINGS	WORDS	ACTIONS
F **E** **A** **R**	TIME	LIVE IN THE FUTURE OR PAST		
		Worried Anxious Distracted	• What if… • I don't want to feel this feeling. • I've got to get out of here.	• Avoid expressing emotions • Be speedy / impulsive / busy • Escape reality through addictions
		OVERGENERALIZE		
		Dramatic Overwhelmed Scattered	• It's always like that. • This is too much. • Nothing ever works out.	• Go on tangents • Exaggerate or minimize issues • Jump to conclusions
	Live in past or future, and over-generalize	LOSE SIGHT OF WHAT IS TRUE OR REAL		
cold shivering quivering laughing nervously breathing irregularly		Indecisive Confused Conflicted	• Maybe this, maybe that. • I don't care. It doesn't matter. • I'll handle it tomorrow.	• Doubt excessively • Procrastinate / fail to take action • Act without regard for consequences
		ATTEMPT TO CONTROL		
		Impatient Rigid Panicked	• If I don't do it, it won't get done. • Things are out of control. • I've got to be in charge.	• Dominate or manipulate • Behave obsessively / compulsively • Plan excessively

When you don't deal with the physical energy of fear, your thoughts are like a pool full of piranhas that haven't eaten in weeks. Frenzied, frantically jumping helter-skelter through time, forwards, backwards, anywhere but the present! And according to your favorite catch phrase, it's always this way, every time.

Residing in the past or future is the first core attitude. You ruminate about the past or attempt to outguess the future. You're a ball of agitation, and it's not hard to spot. Everything that comes out of your mouth sounds like a record from back in the day or a list of 'must-do's' that better get done or the world is going to explode! You might act rashly. You can't stop talking, or you freeze into confused silence. Your thoughts run at hyper speed or blank out from overload. You jump to future what ifs and if onlys, or go wading into the murky waters of the past by rehashing and analyzing, and regretting what was.

Another of fear's core attitudes is to overgeneralize. Always, never, and everyone makes up a large part of your vocabulary. You assume all experiences will be like this one; you weren't good at hockey so you can't play soccer, that kind of thing. All liberals are tree-huggers; blonds have the most fun. You get the picture.

You also become a master at what I call "lumping," dragging other topics into a current situation and drawing sweeping conclusions, such as "everything's always difficult." And if someone's going to argue with you, they better take notes. You'll bring up about 23 topics when only one small thing happened, and by the end of the conversation, neither of you knows what the heck you're talking about. You've brought in dozens of issues and handled none.

The saying should be, 'fear is blind' not love is blind. Because fear causes you to lose sight of what is true or real (the third core attitude), you forget that the current feeling or situation will pass. You forget what you were certain of at an earlier time and place. For example, you might happen to overlook the fact that the double chocolate fudge cake you're about to eat has at least six hundred calories and isn't on your Weight Watchers menu. Or you stay up until two in the morning playing on the computer, forgetting you won't feel sharp for that early-morning staff meeting.

And the fight for control, that's the legacy of fear and the final core attitude. It doesn't matter whether its telling your wife which parking space is better (when you're in the back seat) or hanging out in the right lane ten miles slower than allowed to avoid crazy drivers, you do everything you can to maintain the illusion of control. That uncomfortable, scary, free-falling feeling comes from realizing that some force bigger than you is ultimately running the show. You're not happy about that, so you categorically deny it could be true in all the little ways you can. You delude yourself by having a spotless desk, hiding a microphone in your teenager's messy room, or researching safety records of every airline you fly on.

Joy

Joy's core attitudes spring forth, really honoring who you are from the inside-out. You possess unshakably high self-esteem, and feel gratitude in the smallest of things like the songbird singing you awake in the morning or the hot cup of joe your honey made for you. You feel worthy, knowing you're okay and perfect as you are deep down. You hold your head high and ride the tide of changing circumstances like the champion you know you are. Money doesn't make or break you. You stay grounded in the knowledge that you're whole and complete.

Emotion	Focus	CONSTRUCTIVE CORE ATTITUDES		
Expression	Attitude	FEELINGS	WORDS	ACTIONS
J **O** **Y** smiling bubbling sparkling laughing exuberantly tears	**YOURSELF** Honor yourself	WORTHY		
		Happy Full Lovable	• I am whole and complete. • I'm okay no matter what. • What I am seeking is within me.	•·Identify with your true self • Know you are not your actions, roles, traits, and body • Think well of yourself
		SELF-RELIANT		
		Independent Confident Authentic	• My job is to take care of myself. • Only if I take care of myself can I truly take care of you. • I am alone and I am connected.	• Fulfill your own needs and desires • Speak and act in line with your intuition • Enjoy independent activities
		APPRECIATE AND RESPECT SELF		
		Self-accepting Self-respect Delighted	• Life is for learning. We all make mistakes. • I did the best I could at the time. • I love / accept myself unconditionally.	• Celebrate accomplishments • Learn from mistakes • Be gentle with yourself
		SPEAK UP AND TAKE ACTION		
		Powerful Assertive Capable	• My views are equally important. • I am responsible for what I do, think, say, and feel. • I can do this. I can handle this.	• Set goals and follow through • Speak up about what's true for you • Face obstacles head on

The second core attitude associated with joy is self-reliance and independence, following your inner wisdom regardless of others' opinions. Rather than seeking validation, which puts you at the mercy of real and imagined external pressures, your heart leads the way so sadness can't set up shop. You live your life committed to honesty and personal integrity.

Joy's third mental tendency is to accept, respect, and appreciate yourself even if something sad happens or you do something you regret. When you slip or fail, you deal with your humanness, take it as a lesson learned, and move through it with compassion. You remain your closest ally.

The last core attitude that joy delights in giving you is a willingness to take personal responsibility. You may not always take the easy road, but you do always take the high road. You courageously speak up and take action in line with what you know comes from a place of integrity and honesty. It's not about hanging on to what's familiar. It's about rising up to the best version of who you can be.

Love

You've got a love connection. You're wholeheartedly connected to other people, things, and situations when you're in love — with life. I'm not talking about the gooey-eyed, sticky love fest that happens when you're blinded by that someone special. General feelings of love for everyone and everything is what you get when you operate from an open heart, the first core attitude. Your inner compass guides the journey and decisions come from inside instead of outside, unrelated to what others think or need.

Emotion	Focus	CONSTRUCTIVE CORE ATTITUDES		
Expression	Attitude	FEELINGS	WORDS	ACTIONS
L **O** **V** **E** warm open soft tone happy eyes smiling	PEOPLE AND SITUATIONS Accept people and situations	**OPEN HEARTED**		
		Honest Centered Genuine	• My focus is myself. My domain is me. • What is most loving? What is the high road? • What does my intuition tell me?	• Obey your intuition • Speak honestly about yourself • Act with integrity
		ACCEPT PEOPLE AND SITUATIONS		
		Satisfied Tolerant Forgiving	• People and things are the way they are. • This is the way it is. • We are all on our own paths.	• Have realistic expectations of others • Give opinions only with permission • Encourage others
		APPRECIATE AND RESPECT WHAT IS		
		Kind Compassionate Grateful	• I love you. I like you. • We are all connected. • Thank you.	• Be kind to people and things • Offer praise and show gratitude • Attend to the positive
		GIVE SELFLESSLY		
		Humble Caring Generous	• How can I help? What can I do? • Your viewpoints and needs are as important as mine. • I wish you well.	• Listen lovingly • Serve / support / cooperate • Show friendliness and affection

And what an easier life you're living accepting people and things as they are — even someone's insensitivities, shady political maneuvers, or blatant disregard for another's well-being. That's core attitude number two. No one can call you a pushover. You're just a lover, not a fighter! This doesn't mean you agree with everyone, but it does mean that you fully understand their point of view. Standing in true acceptance, your foundation finds and increases love in every situation. It can't help itself.

Love's third core attitude is valuing everyone and everything that exists as we do ourselves. You work with a global consciousness mentality, appreciating that we're all connected and loving and the value each of us provides. You see beauty in our differences, knowing we flavor the world with our diverse backgrounds, ideas and expressions. Coming from the fluid space that all people are fundamentally the same, you flow in respect, treating others as equals, focusing on similarities, and looking for the good in your world.

And when you're feeling love, it naturally gives rise to selflessly, seeking win-win solutions, and giving without expecting anything in return. How cool is that? Doesn't matter the dispute or situation or issue at hand. You share without any ulterior motive besides generating and feeling more love.

Remember that earlier scene, where you and your daughter had an unpleasant exchange over her homework? That was so the old you! This is what your brand spanking-new self would do when you're feeling love instead of anger: Okay, your mother-in-law was a little testy on the phone, but it's understandable. You remember she's been sick for days (first core attitude associated with love: openheartedness). When your daughter whines, you know she's just feeling anxious (the second core attitude associated with love: accept people and situations) and therefore, choose to view her homework frustration with compassion (the third mental tendency: appreciate and respect other people and situations). You give her a big hug, and then decide to put off dinner for a bit so you can help write a paper on reducing U.S. dependency on foreign oil (the fourth core attitude: selfless giving).

Peace

Finally, we rest on peace. Not 'in' peace, on peace. We're not gone yet. We fully relish the moment and see life in terms of specifics. The first core attitude when we feel peace is that we reside in the stillness, beauty, perfection, and miracle of the present moment. We move gracefully through life, soaking in the smallest of details, not rushing the moment or longing for something else. Connected to our inner knowing, our lives flow gently and smoothly through whatever troubled waters come our way.

Emotion	Focus	CONSTRUCTIVE CORE ATTITUDES		
Expression	Attitude	FEELINGS	WORDS	ACTIONS
P		RESIDE IN THE PRESENT		
E		Calm Content Alert	• Everything is / will be all right. • This feeling is temporary. This situation will pass. • Stop. Breathe. Slow down.	• Deal with emotions constructively • Calmly handle whatever happens • Pause to hear your intuition
A	TIME	STAY SPECIFIC		
C		Clear Focused Effective	• One thing at a time. • I'll handle the future in the future. • Be concrete. What's the specific?	• Think and speak in concrete terms • Focus on one thing at a time • Make and take small doable steps
E	Stay	KEEP SIGHT OF WHAT IS TRUE OR REAL		
calm	present	Stable Committed Directed	• This is what's true for me. • I am responsible for my experience. • My actions have consequences.	• Stay motivated to accomplish goals • Persevere • Act with conviction / passion
silent still	and specific	OBSERVE, ALLOW, PARTICIPATE, AND ENJOY		
alert aware smiling breathing fully		Patient Trusting Flexible	• I am part of a greater whole. • Everything is unfolding in its time. • There is enough time.	• Feel centered and safe no matter what happens • Participate with humor, levity, creativity • Show faith and trust

Razor sharp focus on what is specific is an efficient by-product, and second core attitude of peace. Life is so much more manageable when you remain concrete and break things down into a series of small doable units. Whether it's balancing your checkbook or learning to twirl fire, by keeping things manageable, you can accomplish almost anything, and successfully discuss any topic. Instead of biting your kid's head off when he complains about helping with dishes, you let him focus on the utensils while you get the big stuff.

When you decide something is good for you, you stick with it. You're firmly grounded in what you know and keep your eyes on the goal. The third mental tendency of peace is that anchor in reality, regardless of what's going on. Even if you find a class boring and the assignments unreasonable, you finish them so you can graduate.

You hold fast to your goal of getting in good shape, even when you feel like being a couch potato instead of going to the gym.

Spontaneous participation in our precious lives is the gift of the last core attitude, and with it comes a sense of playfulness combined with responsibility. With equanimity, humor, and passion, you enjoy and make something meaningful out of whatever comes your way. Unexpected minor surgery gives you time to catch up on all those trashy novels you love. A death in the family reconnects you to the sacredness of life, and you finally tell your son what you've always needed to say. You miss a flight, start getting chatted up by a handsome stranger stuck in the airport with you, and marry him two years later. Being fired from your job allows you to pursue your true dream of sculpting lawn art. Every moment is an opportunity.

The Ultimate Attitudes

By now you've discovered I like to reduce things to their most powerful essence.

Remember I took you through the six emotions that rule the life you've created (sadness, anger, fear; joy, love, peace). Then I introduced the supporting cast of attitudes that keep those emotional programs in syndication (the 12 core attitudes). And now, drum roll please... I'm going to take you to the heartbeat, the pearl inside of the oyster: the ultimate attitudes.

An ultimate attitude is a universal truth: an all-encompassing statement that beats the heart and breathes the breath. There are only three!

Joy: Honor yourself

Love: Accept people and situations

Peace: Stay present and specific

By deduction, you understand if you're caging the beasts of sadness, anger, fear, you're going to live the exact opposite of these ultimate attitudes. So you're continuing the journey that leads you down the path to the gold at the end of the rainbow. With each page, one foot will follow the other, and you'll get more tools to bushwhack the weeds and widen the road. We'll do it together.

2

Creating Joy, Love, and Peace

In the last chapter, you saw far-flung examples and close to home scenarios of the ways unexpressed sadness, anger, and fear penetrate every nook of cranny of life. You assessed your own emotional constitution and learned about the destructive core attitudes holding you back. You're painfully aware now of what's dimming your light and what's keeping you from shining your brightest self. That's probably a huge revelation.

You're moving to higher ground now. Soon you'll be learning about tools to turn those destructive core attitudes around, for good. You want a grand life , and it's yours for the taking. But before we go further, I want to share the capstone of my work, the Attitude Reconstruction Blueprint. I've included it here in case you want to skip the explanations and just get the skinny on how to address challenges a.s.a.p.

The Attitude Reconstruction Blueprint

From the baseboards to the pitched roof, remodeling your emotional dream home requires careful, meticulous planning. Oh, and did I mention a lot of details? The Attitude Reconstruction Blueprint lays out the common wiring we all share. The familiar six emotions with their core attitudes are there, along with an entire scope of feelings, words, and actions associated with them. Explore it. Open to it. Study it or just randomly cruise around and see what pops out at you.

ATTITUDE RECONSTRUCTION® BLUEPRINT

Emotion	Focus	DESTRUCTIVE CORE ATTITUDES		
Expression	**Attitude**	**FEELINGS**	**WORDS**	**ACTIONS**
S **A** **D** **N** **E** **S** **S** crying sobbing wailing frowning	**YOURSELF** **Don't honor yourself**	**UNWORTHY**		
		Empty Inadequate Unlovable	• I'm no good. • I'm not enough. • There's something wrong with me.	• Think and talk poorly about yourself • Create false impressions • Feel disconnected from who you are
		DEPEND ON OTHERS FOR APPROVAL		
		Lonely Insecure Needy	• Show me you love me. • I'll do anything to keep you happy. • Tell me I'm okay.	• Please others at own expense • Cling to other people • Seek validation and compliments
		JUDGE SELF NEGATIVELY		
		Self-loathing Stupid Ashamed	• I should have known or done better. • I'm stupid. I'm pathetic. • I hate myself when I make mistakes.	• Set unrealistic expectations for yourself • Put yourself down and beat self up • Demand perfection from yourself
		PASSIVE		
		Helpless Incapable Unassertive	• Poor me. • I can't do anything about this. • I don't know how. It's bigger than me.	• Play the submissive victim • Fail to follow through • Avoid confrontation
A **N** **G** **E** **R** hot aggressive hitting stomping shouting pounding	**PEOPLE AND SITUATIONS** **Refuse to accept people and situations**	**OUTWARD FOCUS**		
		Jealous Blaming Alienated	• You make me so mad. • You are the problem. • What do they have? say? think?	• Blame / ridicule / justify • Make "you" statements • Compare yourself to others
		DON'T ACCEPT PEOPLE AND SITUATIONS		
		Intolerant Disappointed Frustrated	• You should be different. • It's not supposed to be like this. • I don't believe it.	• Have unrealistic expectations • Give unsolicited advice / opinions • Reject others and withhold yourself
		MAKE NEGATIVE JUDGMENTS OF WHAT IS		
		Resentful Critical Disgusted	• You are a loser. • Right-Wrong / Fair-Unfair / Good-Bad • It's not enough.	• Expect the worst • Label people and things negatively • Be sarcastic / critical / cynical
		SELFISH		
		Stubborn Rebellious Arrogant	• Me. Me. Me. • My way or I won't play. • I'm special.	• Act as if you are more important • Be vain / pushy / insensitive • Don't listen / opinionated
F **E** **A** **R** cold shivering quivering laughing nervously breathing irregularly	**TIME** **Live in past or future, and over- generalize**	**LIVE IN THE FUTURE OR PAST**		
		Worried Anxious Distracted	• What if… • I don't want to feel this feeling. • I've got to get out of here.	• Avoid expressing emotions • Be speedy / impulsive / busy • Escape reality through addictions
		OVERGENERALIZE		
		Dramatic Overwhelmed Scattered	• It's always like that. • This is too much. • Nothing ever works out.	• Go on tangents • Exaggerate or minimize issues • Jump to conclusions
		LOSE SIGHT OF WHAT IS TRUE OR REAL		
		Indecisive Confused Conflicted	• Maybe this, maybe that. • I don't care. It doesn't matter. • I'll handle it tomorrow.	• Doubt excessively • Procrastinate / fail to take action • Act without regard for consequences
		ATTEMPT TO CONTROL		
		Impatient Rigid Panicked	• If I don't do it, it won't get done. • Things are out of control. • I've got to be in charge.	• Dominate or manipulate • Behave obsessively / compulsively • Plan excessively

Emotion	Focus	CONSTRUCTIVE CORE ATTITUDES		
Expression	Attitude	FEELINGS	WORDS	ACTIONS
J O Y smiling bubbling sparkling laughing tears	**YOURSELF** **Honor** **yourself**	WORTHY		
		Happy Full Lovable	• I am whole and complete. • I'm okay no matter what. • What I am seeking is within me.	• Identify with your true self • Know you are not your actions, roles, traits, and body • Think well of yourself
		SELF-RELIANT		
		Independent Confident Authentic	• My job is to take care of myself. • Only if I take care of myself can I truly take care of you. • I am alone and I am connected.	• Fulfill your own needs and desires • Speak and act in line with your intuition • Enjoy independent activities
		APPRECIATE AND RESPECT SELF		
		Self-accepting Self-respect Delighted	• Life is for learning. We all make mistakes. • I did the best I could at the time. • I love / accept myself unconditionally.	• Celebrate accomplishments • Learn from mistakes • Be gentle with yourself
		SPEAK UP AND TAKE ACTION		
		Powerful Assertive Capable	• My views are equally important. • I am responsible for what I do, think, say, and feel. • I can do this. I can handle this.	• Set goals and follow through • Speak up about what's true for you • Face obstacles head on
L O V E warm open soft tone happy eyes smiling	**PEOPLE** **AND** **SITUATIONS** **Accept** **people and** **situations**	OPEN HEARTED		
		Honest Centered Genuine	• My focus is myself. My domain is me. • What is most loving? What is the high road? • What does my intuition tell me?	• Obey your intuition • Speak honestly about yourself • Act with integrity
		ACCEPT PEOPLE AND SITUATIONS		
		Satisfied Tolerant Forgiving	• People and things are the way they are. • This is the way it is. • We are all on our own paths.	• Have realistic expectations of others • Give opinions only with permission • Encourage others
		APPRECIATE AND RESPECT WHAT IS		
		Kind Compassionate Grateful	• I love you. I like you. • We are all connected. • Thank you.	• Be kind to people and things • Offer praise and show gratitude • Attend to the positive
		GIVE SELFLESSLY		
		Humble Caring Generous	• How can I help? What can I do? • Your viewpoints and needs as are important as mine. • I wish you well.	• Listen lovingly • Serve / support / cooperate • Show friendliness and affection
P E A C E calm silent alert aware smiling breathing fully	**TIME** **Stay** **present** **and** **specific**	RESIDE IN THE PRESENT		
		Calm Content Alert	• Everything is / will be all right. • This feeling is temporary. This situation will pass. • Stop. Breathe. Slow down.	• Deal with emotions constructively • Calmly handle whatever happens • Pause to hear your intuition
		STAY SPECIFIC		
		Clear Focused Effective	• One thing at a time. • I'll handle the future in the future. • Be concrete. What's the specific?	• Think and speak in concrete terms • Focus on one thing at a time • Make and take small doable steps
		KEEP SIGHT OF WHAT IS TRUE OR REAL		
		Stable Committed Directed	• This is what's true for me. • I am responsible for my experience. • My actions have consequences.	• Stay motivated to accomplish goals • Persevere • Act with conviction / passion
		OBSERVE, ALLOW, PARTICIPATE, AND ENJOY		
		Patient Trusting Flexible	• I am part of a greater whole. • Everything is unfolding in its time. • There is enough time.	• Feel centered and safe no matter what happens • Participate with humor, levity, creativity • Show faith and trust

I'll walk you through the Blueprint now. Check out the left side:
locate the emotions of sadness, anger, and fear. On the right: their opposites: joy, love, and peace. Fairly straightforward, right? You'll also find
the three foci — yourself, other people and situations, and time — as
well as the core attitudes associated with each emotion and samples of
feelings, thoughts, and actions that derive from each one.

Think of the left side as the 'wrong' side (that is unless you're driving in London). Living on the left, or destructive, side of the Blueprint
keeps you on the hamster wheel of trouble that brought you here. Leaning to right, regardless of your political beliefs, in this case is a good
thing! The right or constructive side, builds joy, love, and peace. Anytime
you feel "off," simply locate what you feel, think, or do on the left side of
the Blueprint, and get the 'fix' on the right.

Say, for example, you feel overwhelmed. You scan the left side of the
Blueprint, and find "overwhelmed" listed as a feeling associated with
fear. On closer inspection, you'll see that feeling overwhelmed falls under
the core attitude of "overgeneralize." You think, "Hmmm, I do tend to
lose track of time, and Billy's always teasing me about saying, 'always' or
'never' for everything!" You'll also discover some of the thoughts that fill
your mind when you're overwhelmed, as well as some ways you behave
when in the grip of that feeling.

Now slide on over to the right side of the Blueprint. You'll see that
the opposing mental tendency, "stay specific," is associated with peace.
Feelings that come from staying specific sound almost impossible right
now: clear, calm, or steady. Your fingers settle on the new thoughts, which
you begin to whisper to yourself. **"One thing at a time." "I'll handle the
future in the future."** After a deep breath, you repeat again. And finally,
looking to the "action" list, you start relaxing, little by little. The steps are
small and doable, and you know this time is going to be different.

Your Toolkit

You're a master builder who needs high quality tools to craft a life
of beauty, abundance, and happiness. If you were an electrician, you
wouldn't show up on a job without cords, plugs, and wires. Likewise,

you have to come to work armed with the appropriate tools for creating happiness. You've actually had them since birth. They're powerful. You've seen how destructive they are when handled inappropriately. Now you're going to use them to build a better life.

We innately possess the ability to experience our world. Milky blue skies and the smell of a salty ocean; frosty beer, and a baby's giggles. Sun-soaked skin and gasoline fumes. Without our five senses, we couldn't experience any of these. Sight, hearing, taste, smell, and touch are the doorways into the world of sensation. From subtle to overpowering, they help us perceive and process our environment.

At birth we were also given five tools with which to interact with our world: emotions, thoughts, intuition, speech, and actions. In each moment we use one or several of them.

Our senses and tools are vastly different. Our senses are involuntary. Our five tools are voluntary. In each moment, our senses take in a constant barrage of stimuli. We hear a couple arguing on the corner or see a homeless person huddled under a thin cardboard box. With our tools, we interpret what we take in through our senses. Do we snap at our secretary after hearing the couple or do we tell her how much we appreciate her hard work? Do we think poorly about the transient or do we leave half a sandwich next to him?

The Five Tools

> 1. Emotions
> 2. Thoughts
> 3. Intuition
> 4. Speech
> 5. Action

With these five tools, we choose to express an emotion, ignore or consult our intuition, make a remark, or act out what we're feeling. We've been misusing these remarkable instruments to perpetuate sadness, anger, and fear. Now, we can use them to produce joy, love, peace.

Here's a situation you might actually encounter: say you're marched into a conference room and told that your company is going to downsize. If you want to keep your job, you're going to have to move to another state. Your senses are heightened. Life seems to be in Hi-Def. You smell the musty room. You hear your boss's words. Your heart is pounding, and a wave of nausea rises in your stomach.

How are you going to react? You can burst into tears, withdraw and zone out, become shell-shocked and despondent, or resist and counter-attack. You can tell yourself, "I knew this job was too good to last" or complain to your friends, "I'll never find another position with such good benefits." You can light up a cigarette, have a stiff drink, or decide not to show up to work the next day. Or, you can start thinking about a creative solution, ask copious questions, and make a plan. At every moment, you choose which tools to use and how you'll use them, destructively or constructively.

The first tool, your emotions, seems to be a sticky point for many. It's probably a bit of a new concept, but the healthy way to express these emotions is to emote, physically and constructively. That doesn't mean you get to poison a loved one with your venom. It means you allow the pure energetic sensation to move out of your body. What does that look like? It could involve crying, pounding, or shivering. You're just looking to release pent up emotions so you don't have an internal nuclear meltdown that burns you, and the atmosphere, with toxic waste. Physically expressing your emotions in a healthy way is the fastest method to get rid of the energy and halt the destructive core attitudes.

Thought is your next tool. You can stay in your old rut, or you can replace your negative thoughts with new ones that are unequivocally true, such as **"People are the way they are,"** or **"We all make mistakes."** You'll keep yourself from sinking by repeating helpful thoughts, interrupting destructive chatter, and expressing any emotions. I only half-jokingly tell clients that one hundred thousand repetitions will bring the new concepts into focus and offset all the times they've told themselves the contrary. Repeating constructive truths eventually works magic, even if it just feels like repeating formulas for calculus right now. Just be sure that you're focusing on something that contradicts the old and is indisputably true.

Next is that nebulous thing called intuition. Consulting this well of wisdom allows you to tap into your heart and find what's indisputably true, at lightning speed. It's an unfailing guide for making sound decisions. Intuition helps with everything from simple things, such as what you really want for dinner, to the heavy hitters such as breaking up with your girlfriend after ten years. It's the knowing in your gut of what's right, right now. For example, perhaps you know that even if your company downsizes and offers relocation 400 miles away as the only option, you can't leave your aging parents and move, no matter how lucrative the offer.

Tool number four is your speech. The words and tone you use will either cause separation and fear or create connection and solutions. When you feel upset or off center, your communication skills can go out the window. What can be done to prevent this? Rather than accusing the company of being heartless, you can calmly talk about the implications this turn of events has for your situation.

Finally, with your actions — the last tool in the box — you can counteract those worn out and harmful ways of behaving by taking little steps toward more joy, love, and peace. In the example of the layoff there are several possibilities to consider: you might offer to take a cut in pay, put in applications at other firms, start checking the classified ads, or consider job retraining.

Cycling Through All Five Tools

If you're used to hanging out in the dark emotional corners but find it's getting lonely in there, move to the light side in a flash by using any one of the five tools. For maximum results, whenever you're stuck, cycle through all five. By first using emotions and thoughts (tools one and two) as a base, you can easily hear your intuition (tool three), which will reveal the truth you know within. Then it's easy to speak up and take action (tools four and five). As a result, feel the joy, love, and peace pour into your world.

If you don't have the desire or time to emote (that is, to express your emotions physically), find freedom by aligning your thinking with what is constructive, or by pausing for a minute to consult your intuition. If you already know what you need to communicate, you can just speak up, as long as you abide by the Attitude Reconstruction rules for good communication. If a certain tool isn't working for you, go back around to an earlier one and take it from there.

How to Use Each Tool to Create Joy, Love, and Peace

You get the basic idea now that there are five tools at your disposal in every moment. The rest of this chapter gives an overview of how to put those tools in motion to neutralize sadness, anger, and fear. Each time you contradict old ways of being, you're staying present and specific, accepting what is, and honoring yourself.

You have a silent wellspring inside called pure being, Self, essence, higher self, authentic self, true nature, spirit, or soul. There are many ways to describe this expansive state beyond words, where you are centered, balanced, clear, and on the top of your game. When connected to your true self, you know you're whole and complete, and that nothing is lacking. Using any of these five tools can get you there, if you use them as they were originally intended.

Using Your Tools to Build Joy from Sadness

If you're constantly beating yourself up, not speaking up, or feeling hopeless, chances are your emotional constitution is sadness. Sadness is a natural reaction to hurts and losses. When not expressed constructively, it silently eats at your heart until joy has to pack its bags and move out. Your mind turns against itself. How can you turn the tide and truly honor who you are (the ultimate attitude of joy)? You can use any of the five tools.

On the level of the emotional energy, you can express sadness purely by allowing yourself to cry. Big, wet tears — the more, the better. But while you're crying, keep your mind quiet and clear. Ignore those mean voices, "I'm a loser. I'll never get this right." The emotion of sadness has no words, so if you think anything, it needs to be something simple, something like, "**I just feel sad. It's okay to feel sad.**" Crying in this manner allows the sadness to pass. You'll come back to your wonderful self, and sadness' negative influence will vanish.

Crying cleanly (without indulging any destructive thoughts) is the most direct route to joy, but it isn't the only one. The second tool that moves out sadness is your thinking. First you have to identify the unproductive thoughts you're telling yourself. For example, say you routinely don't assert yourself and believe the views and needs of others are more important than yours. Determine the constructive opposite: **My viewpoints and needs are as important as yours.** Contradict that old thinking and claim your personal power by repeating, "**My viewpoints and needs are as important as yours. My viewpoints and needs are as important as yours.**" Don't worry if you don't believe what you're saying at first.

Some other great truths are: **"I'm whole and complete," "My job is to take care of myself,"** and **"I'm responsible for myself."** Thinking and saying kind things about yourself focuses on the half-full jar and offsets the countless times you've tended to the half-empty one.

To restore more joy, the third tool of intuition also comes in handy. We often give too much power to what others say and do, automatically assuming how they'll react and basing our behavior accordingly. We're not connected to our inner wisdom unless we're checking in. If this is your challenge, take the time to look within. You often find solutions to situations you were convinced kept you in a stalemate.

Rather than repeating "I don't know," take a moment to pause and ask yourself, "What's true for me about this situation? What does my heart tell me I need to do about this?" Listen to the answer. You do know! And this answer, if it comes from a still place — not from your mind — will be in line with the three constructive ultimate attitudes. That is your "I."

Looking within for answers is a habit you'll be happy you've developed. It helps you in every aspect of your life, in every moment. You may have to put in some effort to plug into it. Maybe that will involve slowing down, shivering, or taking a couple of full breaths, so you can listen to your heart rather than your head. When you say aloud what you hear, it will resonate within you when it's correct, and bring a joyous, peaceful feeling. If it's not ringing all the way true, modify it until it does. If you can't hear anything at all, maybe have a good cry, then ask again.

The fourth tool to catch the joy train is communicating what is true for you in a kind way. Rather than asking other people what they want, refocus, find your "I" about the specific topic at hand, and then talk about just that. You can still listen to others. You aren't being egocentric. You're just taking responsibility for yourself and voicing what's in line with your personal integrity.

Questions to ask yourself could be: "What do I need to say about this specific topic?" or "How can I talk about what is true for me?" When you're clear on what that is, the task is to confidently speak your "I." It's time to stop being the perpetual nice guy or unavailable woman. When you assert yourself with kindness and say, "I don't want to do that right now" or "I need this to happen before I'm willing to do that," you are honoring yourself. You'll be amazed by how empowering it feels.

Action is the fifth and final tool to break into living the joy factor. Rather than acting in old familiar ways, you choose to align your behavior with those things on which you are clear. Clarify your goal for a given situation; translate it into small, doable steps and then take those steps one at a time.

Remember the wise adage of Lao Tzu: "A journey of a thousand miles begins with a single step." If you crave a mate, for instance, write out a list of different ways to put yourself into circulation. Decide on a first little step, such as investigating online dating services. When you find a site that seems good, sign up. If that's too much, too fast, determine what actions are in your comfort zone, and take them. Maybe it's enlisting a friend who is also looking for 'Mr. Right' instead of 'Mr. Right Now'. The two of you could join a coed softball team together or sing in the community choir. Praise and appreciate yourself as you venture into new territory, and you'll experience a double shot of joy.

Using Your Tools to Build Love from Anger

Anger bites and barks and tears away at anything it can sink its teeth into, whether it be your stomach, your heart, or any innocent bystander within a hundred mile radius. No one escapes the feelings of anger. Even revered Zen Buddhist monk Thich Nhat Hanh tells a story about his struggle to stay centered while angry, and this guy is the epitome of peace! It's in everyone's emotional constitution to one degree or another. It oozes out in big and little ways, no matter how valiant the attempt to disguise it. It shows up when you act mean-spirited, inconsiderate or bossy, or when everything you say has a negative spin to it. Maybe you attempt to change other people, get huffy when things don't go your way, or just find yourself frustrated about almost everything. When you don't express the anger constructively, you focus outward on people, things, and situations without accepting them — the second destructive ultimate attitude. The result is always the same: you end up feeling disconnected, separate, alienated. Unkind looks, words, and actions follow.

It's human to feel angry when experiencing an injustice or violation. For instance, if a coworker takes all the credit for a project you did, your hackles are going to rise. Anger hits everybody at one time or another, no matter how peachy the upbringing. Think about the injustice you felt when it was obvious your mother favored your sister over you. What did you do when Sis got more new school clothes and you were "too old" to have a tantrum?

Transforming your anger takes surrendering your pride and going for it. The first tool is dealing with the emotion itself by moving the hot, surging, wordless energy out of your body constructively. Think about a small child in the supermarket. When he's denied the sugar cereal he saw on television — an injustice in his eyes — he flops on the floor and throws a tantrum. He doesn't say, "Excuse me, mother dear, I'm feeling angry and need to do some exercise or regulated breathing." He spontaneously moves that energy out of his body in whatever loud and outrageous way it comes. Mother is totally embarrassed (a feeling associated with fear), but the child is just taking care of himself. If his mother takes him somewhere safe, like the car, and allows him to express the anger physically, the energy passes. At some point, it's over. He cries, falls asleep, or gets absorbed in something else. He's then back, fully present with no lingering after taste.

Adults need a physical way to move anger energy, as well. To expel this emotion, you need to do something where you can safely let go, such as yelling into a pillow, stomping around, or pushing against a doorjamb. What is important is that you don't destroy anything of value (including yourself) while getting rid of the physical sensations. Make hard and fast movements with total abandon until you experience a noticeable shift and feel the anger energy dissipate.

What you think and say to yourself while pounding is crucial. Blaming or cursing others will heat things up. Other people and situations are just convenient targets. To move the energy constructively, you need to own it as residing within you. While pounding or pushing, make primal sounds, grunt or growl or say, **"I feel angry. I feel so frustrated."**

Your thinking will neutralize your anger if you can fully accept people, things, and situations. Refocus on what you can do to feel more love. Negative thoughts about external things are born from anger and only perpetuate more. To break the cycle, think the opposite of what you usually tell yourself. Instead of thinking "You shouldn't act like that," or "He should be more considerate of my feelings," remind yourself, **"People and things are the way they are, not the way I want them to be."**

This profound sentence contradicts the "shoulds" and me-me-me thinking that people with anger constitutions have likely repeated to themselves for a long, long time. Think your acceptance thoughts anytime, but especially when you realize you're not thinking well of someone, when you feel like pulling away, or when you're ranting. Then you can remind yourself, **"My focus is myself."**

Use your intuition rather than blaming the world for the conditions you find yourself in. Turn your attention around one hundred and eighty degrees, and ask yourself: **"What's true for me about this situation? What do I need to do here to feel more love?"** If you come back to yourself and listen to what your inner knowing tells you, rather than giving credence to your vindictive mind or self-centered ego, you'll get clear about where you really stand and what you need to say or do.

Find a way to communicate what is true for you, and do it in a kind way. Anger awards us a Ph.D. in telling other people about themselves, so it may seem nearly impossible. But focusing negatively on others doesn't bring love, it only gets you more disconnected and accentuates differences. Rather than fuming over how other people are, how they should be, or what they should do, refocus. Speak about yourself — that is, speak your "I." It's not, "What's your problem?" It's "I was angry when I couldn't catch you on the phone." You don't have to remove the word "you" from your vocabulary. You just have to keep your attention on talking about what's true for you about you.

Another surefire way to move through anger and increase love with your speech is to give appreciations and praise to others, emphasizing the bright side, and voicing your gratitude. The more of this, the better.

Action — as in genuine acts of giving — melt anger and fuel love. Frequently ask yourself, "**What can I give? How can I help?**" Then follow through. Give undivided attention by listening lovingly. When you become the devil's advocate or offer unsolicited advice, you provoke anger. When you listen in order to understand, people feel respected, and you'll feel more love. There's many ways you can give: a greeting card, money, time, or expertise. You can cooperate, compromise, or gracefully give up your preference and do something the other person's way.

Choose any or all of your five tools to move you from anger to love in any situation. As you go along, you see the bright light at the end of the tunnel, drawing you closer to the treasure: the second ultimate attitude of accepting people and situations. Love brings you back to your true centered self. You live in your heart and come from a space of openness and expansion. It's impossible not to love and accept people and situations when you're truly connected to all that is.

Using Your Tools to Build Peace from Fear

Peace is fleeting, especially for those with fear constitutions. Being able to relax into a moment, to feel calm when sitting in traffic, or to experience ease in new situations is probably a foreign concept. Instead, your heart races, stomach tightens, legs jiggle, and sleepless nights are the norm. Held-in fear is the root of the anxiety so prevalent in our culture today. We burn ourselves out, trying to squeeze in just one more errand in the day, speeding from one thing to the next, multitasking, and end up agitated, spaced out, or exhausted.

Fear is a normal reaction to threats to our survival. It is a highly useful emotion to keep us safe and out of harm's way, whether it's a lurking stranger in the parking lot or driving in a neighborhood we know we shouldn't be in after dark. In general, stepping into any unknown situation naturally elicits fear. But that fear takes on new meaning for people with fear constitutions. They react to little events as if they were life threatening, and to them, most events genuinely feel like life or death.

If we want to live in peace we need to embody the ultimate attitude associated with it, and stay present and specific. In situations that push our fear, pulling out the five tools and attacking it from all angles moves us closer to dealing with what's required in the moment, to becoming a witness, and enjoying what life has dealt us.

How can you deal with fear on an emotional level? Here's a hint: think about what your dog looks like when you take him to the vet's office. He cowers and shivers. He trembles and pees in the corner. That's what being scared looks like. Have you ever been in an automobile accident or earthquake? In those threatening situations, your body sends a message to the brain that your survival is threatened. As stress hormones surge, the body starts shaking uncontrollably. Quivering out the fear, rather than tightening up, frees your mind from survival-mode thinking and enables you to deal with the situation.

Expressing fear physically releases the agitated energy zipping through your body. When you're afraid, the body temperature drops, your stomach flip-flops, and your voice quivers. People who have panic attacks know the sensations. To get in touch with that feeling, imagine you're about to give a speech in front of five hundred people. Are your knees knocking? Hands freezing? Is your stomach in your throat?

On a purely physical level, you can dissipate the fear energy by shivering and trembling with wholehearted vigor. Move the energy up your spine, through the jaw, into your neck, down the arms and out the hands, the legs and the feet. Don't tighten up against it. Don't fight it. Shiver it out instead. If you need encouragement, put on music and dance to release the fear energy.

You must be vigilant while quivering and quaking to not give in to fear's core attitudes. Make high-pitched squeals or name what you are experiencing: **"I just feel scared. It's okay. This feeling will pass. I just need to shake."** Sometimes all that's required is a two-second shudder before you focus on whatever needs attention. Shuddering may be something you've only heard joked about or think only happens in vampire movies. But it's exceptionally helpful — and something real — to use right now. I know it sounds a bit strange, but if you try it — especially if you are lying awake in the middle of the night or facing something that feels intimidating — you'll experience the benefits first hand.

Each time you replace the skewed thoughts about the past, future, or present that your mind tries to convince you of, you'll feel calmer and more relaxed. Two of the best phrases to use are **"Everything is all right"** and **"Everything will be all right."** When the mind chimes in and says, "Oh no, it won't," take a strong stance and remind yourself, "Yes it will. **Everything will be all right. This situation is temporary."** When you're feeling nervous or anxious, relentlessly repeat such thoughts as **"One thing at a time. I'll do what I can, and the rest is out of my hands."**

Thinking in specifics also helps to reduce fear. What do I mean about specifics? Be exact. Precise. Here's why: when worrying about the future, your mind usually rotates in circles. The tires are spinning but you aren't going anywhere. If you identify the issue in concrete terms, rather than being hazy and vague, you can deal with what's frightening you. For example, if you have to take a test to qualify for a promotion, instead of freaking out and telling yourself that you'll never pass, make a list of the skills you need to review and set a reasonable study schedule. It doesn't matter what you're doing, as you go through the day, brushing your teeth, drinking your coffee (which you need to go light on because it will agitate you more), or driving your car, repeat: "I'll do what I can, and the rest is out of my hands."

Intuition neutralizes the debilitating influence of fear. Pause and check in with your heart about what is true for you. Instead of doubting your decision to go on an exotic vacation, ask yourself, "What's true for me about this specific situation? What do I need to do?" If you ask yourself specific questions, you'll hear specific answers. When you know precisely where you stand, hold on to what's true for you and proceed.

And remember when I said to focus on specifics when thinking? What comes out of your mouth should also only be about specifics. We rely on specifics in almost every field of endeavor — cooking, architecture, computers, gardening, and so on. If you stay concrete in your words, other people can more easily understand what you're talking about. Using vague or abstract terms, it's easy to get confused or frightened. Instead of saying, "We need to talk," you'll open up communication channels if you say, "I want us to set a time to talk about what you said to my brother last night." Instead of "This situation is out of hand," say, "I want us to look at our budget this weekend, because I'm concerned we can't pay our bills this month." You give more information that way.

Talking in labels like carelessness, immaturity, inconsiderate, or trust invites breakdown and fracture. Focus on specific topics to come up with workable solutions. The more clear you can be about boundaries, requests, consequences, and solutions, the less ambiguity and more safety you will create.

Finally, use your actions to increase peace by zeroing in on exactly what needs attention. Make your steps small and doable, and then take them one at a time. You'll stay out of overwhelming or intimidating situations, and successfully complete each project before entertaining the next. If you want to quit smoking, focus on making another choice when the impulse arises just for one day. Just take one minute, one hour, one day at a time. In this way, you can string together a series of victories and eventually accomplish your goals. I know it sounds a bit strange, but if you try it — especially if you are lying awake in the middle of the night or facing something that feels intimidating — you'll get tangible proof about the effectiveness of physical expression.

JOY, LOVE, PEACE

PART II
Your Toolkit

1

Emotions: Laying the Foundation

Cry
Pound
Shiver

Many of us are more comfortable talking about why we feel something than physically expressing the bodily sensations we feel. It's understandable because none of us, including you, have been taught it's a healthy or desirable thing to deal with emotions in a physical, constructive way. You're caught in a sticky web of your own making. Good thing you're aware there's a choice. Rather than stressing out, acting out, tuning out, or doing other things to avoid what you're feeling, you can take the necessary space and time to move emotional energy out of your body by emoting constructively.

Emoting isn't going to get you a guest appearance on your favorite sitcom, but it may just make you the star of your own life by cleaning out the cobwebs and allowing you to shine. Of course I'm joking about the acting part, but many think of physically emoting as dramatizing or exaggerating what we feel, which isn't what we're aiming for. The word emote simply means expressing emotional energy in a pure, physical, non-damaging way. Sometimes a few seconds of pushing against a wall or shedding some tears is all you have time for. That will be sufficient to skim off surface emotions and change your state. However, a few minutes of sustained emoting will usually drain the energy and produce a significant shift in your awareness that will last much longer. The world will look like a gentler place. And you'll gratefully watch the sadness, anger, and fear pass.

Reasons to Emote

As I mentioned, children point us in the right direction. They do whatever they need to: scream, growl, pound the floor, alternate between stutter sobs and octaves piercing enough to break glass. But the coolest part is they're present. They're present with what they experience and instantly display their emotions - no matter where, no matter who is watching and no matter the results. Their reactions are intense and genuine. And if accepted instead of diverted, judged, or discouraged, children will wail or kick it out for just a few minutes and then go right back to their happy little selves.

If we can get to that place where we feel comfortable with physically releasing a stored-up emotion, it's like life moves into 3D. No longer the dull, empty shell of numbness, we're plunged head first into the vibrantly pulsing present moment. Our minds are sharp, free to process an event, thought, or impression so we can use the information in the future. Our thinking becomes more flexible and creative, setting the stage to hear the spontaneous wisdom of our intuition. We have freedom to make more constructive choices, causing us to feel empowered and take responsibility for ourselves. We speak and act constructively.

Who would have thought pounding and crying could also make you look younger? Well, I'm not totally sure it will get rid of your wrinkles, but for sure it will add years of quality to your life by purifying and balancing your body. Every part of your body softens and expands when you physically express. The diaphragm, chest, and lungs extend during crying. The jiggling of shivering when afraid releases the tension. The liberating exertion of pounding out anger removes that hard edge. All three realign your spines, relax muscles, soothe organs, improve posture, increase all-around energy, and make you look more radiant, healthy, and attractive. Even your facial expressions relax.

Emoting has another upside: the quality of your social interactions with family, friends, coworkers, and even strangers will improve. Those warm feelings of connection and intimacy skyrocket when sadness, anger, and fear are no longer percolating. The inner turbulence of unexpressed emotion stops causing your stomach to do belly flops. It's easier to cooperate, share, and lend a helping hand to your community. Ultimately, handling your own emotions is one big thing you can do to make the world a more harmonious place.

What Constructive Emoting Is and Isn't

What we think and say while emoting is key. It's about owning the emotions inside of you. You take personal responsibility and stop entertaining the victim mentality that makes your life a helpless mess. Remember that expressing sadness, anger, and fear can involve a vocal component, but no words. You enter a wordless zone of emotions. Make sounds that express the intensity you're experiencing, such as "ooooowww", "ohhhh", etc. If you need some words, stick to naming the emotion: state what you feel right now or recount the facts of the event that triggered your emotion. Say things like:

- **I feel sad. I feel angry. I feel afraid.**
- **I just need to cry. I need to stomp.**
- **It's okay to express this.**
- **These feelings will pass.**

Consider the distinction between saying or thinking, "You make me so angry" and, "I felt angry when you left the room while I was talking." Or the difference between "He's freaking me out" and "**I feel scared right now.**" These are subtle but very important distinctions. State what you're feeling when you release emotional energy (e.g., "I feel angry") because it gives emoting its full weight. You're the owner of your emotions. No one can make you feel anything or say anything. You stop blaming others for what is happening in your world.

EMOTIONS

And getting even more into semantics, it's not "I'm angry," but "**I feel angry.**" Anger is an emotion, not an identity. Tell yourself, "**It's okay. I'm all right. I just feel angry right now.**" Whatever you're feeling, remember that you are all right; your emotions are separate from your essential being.

Resisting What's Natural

Physical expression might be easy when you're at a ballgame or when you're moving to some saucy Latin grooves, but it's a different story when it comes to emotions. If you're thinking you like the concept, but can't really get into the 'physically expressing yourself' thing, don't worry. Almost everyone resists the idea of physically expressing sadness, anger, and fear. It seems a bit silly or even intimidating at first, but that's only because you haven't done it before.

Breaking through the mental chatter and releasing our emotions intentionally takes a little practice and a lot of courage. It requires ignoring ego, pride, and the stubborn desire to be "in charge." So here's my question to you: Do you want to be cool or do you want to be healthy? Just to humor you, here are some typical comments that my clients and students make to justify not expressing their emotions:

- I'm not that angry right now.
- Crying is a waste of time.
- What would people think of me?
- I won't do it right.
- It's too disruptive.
- I've got my pride.
- This is really stupid.
- I'll look dumb.
- I'll be out of control.
- It makes sense, but I'll do it at home.
- I just put on mascara.

As a psychotherapist, I've heard just about every excuse. You'll admire your own creative endeavors to get out of what you know is right. Understanding that excuses come a dime a dozen (and appear to be in endless supply), practice what you read on these pages, and have an image in your head to combat those negative Nelly thoughts. How does a kid react when he drops his ice cream cone one bite in? Or think about the Western (Wailing) Wall in Jerusalem where people can truly mourn their losses and acknowledge their pain and sorrow aloud. Be bold. You can do it…and you will feel the benefits.

Crying

Cathy Cries

At last, after a hectic week, Cathy found herself alone. Her husband had gone out with friends, and her son was away for the weekend. She cherished her private time and had three hours of a distraction-free household. Cathy was aware of a number of upsetting incidents that she had shrugged off but that still lingered. Before diving into a pile of chores that she had postponed, she sat down with a cup of tea and flipped through the TV channels.

She found herself getting pulled into a story about a woman who had just reunited with the daughter she had given up for adoption. For twenty-five years, the mother had thought she would never see her daughter again. Cathy hadn't planned on getting sucked into television that night, but there she was, glued to the set, tears streaming down her face. She settled into the show, pulled out her hanky, and wept. She'd known for days that she needed to cry and hadn't made the time. "I'm just so sad," she said as she sobbed. "I just need to cry."

Cathy understood that crying hard was a kind of inner cleansing, a beauty treatment that would renew her from the inside out. She knew she wasn't just crying about what was on television. She was crying out the tears that had been accumulating in her over the last few weeks. The exact causes weren't really important.

Were you ever told that tears were nectar? They are the natural expression of hurt and loss. In North America, crying openly has become only slightly more acceptable in recent years. We're only just beginning to feel comfortable with tearful displays of grief or happiness in public. Many of us still believe others will judge us if we cry and so we avoid it at all costs, choking back tears and fighting the lumps in our throats.

Infants are great role models for truly effective crying. When something happens that they perceive as a hurt or loss, they sob and shriek. After just a few minutes, they return blissfully back to the moment. No repercussions or lingering moods. It's over and done. Their sparkling eyes instantly return, innocently observing the beauty of the world, in joy, delight, and wonder.

As you know by now, sadness manifests as internal sensations in our bodies and that means a tender heart can literally ache as well. Hurts are inflicted by mean words, broken promises, prejudice, or physical injury. Losses can include unrealized goals as well as the loss of innocence, opportunities, a loved one, money, or freedom.

When we don't release our sadness, it's easy to get down on ourselves. We fall into self-pity, helplessness, or self-reproach. Over time, our sadness can manifest as depression and despair. But if we truly express our sadness by crying instead of bottling it up inside, its influence will dissolve, and we will naturally honor ourselves and feel more joy. (Part III, Chapter 2 disarms sadness-based attitudes and instructs you on how to overcome them.)

How to Cry Constructively

"Clean" crying — that is, crying without criticizing yourself — is the most efficient way to release sadness. When your eyes start to well up and you sense a heavy constriction in your throat, try something different. Regardless of why you feel so sad, just allow yourself to cry — the harder, the better. Say yes to the runny nose and red eyes. Don't apologize or be ashamed. Simply return to how you expressed yourself as a child before you succumbed to the pressures of family and culture. Jump back into that little kid mentality and feel the loss, the sorrow, and the rejection. Whatever it is, let the healing tears flow. You'll feel the benefits. Other people really won't mind as much as you think. If they do, that's their problem, not yours.

No matter why you're feeling sadness, you just need to cry. Since self-criticism only increases your sadness and reinforces bad feelings about yourself, it's crucial to refrain from thinking or saying anything negative about yourself as you cry. Interrupt any thoughts about how inadequate, unlovable, or pathetic you are. You need to intensely express your sadness, so turn it up a notch. Wail! Get into it. This is your time to unplug the dam! If you do use words, stick to naming the emotion, stating how you feel right now, or recounting the facts of the event that triggered your sadness. Say things like:

- **I feel sad.**
- **I just need to cry.**
- **I feel so hurt.**
- **My sadness will pass.**
- **My mom died last month. I really miss her.**
- **Dave just told me he wants a divorce.**

If you haven't cried in years, it's never too late to start. If you feel sad, set aside some time to ignore all the excuses you've made up to avoid tears and let yourself cry. Find a safe place — maybe a darkened movie theatre. Or wait for nighttime, when you can curl up and be alone. Turn off the phone, think about the sadness you have been carrying and turn on the spigot. Light a candle if you're so inclined. One tear falling down your cheek during a sentimental song is a fabulous start, but crying means really letting the tears flow. If you want to siphon off your accumulated sadness, you'll have to give yourself permission to cry for a few minutes when you experience that weighted-down sensation.

Set aside some time, and with a box of tissues, do one or more of the following:

- Watch a movie that touches you.
- Listen to a song that stirs your heart, over and over.
- Look at photographs of loved ones, pets, or places you've been.
- Lovingly say good-bye, over and over, to acknowledge the many losses in your life.
- Hug a pillow, pet, or teddy bear.
- Press your chest, curl up, and rock back and forth.

EMOTIONS

- Make sounds, say and think, "**It's okay. I feel sad. I just need to cry.**"
- Confide in a friend about your troubles.

Whether you decide to go it alone or cry with a supportive friend, let go of the critical voice and remind yourself it's okay to let the tears roll. If you're trying but nothing is happening, shift to shiver or pound — the other two expressions. Pretty soon, the true emotion begging to be expressed will rise to the surface, making itself known.

As unpleasant or weird as it might sound at first, crying is rejuvenating. It restores openness, clarity, and receptivity while washing your every cell clean. A feeling of lightness will wash over you when you're finished: this is a divine shift.

Because emotions and thoughts are so inextricably linked, I want to briefly mention a concept that is covered in detail in the next chapter. In addition to simply stating what you are feeling, or describing your hurt or loss while crying, you can also repeat a phrase that contradicts your well-worn commentary about your own failings, such as "**I am whole and complete**" or "**What I'm seeking is within me.**" It's important to get this part. Sometimes you'll be surprised at how repeating 'a truth' helps kick-in the emotional release. Your crying may intensify, which is a good thing allowing you to finally let go of what you've stored inside, often for years.

Pounding

Peter Pounds

*Over the past few years, Peter had become more and more disagreeable. He recognized that his irritability was a real danger and found that he was most outrageous when he was in his car. "**It's me against the world! Other drivers are my enemy!**" he would think. Peter had a huge case of road rage, but unfortunately, it didn't stop there. Whoever crossed his path got the worst of his anger. At his office, this was usually his hardworking assistant. At home, it was his wife. Some days, all it took was a moment stuck in traffic to set him off for the day.*

Following the principles of Attitude Reconstruction, Peter learned how to push on a doorframe with his hands, shoulders, and legs to express his anger. The first time he tried it, he worked up quite a sweat. Traumatic events from his past, as well as minor incidents from his present, popped into awareness. He grunted, yelled, and pushed with all his might. After a few minutes, he found that he was less crazed and more willing to look at things differently. For the first time, he could see how childish, mean, and selfish he was to take his anger out on the world and other people.

Pushing walls, doorframes, and even trees now helps Peter accept that people aren't the way he wants them to be. They drive the way they drive. They make the decisions they make. That's just the way it is. Now he laughs and ignores other drivers instead of doing what he used to do (which he says is unmentionable and incriminating). As a result, he sees the world as a better place.

"I seem to have new circuitry inside me ever since I started to release my anger physically," he told me. "Dealing with my anger is going to be a lifelong activity, and I've given up resisting."

It is human to feel anger. But the velocity of that turbulent energy stored in our cells can only create heartache. When we don't handle anger in a constructive way as Peter learned to do, we take it out on other people and situations. In a split second, as the anger surges in our bodies, we think, say, and do hurtful things. Unexpressed anger shows up as disgust, grumpiness, sarcasm, frustration, or hate (Part III, Chapter 2 elaborates on these and other anger-related topics).

Events we perceive as violations and injustices naturally evoke anger. Maybe we were lied to. Maybe we were abused. Maybe we were neglected. A violation occurs when an agreement is broken, or when someone inflicts harm upon us or on others. Verbal violations include unkind words, harsh criticism, and lies. Certain actions can also be violations, such as when someone infringes on our personal space or flagrantly deceives us. Discrimination, neglect, unreasonable punishments, crimes, economic inequities, and even natural disasters are just a few examples of injustices. Violations and injustices are an inescapable part of life.

Years of suppressing anger has led to withdrawing in cold resentment, flashing looks of contempt, lashing out with cruel words and actions or even violence. Anger is strong energy in the body, and the best way to douse the firestorm is to constructively move it out of our bodies physically. When we do, we're too tired to argue and have more room for authentic, intimate contact. We can communicate from that place, and gracefully accept other people's differences. We'll enjoy our lives more if we hang out in love. When we tap into our hearts, it becomes clear there's no difference between us and them.

Some people, especially women, have a history of being subjected to misdirected anger. This history elicits so much trepidation that they may reject the very idea of expressing anger. Others consider anger to be unfeminine or unspiritual, believing they should be able to transcend their emotions. Regardless of your bias, find a constructive, physical release for anger that best accommodates your own style. Do what you secretly yearn to do with sustained gusto. You'll be amazed by the effects!

When you start to notice you repeatedly feel frustrated, find your negativity building, or a judgmental voice ridiculing everything in sight, recognize these as signs that it's time to get rid of some anger. Regardless of your age or physical condition, select an out-of-the-way place and activity that can work for you. Even if you are physically limited or delicate, you can find a constructive way to express this energy outwardly, such as loudly screaming wordless sounds or words like "broccoli" or "Hawaii."

How to Pound Constructively

I first saw people pounding on old telephone books at a Dr. Elizabeth Kubler-Ross workshop in the late seventies. She successfully incorporated the active release of anger into her groundbreaking work on death and dying because she understood the necessity of embracing our emotions and moving them out of our bodies in order to heal.

If you're an adventure athlete thinking you properly release your frustrations on the obstacle course, think again. Exercising or working out regularly, even excessively, only dissipates a small amount of anger energy because the repetitive movements of most exercises are vastly different from the erratic expression of true anger. Visualize you're 5-years-old again and having a meltdown over the Mr. Potato Head at the toy store. With the same intensity, express your anger by pushing, yelling, pounding, stomping, or kicking something inanimate until you feel exhausted. The operative words are "hard, fast, and with abandon." Simply make sure that no one and nothing of worth is damaged. Remember that emotions are wordless — you're just releasing the energy of the emotion through sound and movement.

Set aside some time, and in a place where you feel comfortable, do one or more of the following:

- Push hard against a doorjamb, fireplace mantle, or wall with the full weight of your entire body.
- Scream or yell into a pillow with all your might.
- Take a twenty-inch piece of garden hose or flexible tubing (available in the plumbing section of your local hardware store) and destroy a stack of phone books by pounding on them.
- Wrap both hands at shoulder height along the side of an open door and vigorously move it back and forth on its hinges.
- Punch the air with your fists.
- Lie on your back on a bed and flail your arms, legs, and head.
- Tear up old magazines.
- Put a towel in your teeth and pull, growling like a dog.
- Strike a bed, sofa, or old cushion with a plastic bat, bataca, or tennis racket.
- Pound a boxer's heavy bag (use gloves to prevent injury).
- Stomp on empty cardboard boxes.
- Get in your car, shout, beat the seat, or push against the steering wheel (not while driving).
- Make loud sounds, or say and think, **"It's okay. I feel angry. I just need to pound."**

Regardless of what method you try, think of it as an emotional fitness regimen and go at it until there's no anger left. Break a sweat! When you feel exhausted, catch your breath, and then do it again. You may need to go at it for five to seven rounds. Do this until the anger is completely gone, or until you experience an obvious release — a divine shift. If uncertain, go one more round for good measure and see how you feel the next day. Make sure to use both arms equally to protect your back and shoulders from injury.

You can do something less primal to dispel the energy, like vigorously throwing rocks into a lake or open field, or smash tennis balls hard against a wall without windows. Pound on dough or clay. Yank weeds. (Be extremely careful, however, about using sharp equipment such as an ax or shovel!) The salient point is to constructively move the energy hard, fast, and with abandon until you're genuinely tired. The next morning, you'll discover muscles you never knew you had! These physical effects will be a virtuous reminder of why you feel so much better.

As with crying, what you think and say while expressing anger is of utmost importance. Limit your words to describing the emotion and how you feel. Stick to such statements as:

- **I feel angry.**
- **I feel frustrated.**
- **I just need to move this energy out.**

Avoid swearing, name-calling, or condemning ("You shouldn't have done that," "She's a tramp"). No matter how much you pound, if you continue to target your anger at other people or situations, you will only fan its flames and miss the liberating experience of a physical release. If you say anything, repeat a statement that contradicts your negative thinking, such as **"People and things are the way they are, not the way I want them to be"** (a phrase coined by Dr. Albert Ellis, a pioneer in the field of cognitive behavioral psychology).

Shivering

Sam Shivers

Sam was a "fear man." He obsessed about the future, especially what might happen at work. He lay in bed at night and conjured up all the things that could go wrong. Sam couldn't see that he was driven by fear until he realized how much of his attention was focused on dreading days to come. Sam was wound up like a clock, viewing the future "like an enemy or something."

One night, Sam bolted out of bed. His heart raced, palms were sweating and waves of nervousness surged through his body, head to toe. He was overloaded. Instead of pacing around the house and worrying about the next day as he usually did, Sam shivered it off in fewer than three minutes. As he told me, "That's right, I stood up and shook, wiggled, and jumped until I felt the fear drain right out of me. Then I went back to bed, feeling light, relaxed, even cozy, knowing everything was really all right. I immediately fell into a deep sleep."

Now, no matter where Sam is, when he notices that he is talking, thinking, or moving too fast, he lets himself shudder for a few seconds. "Like a dog shaking water off, I shake off my fear," he told me. "It transforms me instantly, every time."

Remember that little metal lunchbox and the chocolate milk cartons? You probably wish you could say your first day of school was as memorable. For many of us, the first time the yellow bus dropped us off at the 'big school' was terrifying. Perhaps we even trembled uncontrollably. It only took a few comments or a disapproving look to conclude that fear was an emotion to hide. We quickly learned to pretend not to be afraid, in order to escape ridicule. The reality is that fear is an innate reaction to perceived threats to our physical survival. For example, when our plane goes through severe turbulence, it triggers our survival instinct. For some of us, taking an entrance exam or giving a presentation is enough to make us break out into a sweat or have nervous coughing fits in the bathroom. It seems reasonable to think that we should be able to get through ordinary life events without fear and that only severe trauma and violence warrant being scared. But that's not real. What is real, are feelings of panic or terror, even if others downplay the threat. This is especially true for those with a fear constitution.

Shiver. It's a universal practice. That's what the Bushmen of the Kalahari do before heading out on a hunt. It is also prescribed as part of the ritual ceremonies performed by indigenous shaman to heal the sick. It's part of the war dance that Native American warriors used to do before battle. It's becoming a current practice, too. Bradford Keeney, Ph.D., is a renowned scholar, therapist, and shaman who advocates "shaking medicine" as a way to heal physical and mental ailments — that is, moving the fear energy until there is deep relaxation. Dance events, raves, and rock concerts are unknowing ways people seek to shake out their bottled-up emotional energy.

Instead of releasing fear, we generally hold our breath and attempt to keep functioning, tightening up rather than letting the sensation out. We freeze. We're paralyzed. We become frantic. This was Sam's problem. His unresolved fear spawned doubt, confusion, and indecision. It led to rushing and feeling overwhelmed and anxious (Part III, Chapter 3 addresses the full range of fear-based attitudes.)

What is your body telling you when you feel jittery or wired? You're feeling fear. Think again of how pets act during fireworks or when strangers are present. I watch my cat quiver in fear upon hearing the garbage man rattle the cans. People experience the same kind of physical reactions to fear as animals. Our bodies instantaneously shiver when we perceive danger or are thrown into shock. I recently witnessed uncontrollable fear as a client of mine sat on the couch and heard his wife say she wanted a divorce. His legs shook like leaves on a tree.

Regardless of the cause, when you feel nervous or agitated, tap into that physical, emotional reaction, and let your body do what is natural. Give yourself permission to vigorously tremble, and the wordless energy of fear will quiver itself right on out of your body. Within a minute or two, calming energy will flow through you. It might be subtle at first. Keep going. Eventually, you'll come to remember everything is okay. You're going to be all right.

How to Shiver Constructively

No matter what your physical condition, you can shake and shiver. Some of us may be a little stiff, and most a little self-conscious about shivering. Make it a fun experience! To get started, simulate a quivering movement. Isolate your body parts, focusing on shivering in each section. Tremble up your spine, out your arms, hands, legs, feet, shoulders, head, jaw, and neck. Intensify the movements for several seconds or, better yet, for a few minutes. With practice, the motion becomes spontaneous. Your body recognizes these movements: they feel natural because it's what you were designed to do.

Keep going. It's okay to laugh. Nervous laughter loosens the tightness and releases the fear underneath your anxiety or embarrassment.

Here are some tips for releasing fear physically and constructively:

- Jiggle, shimmy, quiver, tremble, and quake.

- Mobilize all parts of your body, including your neck and jaw.

- Keep your eyes open so you don't lose your balance.

- Put on music and shake all over.

- Exaggerate the wild movements. Make them hard and fast.

- Shiver with abandon (but be careful not to hurt yourself).

- Make high-pitched sounds: "Eek!" Laugh.

- Repeat, "**I feel scared. It's okay. I just need to shake.**"

Shiver like you have ants in your pants. No joke. Try to imitate it. You might feel silly at first, but just gaining that momentum will start an avalanche. If necessary, hold on to something stable, lie down, or sit. If vigorously shivering your neck gives you a headache, hold it relaxed and upright and simply shake your legs, arms, hands, and spine. The operative words for releasing anger also apply to fear: "hard, fast, and with abandon." No holds barred. Accentuate the movement and use different body parts. But please, keep your eyes open so you maintain your balance. If you need prompting, think about something uncomfortable like hearing fingernails run up a blackboard or talking in front of a large audience. As your body shakes, stick to acknowledging what you're feeling or naming the emotion:

- **I'm feeling afraid.**
- **I feel scared.**
- **It's just fear.**
- **It's okay to feel my fear.**
- **I just need to shiver.**

Thinking reassuring thoughts during and after shivering will help to restore your perspective and peace. Try a phrase such as **"Everything is all right. Everything will be all right."**

You can shudder anytime, any place. Try it *before* doing something you find scary, such as speaking up about something controversial or competing in a contest. Do it *after* something scary, such as seeing someone in a rage or falling off a ladder. And do it *during* a scary moment, like hearing a noise when you're alone at night or watching a frightening movie. People whose very survival has been threatened, such as survivors of a natural disaster, need to shake especially intensely and frequently until they can think about what happened without fear. (To fully process their trauma, they probably need to cry and pound to release the sadness and anger as well.)

Depending on the circumstances, you might need to postpone a full shiver until you find an appropriate place, but you can almost always let out a few "involuntary" twitches. Performers and athletes often use shaking as part of their preparation. It's not uncommon to see an actor outside of an audition room shaking like the tin man in the Wizard of Oz, rolling around, flapping their arms and legs and everything in-between. It eases their bodies and minds, allowing them to fully focus on the present and perform at their best. We all need to allow our bodies to tremble when we notice the signs of fear. If we do, we'll feel more calm and relaxed. With our senses heightened and our minds clearer, we can identify what needs attention, set a course of action, and follow through to reach our goals. And along the way, we definitely feel more peace.

The longer and harder you shiver, the more fear starts shaking loose. Shiver a little past the point where you think you're finished. Keep going longer for good measure. Sometimes a wiggle or jiggle will do. Other times, you may need to shiver many times a day for a couple of minutes.

Other Ways to Pacify Fear

Although physically expressing fear is the most efficient and natural strategy, these techniques may also help you out. Try one or more especially when shivering feels too disruptive.

- Regulate your breathing. Fear disrupts the depth and evenness of your breathing, so to get back to a peaceful rhythm take several deep, measured breaths. Put your attention on your inhalation and exhalation while thinking calming thoughts.

- Step back and witness the physical sensation of fear itself. Observe the physiology of fear without getting involved in the stories you're telling yourself. The internal sensations will pass in a few minutes. Bring your awareness to the present and pay attention to what's going on in your body. If your heart is racing, let it race. If your inhalations are quick, let them be quick. Just observe whatever happens without trying to fix it.

- Make a conscious choice not to indulge in "freak-out" thoughts that only perpetuate the fear energy. Interrupt them with reassuring statements: **"It's okay to feel fear. This feeling is temporary. I'll do what I can and the rest is out of my hands."**

- Gather information. Pertinent information reduces fear of the unknown, produces valuable insight, and clarifies reality so you can determine how to handle a situation constructively.

- Seek nurturing comfort from others. It's okay to ask for help. You allow others the opportunity to support you, which can bring them joy and love. Genuine reassurances from loving people provide feelings of safety. Like a healing salve, an accepting demeanor and reassuring words can diffuse fear and create a state of ease.

EMOTIONS

- Take action. Instead of stewing in your juices and creating more fear, do something little, even if it's not perfect. Put an end to your immobility. Doing something rather than nothing will at least get you off the sidelines.

Joy, Love, and Peace Boosters

Joy Happens Even in the Midst of Grief

Frank, a man in his early seventies, lost his wife unexpectedly. He did his mourning: crying buckets of tears, attending a hospice support group, and seeing me regularly. After a while, he realized as hard as it was to imagine, he needed to resume some activities that he enjoyed. He started by rejoining his hiking club, getting small glimpses of the joy that nature once brought him. A month later, he pushed himself to start traveling, beginning with short trips to see old friends whom he dearly loved. Although he missed his wife terribly, gradually he understood he was still alive and needed to continue activities that brought him pleasure. His range of interests eventually broadened, and Frank learned how to balance his pain with his essential love of life, and his sadness with his joy.

Freely and physically expressing your sadness, anger, and fear is like taking the Yellow Brick Road to joy, love, and peace. The wonderful thing about these emotions is that they are contagious. Just by watching someone being surprised, seeing people reunited after a long separation, or being around a calm teacher, we can experience their emotional state.

Joy, love, and peace or a combination of the three can be triggered by specific events or by engaging in uplifting activities with a focus on the present. You'll treat yourself well, increase the good vibes you feel, and influence the world around you each time you engage in activities that elevate your state. A few examples include:

- Engaging in a constructive activity, whether it's gardening, dancing, or playing a game

- Indulging in pleasurable activities such as cooking or sex

- Recollecting cherished memories, such as the affection of our peers when we lead a team to victory

- Focusing on uplifting images like nature photographs, art, or holy symbols

- Being in nature

- Taking care of pets and other people

- Reading inspiring stories, poetry, and scriptures that glorify universal truths

- Engaging in spiritual practices, such as prayer, chanting, meditation, yoga, or martial arts

- Repeating and contemplating the very words joy, love, and peace, because they will fill us with the experience of their meaning.

We jump for joy, we double over in uncontrollable laughter, we squeal with delight. Joy is a physical experience in our bodies. Try on some joy-makers such as amazing art, inspiring music, healthy exercise, and tasks done well. Thrills and robust laughter spontaneously arise from watching the innocence of children and animals, becoming absorbed in any kind of creative project, or winning a prize. Dancing, singing, spotting a beautiful bird, running with a loved one through a summer rain, our bodies hum with pure bliss.

When we experience the unity that resides underneath all differences, feeling love is natural. This connection with another human being blossoms through acts of giving, affection, and tenderness. Love is kindled when we unselfishly cooperate with others, lend our help to a person or cause, or take time to genuinely understand another person's position. Forgiveness, gratitude, compassion, generosity, and unequivocal trust all evoke rolling, warm waves of love in our bodies that ripple out into our world.

We can invite peace into our lives at any time by making mindful choices that honor our intuition and are beneficial to the greater whole. We feel peace when we're in a non-threatening and nurturing environment where security and trust is a given. Think of being back home after a long time away, smelling home-cooked food wafting through the house, hearing familiar laughter, getting big, warm hugs from those who know everything about you and love you anyway. Likewise, when we intentionally engage in activities that quiet our thoughts and soothe our bodies, such as massage or meditation, we feel peace fill us.

Big Picture Thoughts about Emoting

Before concluding the topic of emotions, I want to look at Attitude Reconstruction's approach to expressing emotions within the context of other philosophies and schools of thought. Through the last centuries, the Western attitude regarding emotions amounts pretty much to plain denial, and many people still choose that mindset.

In the sixties and seventies, it became popular to let it all hang out, to let the emotions fly, regardless of the repercussions — the wilder, louder, and more dramatic, the better. But that philosophy was replaced in some circles by a spiritual stance suggesting we needed to "just breathe" and witness the sensations in our bodies without giving voice to them. Attitude Reconstruction is rooted in the belief that we need to give ourselves permission to express our emotions in a physical but constructive way to validate them and ourselves. The benefits are many, and you'll experience overall good health by reducing illnesses caused by bottling up emotions or tamping them down with alcohol or drugs.

Don't underestimate the power of emoting. You may think it sounds simple. But it's a powerful and profound tool, and particularly effective in dealing with physical conditions. Recently, a client who came to see me for anger management told me that pounding a punching bag with a plastic bat on a regular basis had not only dissolved his anger energy, but had also led to a significant decrease in his high blood pressure. Another client shared that giving herself permission to cry, pound, and shiver had remarkably reduced her longstanding intense headaches. I wasn't surprised; frequent and intentional emotional release unfailingly allows the entire body to come back into balance.

Contrary to our expectations, the people around us appreciate seeing us handling our emotions responsibly. Young children, in particular, will be delighted to see you take a hose to a stack of telephone books or find other creative ways to let your anger fly instead of yelling at them about too many hours of video games. So you can save your offspring and others around you from excruciating unhappiness if you legitimize the expression of emotions as a normal human activity. Constructive emoting is a precious legacy that you can pass on to your children, loved ones and everyone else you meet. If you model constructive emoting, you can lead your household, friends, and acquaintances to joy, love, and peace by example.

A safe space to emote is as essential as a bathroom. I contend that all public and private institutions, including homes, schools, workplaces, hospitals, and prisons need a designated room where people can cry, wail, pound, push, and shiver freely. The constructive expression of anger on a mass scale would do wonders to reduce negativity, violence, and abuse in the world. Releasing fear physically would bring clarity and calm. And more constructive crying would increase everyone's ability to connect to his/her true self.

Hey, Jude!

1. *Are you saying that the only way to handle my emotions is to express them?*

No, but it's the fastest and most direct way. Some people resolve their emotions by talking about their conflicts until they come to a satisfying resolution. Others have laughing fits. Still others release emotional energy through free-form singing or dancing. Any activity can be effective if it truly dissipates the pure emotional energy in a nondestructive way.

2. *I'm confused about when to express my emotions in my everyday life. Any suggestions?*

The trick is getting good at knowing when you need to emote. Certain bodily sensations or feelings (e.g., spacing out, becoming impatient, having a tight stomach, or a surge of heat) indicate that you're feeling some emotions. Negative repetitive thoughts such as berating yourself, worrying, or making negative judgments are also cues. You'll get better at recognizing the signs, and you can stop to emote before you revert to familiar forms of distraction.

3. I'm afraid someone will hear me pounding telephone books and call the police. Is there something less noisy I can do?

Your ability to release anger will be compromised if you're concerned about the effect of the noise. I suggest you dedicate an area to your emotional fitness training. Where can you safely go and not disrupt others? The garage? Back bedroom? Have a little talk with the people living nearby so they don't think your life is in danger and become alarmed. If this feels too personal to share with a neighbor, reduce the noise by trading the telephone book for your mattress. Or try pounding the air, lying on a bed and thrashing your arms and legs, or shaking a door on its hinge.

4. When I heard that my friend had had a serious accident I felt very sad, but I couldn't cry. Why?

The sadness isn't going to go away on its own. Believing it will is just going to make things harder in the future. Unexpressed emotions pile up, and we start to feel bad about ourselves. Those voices become stronger and bigger and louder than anything else. You have lost sight of the severity of your friend's accident and deny something has happened. Remind yourself, **"I'll feel better if I cry. It's okay. I just feel sad."** Set aside some time to acknowledge your friend's situation. Think about the particulars. Putting yourself in her shoes will bring up sadness, anger, and fear. Shiver about what it would mean if it were you. If you find yourself resisting, be gentle but persistent, and you'll tap into your sadness.

5. My adolescent son is beating up other kids at school, and I'm at a loss about what to do.

All children have reasons to feel angry, because injustices and violations are part of being alive. Your son has decided to deal with his anger by acting out against his peers. He needs a physical outlet for his anger that neither gets him in trouble nor hurts others or himself. If your child learns to vent his emotions physically and constructively, he will be more likely to talk about what's really bothering him. It's likely he doesn't even know either, or might not be able to confide in you unless you take a stance of genuinely listening to what he has to say. When he does speak, patiently listen to what's going on in his world. After plenty of uninterrupted listening, you'll discover the source of his emotions and together can find a workable solution.

6. *Before big golf tournaments, I get so anxious that my hands get numb and I feel like I'm going to throw up. Do you have a suggestion?*

Absolutely. Shiver. Golfers, swimmers, game-show participants, debaters — anyone in a big competition should do some shivering to stay present and alert.

7. *Is laughter an emotional release?*

Yes. There are many varieties of laughter, and all of them dissipate some emotional energy. (Laughing therapy isn't getting popular without reason! We all need to laugh more!) Laughing is a wordless physical expression for every emotion except sadness — though sometimes people laugh in the midst of crying when recalling a story about a loved one who has died. Nervous laughter is a release for fear. Sarcastic laughter is a release for anger. Genuine melodious laughter expresses joy and love. Opening your mouth and letting out the sounds of joy can open almost every door that's been closed to you. A peaceful chuckle indicates that we relish the humor and unfathomable nature of life.

8. *I've seen several therapists, but still haven't gotten any resolution about my parents' divorce.*

The trauma of your parents' divorce is lodged inside you. If you ignore the emotional component of specific past events, it's going to show back up one way or another. Few treatments put sufficient emphasis on releasing emotions physically. Keep talking about how you remember feeling back then, and when emotions begin to surface, let them come out. Emotions are at the root of virtually all psychological issues, and honoring them is a necessary part of the healing process.

9. *What if I feel weird or have intense images while I emote?*

You might experience powerful thoughts or images in the process of physically expressing your emotions. They can be distractions or revelations. Emoting is not the time to get cerebral or intellectual. Being a member of MENSA isn't going to help your cause while crying, pounding or shivering. However, while your muscles, heart rate, breathing, and entire body rests between rounds of expressing your emotions, it can be revealing to go back and note any thoughts that surfaced.

10. *I cry often, usually when I feel sad or watch a romantic movie. But I also cry when I'm really angry or even really happy.*

Crying is actually a physical expression of every emotion except, perhaps, peace. If you already cry often — lucky you! You have given yourself permission to cry when you feel touched. Tears keep your heart open, provided that you think constructive thoughts when you cry. Be aware, however, that you may have anger or fear waiting to be acknowledged and expressed.

11. *My sister yells at me all the time. What's her problem?*

When your sister feels angry and takes it out on you, remember that her emotions belong to her. You're not the cause, no matter how much she says the opposite. External people and events are just convenient triggers for her stored-up anger. What other people think of you is none of your business. Don't take it personally. Don't try to be logical. Walk away. Cry if you feel hurt.

12. *How can my partner and I get our anger out together?*

When you are both calm, decide what you'll do at times when you are upset. One way is to have two stacks of phone books and simultaneously pound the heck out of them. It's the perfect thing to do when tempers flare. If you're an adventuresome couple who want to drain your anger buckets together in a way guaranteed to foster love, I suggest that you stand with your arms fully extended at shoulder height, facing each other. Use your legs to brace yourself (the physically weaker partner can use a wall for added support). Make sure both of you are ready before you push against each other's hands while making sounds of anger. Don't try to manhandle your partner. You're not trying to overpower them. Both people are simply moving their anger energy out by pushing against one another. To take this exercise a quantum leap further, I encourage you to shout, **"I love you"** at the same time!

13. *What does Attitude Reconstruction say about emotions and dreams?*

Your emotional condition is mirrored in your dream life. A dream can send you a message before you even realize what you're feeling. Dreams are rich repositories of information if you're willing to look at what can sometimes be really erratic or crazy concoctions of scenes! Attitude Reconstruction doesn't analyze the storylines or symbolic meanings of dreams too much. Rather, it focuses on a dream's emotional flavor. A dream is a reliable indicator of what is currently going on in your emotional body, and it points to what kind of emoting would be beneficial to you. A dream in which you're frantically running through the airport points to fear; acts of violence indicate anger; a happy, carefree dream reflects joy; and a feeling of being safe and nurtured indicates peace. If you dream you get what you've always wanted and then wake up feeling sad because you don't have it in real life, that might mean you need to cry and mourn so you can embrace what is, or that you need to change your situation to get more of what you need.

14. *Can emoting help my PMS (premenstrual syndrome)?*

Absolutely. If you undergo a radical personality change before your menstrual period, move that hard-to-be-around, testy energy out with some major pounding on telephone books. If you tend to get hypersensitive or super vulnerable, devote some extra time to crying constructively, and that heavy sensation in your heart will recede. Emoting will help you feel more "normal" again.

15. I'm experiencing PTSD (post-traumatic stress disorder). What would Attitude Reconstruction suggest?

Here's a situation that calls for professional help, extra social support, and tons of emoting. Whatever the trauma, whether it's a natural disaster, sexual assault, or military combat, there is a lot of unexpressed fear. Shiver as you recount the event(s), or what you remember so far. You probably also feel a great deal of anger at the injustices you witnessed and sadness at the losses and hurts. If you keep talking and emoting in a protected environment, over time, your mind will slowly integrate what happened, and you'll find your symptoms lessen and the events lose their charge.

16. What emotions are associated with great sex?

Sexual intimacy is a potentially great activity for joy, love, and peace. Joy at pleasure; love at connection, openness, and selfless giving; peace at feeling safe and playful in the present. Rigid roles, expectations, and routines exponentially diminish the possibility for these emotions.

17. Is there a correlation between different kinds of illnesses and unexpressed emotions?

There is more and more evidence stating that when we don't deal with our emotions constructively, they manifest in our bodies physically. Ayurvedic medicine from India views diseases in terms of the three doshas (Kapha, Pitta, and Vata) being out of balance. I suggest that sadness, anger, and fear influence our bodies and minds in the same way. Check out the table in the appendix where I've listed some of the diseases and illnesses associated with each of the doshas and emotions.

2

Thoughts: Rewiring the Electrical System

Honor yourself.
Accept people and situations.
Stay present and specific.

Your inner electrical system is a complex collection of love-makers and war-mongers. Its intricate connections allow you to view the world and communicate your interpretations at the speed of light. You jettison throughout time and space, living whatever reality you choose in any moment. It's unparalleled technology, and something to harness with care and reverence.

You're starting to install a new program into the motherboard. You're looking inside your body, feeling the emotional sensations, and giving them names. You know how to express sadness, anger, and fear physically and constructively. You've got a priceless tool in the toolkit and are ready to add another one. Next on board, tool number two: your thoughts.

I gave you some examples of the most expressive (and fastest) ways to emote constructively through clean crying, pounding, and shivering. But sometimes, it's not convenient, appropriate, or safe to emote. If it's more comfortable for you (or perhaps the only option) to work on a cognitive level, it's fine. That's why this chapter is about thoughts.

Maybe you're a little too familiar with that onslaught of mean comments swirling around your head, getting louder the angrier you feel. You might be finding yourself ruminating a bad business decision, rehashing the reasons why it happened and what you could have done differently. You just can't let it go, even when everyone is begging you to. Reflecting on past events can help you learn from mistakes and move into positive action in the future, but not if you're making yourself a monster in the meantime. This section is dedicated to getting you out of the mental trap, that steel padlock that keeps your best self under lock and key. You'll learn how to harness the power of your thoughts to come back to the three constructive ultimate attitudes: (1) honor yourself, (2) accept people and situations, and (3) stay present and specific.

Sound difficult? You're already doing it! Thinking is something we do all the time — even when we don't think we're thinking. We evaluate, organize, and plan. You already know how much easier life is when you have those skills as companions. Those kinds of thoughts are constructive and necessary, but there is another kind of thinking — a running commentary that plays inside our heads — that is neither helpful nor necessary. This self-defeating mental chatter, self-talk, or old tape recording, is born of unexpressed sadness, anger, and fear.

People of all cultures and classes talk to themselves in the same way. You're not alone. Regardless of what we're doing, we spew out an endless litany of complaints, excuses, put-downs, and fantasies. Depending on our unresolved emotions, we repeat certain predictable thoughts. We might tell ourselves, "I'm always screwing up" whenever we start to feel sadness. Or if it's anger, we might think, "That person is such a jerk." With fear, we might repeatedly chant, "This is too overwhelming. I can't handle everything I've got to do."

Mental monologues may be the way you try to keep sane, but they numb you out or push you over the edge so you can't relax in the here and now. They affect how you feel, speak, and act. Let me give you a couple of examples. My client Kay was reeling after being passed over for five different jobs she considered herself perfectly qualified for. Kay told herself, "I must not have been well enough prepared. They must have felt that I wasn't smart enough." This kind of thinking spawned such self-doubts that Kay was afraid to go on another interview. When she did, she found herself tongue-tied, struggling with questions she knew the answers to. Her self-esteem plummeted even further, and she slid into feeling depressed.

Kay's reaction reminded me of a former boss of mine who dealt with setbacks in the opposite way. A true scientist, he handled roadblocks to his research projects with a grin and a wink. He stayed positive even when he got ambiguous results, seeing them as vital data for designing his next study. Whenever difficulties arose, he looked at them as chances to learn something new. "Research is all about learning," he'd say. "A few 'lost' weeks are worth it if they eventually put us on the right track." His coworkers found his optimism so infectious, they adopted his upbeat attitude and became skilled at looking for creative solutions to so-called obstacles in their own work.

As these examples demonstrate, how you think about your experience affects what you feel, say, and do. If your thoughts can cause you to feel bad, they can also cause you to feel good. You're about to transform your destructive core attitudes. Rewiring will make you an anchorman or anchorwoman who consciously chooses a constructive voiceover for your life's news.

You Choose How You Think

Was it a good experience or a waste of time? Is that overtime bothering you or are you reminded how blessed you are to have a fat check coming in? Are you bummed out because it's a rainy day or happy snuggling up in your pj's and watching 'ET' again? What you make of every situation is ultimately up to you, and you get a hundred opportunities a day to look at things positively or negatively. Even when circumstances are beyond your control, and you're convinced you don't have a choice how to react, you absolutely do.

THOUGHTS

Here's an everyday example: Imagine you have just a few minutes left to mail an important package that must go out today. When you enter the post office, there's a long line of customers and only two clerks. How you interpret this situation will differ depending on your past experiences, current condition, and basic emotional constitution. If you are feeling great, you'll be flexible enough to flow with the circumstances. You'll automatically tell yourself, "**There's enough time. This is not a life-or-death situation**." But if you come in carrying unexpressed emotions along with your package, you'll most likely react in one of three ways.

- **1. Sadness.** You sigh, shake your head, and with a look of resignation, trudge away. Then you begin to berate yourself: "I'm such a dope. I should have known better and gotten here earlier. I'm never going to get my act together." Lingering sadness forces you to see the situation as too big and to focus negatively on yourself.

- **2. Anger.** You swear (only half under your breath), join the line, and start on a tirade about the decline of the postal system with the person in front of you. Your mental and verbal barrage includes: "They should have more clerks. These people are so incompetent. Our postal system is a joke." This voice of unresolved anger will cause you to judge other people and situations in a less-than-favorable light. Your anger not only makes your wait unpleasant, but also infects the people around you, who start to feel irritated at having to listen to you mouth off.

- **3. Fear.** You check your watch, feel the knot in your stomach tighten, and begin to panic. "I'm going to be late for my next appointment. I still have three other errands to run. What if my boss is looking for me?" In this case, fear catapults you out of present time and directly into overwhelmed mode.

You can laugh (because maybe you've been there before) but I'm sure you weren't amused at the time. In fact, I'd bet money you were absolutely miserable because none of these options improves your circumstances or your emotional state. Ideally, you'd take a moment to express some emotional energy but standing in line at the post office, probably isn't your best bet. That doesn't get you off the hook, however. You can always choose to change your inner state, just by replacing destructive thoughts with constructive ones.

Let's begin with the example of the angry person. You look at the queue and start to feel frustrated (anger). But then you realize that this moment is a perfect opportunity to practice a new kind of thinking that will neutralize your anger. You start repeating, **"People and things are the way they are, not the way I want them to be."** As you repeat this thought in a focused way, you notice that your aggravation dissolves. You accept the reality that there are only two clerks on duty and twenty people ahead of you. Repeating the phrase over and over, more often than not, will shift you from anger to love. There's also a good chance you'll smile, (believe it or not!) because you just saved yourself from ruining the rest of your day. Your easygoing demeanor might even prove contagious to other customers.

Rewiring Your Destructive Thinking

To uproot destructive thoughts, you must systematically replace them with their constructive opposites, a technique I call "powering." Patanjali's Yoga Sutras instruct us to focus on a single thing with devotion and a desire to experience its meaning while ignoring any intruding thoughts. Patanjali was a preeminent psychologist of ancient India, who lived sometime between 400 BC and 400 AD. During this time, Hatha Yoga practices, including meditation, physical postures, and breathing techniques became the means to attain enlightenment. Patanjali believed that transformation and liberation come through mastery of our thoughts.

Powering follows the same principles: you vigorously repeat new thoughts that contradict your old thinking while expressing any emotions that surface. Powering differs from cognitive therapy techniques because it uses both your thoughts and emotions to change how you think. In other words, you use both your heart and your head.

THOUGHTS

Powering may seem like an intellectual exercise, but repeating state-ments that contradict old mental chatter usually stirs up a whirlwind of emotions. They're often the same emotions you suppressed as a child when you first started thinking destructively. Expressing your sadness, anger, or fear physically while you power dissipates the emotional energy and loosens the rigidity of those crusty old beliefs. You'll change your current emotional state, and destructive thoughts start to weaken their grip. They retreat, and, finally, surrender. Victories will happen fairly quickly, but remember you're launching a full-blown assault on atti-tudes that have dug in their heels and plan to stay. Have your mental battle gear polished and ready because you're guaranteed to have repeat confrontations. Strap on the belt, so your tools are within easy reach. Sharpen your senses so you can pinpoint exactly what's happening in your body. And get ready for the battle of your life, because this is your life you're fighting for. You only get one (for now). And you want to make every precious moment count.

Destructive vs. Constructive Thoughts

Constructive thoughts help you rewire thinking because they're valid regardless of your current emotional, mental, or physical situation. They are the real deal. Truths are outside the black-and-white, good-and-bad polarization that characterizes destructive thoughts. They reflect what we naturally know when we're not under the influence of unexpressed sadness, anger, and fear.

For example, "**Everything is all right**" is a truth, even though you might not feel it's true if you've just found out about your husband's illicit affair with a neighbor. The whole world may seem to be crashing in, but what do you really know in the moment? You can speculate about the embarrassment you'll feel when everyone else finds out, worry how a divorce would affect the kids, or wonder how it's possible to ever make love to him again knowing where he's been. But none of that is real. It's all just story. Truths are in line with the three ultimate attitudes we want to live by: honor yourself, accept people and situations, and stay present and specific. It may take work to calm down enough to think clearly, but your trusted 'truths' will be there to help.

To get a feel for the difference between destructive and constructive thoughts, turn to **page 296** in the back of this chapter, and look at the Destructive Thoughts versus Truths chart. These are self-defeating statements I hear frequently from my clients, together with truths that oppose them. Read each list aloud to immediately get a feeling of the power of words.

Affirmations vs. Truths

As will become clear, a truth is not necessarily the exact opposite of what you're used to telling yourself. When you do something you regret, for example, you might automatically tell yourself, "I'm a loser." The accurate opposing statement is not "I'm a winner." More accurate is, "**Making mistakes is human,**" which goes beyond the loser/winner dichotomy. This statement reflects what's really true. Other possible alternatives could be: "**Life is for learning,**" "**We all make mistakes,**" or "**I did the best I could at the time.**"

Truths differ from "affirmations," because truths are undeniably true. Affirmations are often simply desires or ideals that we wish were true. Examples of affirmations are:

- I am rich and thin.
- I see only peace and love around me.
- I am over the fear that I never have enough.

Truths give you unfailing support. They'll be there to back you up when the chips are down, and you're curled up on the bathroom floor with your heart in pieces. They're more effective than affirmations because they speak what is true and real, and what we know deep inside of us when we're clear and centered. I see truths as potent medicines, each one an effective remedy for a different mental ailment. You can be your own doctor. Just as a physician diagnoses a particular ailment and prescribes a medication, you too can select a truth and heal your nonproductive thoughts.

After one remedy does its healing job, you will most likely find another destructive thought that calls for a different prescription. With practice, you can become a master physician and successfully "heal thyself."

THOUGHTS

Reliable Truths

Are you ready to select some helpful truths? Here's how: Write down a list of your most recurring negative comments. The ones you never seem to leave home without. To free yourself from your old tapes, you'll need effective contradictions for each. If you require a little assistance identifying your destructive chatter, check the left side of the Attitude Reconstruction Blueprint for some sample thoughts and see what stands out for you.

There are two ways to find replacements: either select generic "reliable truths" that oppose your destructive thinking, or construct your own truths. I'll go over them one at a time. The easiest way to find a contradiction to your old thinking is simply to pick a reliable truth from the list I've provided. They're well-worn and time-tested throughout the years by my clients, my students, and myself. This list mirrors the sentences on the right side of the Attitude Reconstruction Blueprint under "words."

Recognizing your current emotional state and where your attention is focused, makes it a lot easier to identify the kinds of truths that'll be most useful. As you will see, there are three groups of reliable truths: (1) truths about yourself that help you move from sadness to joy, (2) truths about other people and situations that help you move from anger to love, and (3) truths about time that help you move from fear to peace.

Reliable Truths

Reliable truths to honor yourself and move from sadness to joy:

- I am whole and complete.
- What I'm seeking is within me.
- My job is to take care of myself.
- I am alone, and I am connected.
- I love myself regardless of what I do.
- Life is for learning. We all make mistakes.
- I'm doing the best I can. I did the best I could.
- If I knew then what I know now, I'd have done it differently.
- My viewpoints and needs are as valid as yours.
- I am responsible for what I think, feel, and do.
- I can do this.

Reliable truths to accept people and situations and move from anger to love:

- People and things are the way they are, not the way I want them to be.
- That's the way it is.
- My job is to feel more love.
- My focus is myself.
- What he/she thinks of me is none of my business.
- He is doing the best he can. She did the best she could.
- We are all on our own paths.
- We are the same. We are all connected.
- I wish you well.
- Your viewpoints and needs are as important as mine.
- We can handle this together.

Reliable truths to stay present and specific and move from fear to peace:

- Everything is all right. Everything will be all right.
- This feeling is temporary. This situation will pass.
- Stop. Breathe. Slow down. Be here now.
- Stay specific.
- One thing at a time.
- I'll handle the future in the future.
- My actions have consequences.
- I'll do what I can, and the rest is out of my hands.
- Everything is unfolding in its own time.
- Let go.
- We'll see.

THOUGHTS

Having reliable truths geared to each of the three pairs of emotions will give you a well-stocked arsenal to battle your barrage of destructive thoughts. Look at the list of truths and choose two or three from each category that strike a chord with you.

Put them on a Pocketful of Truths Worksheet which can be found on **page 297**. You can add more Truths to this master list as you come across ones that appeal to you. Try writing your truths on note cards and put them in places where you'll see them often. Keep them in your pocket, nightstand, or day planner for easy reference. Put them in your car, purse, or on a mirror or the refrigerator.

Catherine Gives Herself a Tune-up

Catherine came in for a tune-up. It had been just over a year since I last saw her. After hearing all her glowing news, I asked, "What brings you here today?" She looked down and said, "I feel really bad about myself. I constantly compare myself to everyone. I've worked on this before, but that little voice has crept back into my head."

"Let's put your old thoughts out on the table," I said. "I'll write them down."

After a moment of silence, Catherine laughed and said, "I'm lazy. I'm weak. I lack discipline and don't follow through with commitments, like emoting semi-regularly or powering before bed. Come to think of it, there's not much that's good about me."

"Who do you sound like?" I asked.

*"I'm being as critical of myself as my stepfather was of me," Catherine said. "I hated how he continually put me down. I'd never talk to a child like that so it's probably not such a good idea to talk like that to myself. Ah! Now I'm remembering an old truth of mine: **I love myself unconditionally**." Catherine was smiling. "I feel better already."*

*Catherine had dusted off a truth that most of us could use, especially when our self-deprecating commentary begins to play: **"I love myself unconditionally**."*

Powering

To make a truth an integral part of your mental repertoire, you must saturate yourself with it by "powering". As I mentioned, powering requires gentle but tenacious repetition of your chosen truths while vigilantly ignoring any distractions. You're literally excavating ingrained messages, etched like ancient writing into your soul, and replacing them with their constructive opposites. To fully own your new thoughts, say them with genuine feeling and with an intense desire to know their meaning. For example, if you power on, "That's the way you are" when you're angry and say it with significant feeling, these words will melt your anger at some point.

There are two kinds of powering to rewire your old thinking. You can do "regular powering" where every time a destructive thought pops up, you interrupt it with a contradictory truth. Or you can do what I call "focused powering," where you repeat a truth as a focused activity for a preset amount of time, much like meditation.

Either way, powering requires devotion, conviction, persistence, and a concerted effort over time. Lip service isn't going to do it. Doggedly powering on a phrase is the only way to internalize that constructive thought so that it permeates every cell. As you power, notice what you're feeling in your body. If you're experiencing emotions, good. You're doing it correctly. You're unearthing messages internalized long ago. Laugh, cry, pound, or shiver and continue to power. Keep going. As you persist, you'll connect with what you're saying and experience a divine shift. During those moments, the truth will come alive within you from your head to your toes, creating tangible change in its wake.

Why does powering work? Powering opens the gate to honoring yourself, clear-cutting your path to accepting other people and situations, and helping you find greater enjoyment in each moment. It contradicts your destructive core attitudes, putting them in their place and forcing them to back off. I think it's worth repeating that I cheerfully tell clients that one hundred thousand repetitions should do the job (it's a conservative estimate of how often most of us have proclaimed the opposite!) The more consistently you interrupt the old and repeat the new, the sooner you'll own it. With practice you can say a truth just once or twice and shift your thinking. Until then, I recommend a merciless assault.

To do focused powering:

1. Select a truth that contradicts your old thinking. For example, if you feel overwhelmed, select a reliable truth about time to take you from fear to peace such as, "**One thing at a time.**"

2. Say your truth out loud over and over with a desire to deeply understand what you're saying. (If you find yourself shaking your head side to side as if some part of you is rejecting what you're saying, nod your head up and down.)

3. Vary your tone, inflection, volume, tempo, and speed. Slow is best, because you absorb the meaning of every word. Fast repetitions make sense when your mind is racing.

4. Once you find a truth that feels good, stick with it. Each word is important. Try placing the emphasis on different words.

5. Ignore all other thoughts and continue to repeat your truth. That means not indulging the yeah buts and oh sures that automatically arise. Treat any sounds or visual images as you would a destructive thought. Similar to meditation, focus on one thing only and gently bring your attention back to a truth whenever your mind wanders.

6. When feasible, close your eyes to reduce distractions. You'll feel the effect of what you're saying more completely.

7. If emotions arise, emote while continuing to repeat your truth.

8. Sitting or standing are the best postures, but any position will work.

9. If a truth doesn't sink in, figure out whether you're saying it half-heartedly, if you need a different truth, or if unexpressed emotions are overriding your ability to own what you're saying. Then make the necessary adjustments.

Ignore the discouraging thoughts that I assure you will arise. Be like a giant, strong elephant. As the elephant ignores a barking dog, so you can ignore your negative thoughts or other people's words or actions.

To rewire your faulty circuitry, power on a contradictory truth whenever you hear your old thoughts playing and establish a regular routine for powering as a concentrated activity. Make it a part of your day like taking vitamins or drinking enough water to stay hydrated. It takes effort to put it in the 'schedule' and make it habit, but it's worth it. Maybe powering first thing in the morning is your thing, or try it whenever you need a break or at the end of the day. 10 minutes a day in two-minute blocks works well (use a small electronic timer). Repeat a truth at least 11 times in a row for maximum results. Reciting it aloud is doubly effective, because you hear yourself verbalizing the concept that you are attempting to grasp.

Power anytime, anywhere, out loud or silently. Powering can accompany daily routines and mundane tasks, such as driving, vacuuming, shaving, or waiting in line. You can power while walking your dog or working out. Power, power, power. Power in the shower. Power when you can't sleep at night. It's more effective than counting sheep!

Rita Reclaims Herself

Rita raised six children as a single mother in an era before divorce was commonplace. Long out of the nest, her brood had spread across the country, each with families of their own. One night, her son Chris called. "You didn't allow me to show my anger as a child," he said accusatorily. "You visit my brothers and sisters more than you do me. You're the reason I'm so miserable."

The avalanche of complaints seemed to come out of left field, and was devastating. For years Rita had been guilt-ridden about the effect her divorce had had on her children. That guilt was compounded by her biggest fear: that her children would stop loving her. With Chris's call, that fear seemed to be coming true.

Rita waited for an apology, but none came. "It's been four months since the call," she said, "and I just feel so sad all the time. All I can think about is Chris. I hesitate to talk to any of my children, and when I do, I'm hypercautious. That phone call has made me see just how dependent I am on my children's approval. No, not just them — I'm actually after everyone's approval!"

Seventy years old, Rita had sacrificed her own needs out of a desire to please her children. Since she now saw that this tactic hadn't worked, she was willing to try something new. She realized that the opposite of being dependent on others for approval would be to learn to keep her focus on herself — a big but necessary task!

*Rita had suppressed many emotions throughout her life. I talked with her about their natural functions and, in particular, the value of crying. I encouraged her to shed some tears, because the rejection by Chris was both a hurt and a loss. While crying, she needed to interrupt her disparaging thoughts and remind herself, "**I just feel sad. It's okay to cry.**" We created a pocketful of truths to power on over the next days: **It's okay to cry. I'm fine. My job is to take care of myself. We are all on our own paths.** Rita repeated those words diligently.*

Over the next weeks, she talked about her progress: "Every day I set some time aside to cry and power. As I did, I felt myself detaching from my deep sorrow, as though the sadness had been stuck in my heart and somehow the tears melted the glue. Whenever I could, I would sit in my favorite chair and allow myself to cry. At first, it was difficult. However, as I persisted, I noticed my heartache slowly subsiding. It was remarkable. My energy came back, and I no longer felt so delicate.

*"I realized I had to accept the choices Chris was making and respect his path. Trying to change him was out of the question. Over and over, I had to remember that I'd raised my children as well as I could, and that they might never understand how much I'd tried. All I could do was tell myself what I so desperately wanted to hear. I worked hard on these truths: **I love myself. I did the best I could. I was and am a good mother. What my children think about me is not who I am. My job is to take care of myself.***

"Those statements rejuvenated me like rain revives a thirsty plant. I would take walks in the park and repeat the truths over and over. At first they made me cry. Then they made me smile! I can't convey how good I felt after saying these words all day long.

"Once, while I was powering, I clearly realized that all my children were in fact, creative, caring, and independent. They were living full lives as good husbands, wives, mothers, and fathers, making significant contributions to their communities. I had done a good job! I felt proud of my part. To be honest, I felt more than proud. I felt absolutely free!

"Today, whenever I start to fret about what any of my children think or say about me, I power on my truths. I'm enjoying my friends again, my hobbies, and volunteering at the hospital. I even started dating a wonderful man. No matter what happens in the future, I truly know I don't ever have to make another apology or excuse for who I am."

As Rita gave up her need for approval and accepted Chris's process, she gave him the space to come around, which he eventually did.

Powering with Others

In addition to powering alone, many people find it productive to do concentrated powering in groups. This isn't for everyone, but powering with others — a spouse, friend, family member, or group — can be surprisingly effective. There's a special kind of energy that's created when a group of people get together with the same intention. It's almost palpable. Group powering creates synergy and sets an uplifting tone for any ensuing activity, as everyone gets a connective jolt. Everyone can power on the same truth or repeat different truths. (When everyone powers on the same truth, it's not necessary to say it in unison. Repeat yours in a way that is comfortable for you.) Try powering together for just a minute, or for several blocks of one to two minutes each.

It's true that many people are initially self-conscious about voicing truths in a group. If you feel a little embarrassed, give a shiver or two, then do it anyway with the intention to really "get" what you're saying, and see what happens.

You can also try what I call "connecting powering." You repeat a truth, and another person reflects it back to you. Continue alternating.

I'm doing the best I can.

    You're doing the best you can.

I'm doing the best I can.

    You're doing the best you can.

For those who are drawn to it, connecting powering accelerates their ability to rewire old thinking.

Michael and Brittany Get on the Same Team

Michael and Brittany came in and plopped down on opposite ends of the couch. Their son, Jake, had thrown a party while they were out of town, and a neighbor called the police. Michael and Brittany disagreed about the consequences for Jake's actions. Michael was taking a very hard-line approach and felt Jake should be grounded for the rest of the semester. Brittany believed that Jake had already been punished enough by the humiliation of interrupting his parent's anniversary getaway.

*Before they could decide on a strategy for Jake, they needed to get on the same team. I suggested that they repeat the following statement out loud together about a dozen times: "**We'll come up with a solution together.**"*

*When they were done, each took a couple of minutes to voice what they'd experienced while repeating the phrase. Michael got stubborn and didn't change his position. It seemed compromise might be impossible. Michael's father had reprimanded Michael when he'd been out of line as a teenager, so he believed Jake wouldn't understand the consequences of his actions unless he was severely punished. We listened to Michael's concerns without interruption for a few minutes, and then I suggested that they repeat the phrase together again: "**We'll come up with a solution together. We'll come up with a solution together.**"*

It was then Michael understood it was going to be more beneficial to work as a team. The effect was almost magical. He extended his arm across the couch. Brittany reciprocated and they shared a sweet kiss. Now the foundation had been laid to talk about Jake and the party.

Hey, Jude!

1. There are so many truths. Where do I start?

There are an infinite number of truths because they contradict the entire range of our destructive thinking. Just pick one reliable truth that resonates, and stick with it. Or select one that honors yourself, one that accepts other people and situations, and one that pertains to staying present and specific.

2. My mental commentary is relentless. How do I get a truth to sink in?

Express some emotions! That will help you cut to the chase almost immediately. The second is to keep powering. Select a truth and immerse yourself in it as often as you can throughout the day, during preset blocks of time and any other time as needed. Designate times when you will repeat your truths such as when you first wake up, before going to bed, each time you climb stairs, or when you're waiting for a green light. Another great way to really take in what you're saying is to repeat your truths out loud, over and over, while looking at yourself in the mirror.

3. My husband can say the right thing when I'm stressed out, and it always calms me down. How can I learn to do this for myself?

I'll bet that when you're freaking out, your husband says reassuring things such as, "Everything is okay," or gives practical advice to stay specific, "Just do what you can right now." Instead of depending on your hubby to temper the atmosphere every time you feel stressed, write down what he says or pick a couple of the reliable truths that calm your fear and increase your peace. When you feel ruffled, shiver and lovingly power on your phrases, and you'll be able to reassure yourself and experience the same calming effect.

4. I tend to be really hard on myself, especially when I cry.

You're lucky that you can cry easily because tears are a great purifier that wash you clean. Keep them coming. But be sure to keep your attention on naming what you're experiencing in your body, a specific hurt or loss, or loving yourself. Your crying might intensify at first, but sooner or later you'll get that you did the best you could at the time and that you're okay no matter what.

5. *What can I do when I find myself making my grocery list while powering?*

Your mind, like everyone's, tends to wander. When you realize your focus is elsewhere, don't indulge the other thoughts. Instead, come back to repeating your truth. Try changing the speed, tempo, tone, or inflection of the words you're saying. Play with it. Repeat your truth louder and slower, with vigor and devotion. If this tactic doesn't work, consider shivering, even if you don't think you are feeling fear. Shaking will bring you back into the present. Or try powering on a truth like, "**Be here now.**" If a certain thought consistently pops up, check to see if you need a truth to combat it.

6. *I started to feel faint when I powered for about half an hour. Am I doing something wrong?*

Feeling faint or tired is an indicator that you're about to make a breakthrough. It's as if you are frying some of your old circuitry. However, make sure to remember to breathe normally when you power and don't hyperventilate or hold your breath. Stretch your body and walk around, getting some fresh oxygen into your lungs. Drink some water. Shiver. Take full, deep breaths and remind yourself, "**It's okay. This feeling will pass.**" When you no longer feel lightheaded, go back to what you were originally powering on.

7. *Is powering like meditation?*

Focused powering is similar to meditation in some ways, in that you stay gently and firmly focused on one object or phrase and continually turn your attention away from what's going on in and around you. But it differs from most meditation in that you speak a truth out loud and you know the meaning of what you are saying. Another difference is that you select a particular truth to neutralize your specific emotions, fit your actual situation, and produce a constructive effect.

8. Can you elaborate on the philosophy behind Patajali's Yoga Sutras that you referred to earlier?

Patajali's Yoga Sutras, his aphorisms, are the foundation of powering. They provide instruction on how to quiet our minds, change our thinking, and realize our fullest potential. According to Patanjali's Yoga Sutras:

- To be free from thoughts that distract one from yoga, thoughts of an opposite kind must be cultivated. (Sutra II:33)

- Repeat it and contemplate upon its meaning. (Sutra I:28)

- Practice becomes firmly grounded when it has been cultivated for a long time, uninterruptedly, with earnest devotion. (Sutra I:14)

As you repeat an eternally true statement aloud while focusing on its meaning and ignoring all other thoughts that arise, your mind's chatter will subside. You'll experience a profound shift to clarity.

Custom High-Voltage Rewiring

You're gaining ground on the battlefield, and the enemy is starting to retreat. Each time destructive thinking advances, you fight back with all you've got, a strike here, a strike there. Those old thoughts are taking a beating. You're scraping, burning, and cutting gashes into their best lineup. You're beginning to rip their strongest patterns apart. But don't be fooled. They'll regroup with a surprise attack the moment you turn your back. You can fight back better and faster by customizing your weapons, thereby leveling the playing field. That's what this chapter is all about.

Now that you're clear on replacing destructive thinking by powering on reliable truths, it's time to up the ante. I'm going to explain how to build your own truths so you have spot-on antidotes for your particular mental chatter. You'll also find lists of additional time-tested truths to keep you grounded, support you in taking action in challenging areas, and connect you with your spiritual beliefs.

The more you power, the less mental airtime will be occupied by your destructive messages, and the more often you will find yourself in the vicinity . The next time you feel sad, angry, or afraid, you can indulge your old thinking or choose to promote your own happiness.

Think of your truths as trusty companions. Repeat them until they outshine your stockpile of old messages. Just find the contradiction to your current mental chatter and practice, practice, practice. Rewiring involves waging a battle — remembering to power, forgetting, and remembering again.

Adam Learns How to Accept What Is

Adam came in angry. He was fed up with everything that happened in the last week and even considering leaving his job. We re-wound the clock back through time to when his anger began: his boss went on vacation and had handed over all responsibility to him. That specific event had triggered his mood.

Before Adam could get some clarity about his work situation, he needed to accept the current reality. He had pulled a muscle in his shoulder while mountain biking the previous day, so he wasn't up for pounding phone books. I encouraged him to growl for a couple of minutes to mobilize his energy. At first he resisted (and came up with some of those creative excuses you've smiled at earlier), but when he finally tried it, he started to laugh. Growling made him feel better.

Then I asked Adam to tell me all the things that were really bothering him about work. "Got a huge piece of paper? There are a million things that drive me crazy." I took out my pad of graph paper and wrote down the items he rattled off:

1. People blame others for their problems.
2. Coworkers and clients don't do what they're supposed to.
3. The temperature in the office is too cold.

4. *My boss left a mess for me to deal with.*

5. *I can't do everything.*

6. *Margaret never gets her paperwork done on time.*

7. *My secretary makes questionable decisions.*

8. *People leave their trash in the coffee room.*

9. *Colin is always negative.*

It was time to begin rewiring Adam's old thinking. In this case, he started with a reliable truth: **That's the way it is.** *I suggested we go right through his list and apply this truth to each of his complaints to reflect an attitude of acceptance.*

We began with the first item. **"People blame others for their problems. That's the way it is."** *Adam began to repeat this statement, but resisted the reality. He repeated the sentences at least a dozen times until he quit resisting and "got" it. He smiled and said,* **"People do blame others for their problems."** *Now we were ready to move on to the next item.*

"Coworkers and clients don't do what they're supposed to. That's so true. Clients and coworkers don't do what they're supposed to." *I could hear in the tone of his voice that he was beginning to understand. We moved on.*

He continued like this with each item that bugged him. As he worked on accepting that his secretary made questionable decisions, his eighth complaint, Adam experienced a divine shift. "I know I'm not ready to quit my job," he said. "I really do like my coworkers, and most of the time we work well together. I'm just under a lot of pressure right now because my boss is out of town. You know what? **That's the way it is. People and things are the way they are."**

Several months later, I ran into him at the grocery store. Without any prompting, he said, "I can't tell you what a difference that acceptance session made in all areas of my life. Whenever I take the time to power on those acceptance truths, I can feel my anger dissolve. I realized that I have a choice whether or not to feed my anger monster."

Customizing Reliable Truths

Assault your self-imposed sadness, anger, and fear by making up your own truths. One way to do this is to customize reliable truths such as, **"People and things are the way they are, not the way I want them to be,"** to help you better accept a specific person, thing, or situation. For example:

- **My car is running the way it is, not the way I want it to.**
- **Laura is the way she is, not the way I think she should be.**
- **Our legal system is the way it is, not the way I think it should be.**

Acceptance is not passivity. It invites clarity, empathy, and compassion — qualities and attitudes associated with love. You accept the reality and then, from this centered place, determine what needs to be said or done to honor yourself and the situation. When you determine what's appropriate, you'll be able to speak up and take action from a loving rather than angry stance. For example, accepting your spouse's snoring means the next time he does, you won't be angry and want to pummel him. You can figure out what might work instead, like going to the guest room so you don't have to listen to his snore concert.

Any reliable truth can be finessed in order to reflect your vocabulary, mindset, or situation. Sometimes it means starting with phrasing that feels more immediate and building towards a reliable truth. Suppose you have a tendency to make snap negative judgments about people. These judgments are born of unresolved anger. It can be difficult to leap from biting words directly into acceptance. Let's say your initial reaction to an unshaven and shabbily dressed person is, **"He should have more self-respect."** You may find the phrase **"We are all the same"** too far a stretch, so start with **"I don't know his situation."** After you've powered on that for a while, you might be ready to switch to **"Everybody does things their own way."** Then you can say, **"We all have our own idiosyncrasies,"** before you finally can take on **"We are all the same."**

Contemporaries, pundits, or clergy may offer some inspiration in helping to personalize a statement. You can also personalize a constructive statement that you hear. For example, to deal with self-deprecating thoughts, you could take the great truth coined by Terri Cole-Whittaker, "**What you think about me is none of my business,**" (the title of one of her books), and adjust it to fit your own circumstances: "**What my mom thinks about me is none of my business**" or "**What the salesclerk thinks about me is none of my business.**"

Truths about What's True for You

Fear can be paralyzing. It can stop us frozen in our tracks, unable to move, speak, or function with any clarity. When we're under its spell, we have a tendency to lose perspective and forget what's really true beneath all our mental noise. You can create a truth by remembering what you know when you feel centered and clear.

Many times, after hearing a client's predicament, I ask them, "What's really true for you about this?" or "What do you know when you're feeling good?" Most of the time, an answer comes tumbling out of their mouths before doubts and "shoulds" take over. Take a moment to look inside. You'll find that more often than not, you really do know what's true for you about a given situation. Here are some examples of clients' truths.

- **I was hired because I could do this job better than anyone else.**
- **It's better to be alone than with someone who treats me badly.**
- **Nothing is more important to me than my spouse and family.**
- **This relationship is over.**
- **I feel good when I'm honest.**
- **I need to be truthful with my son.**
- **I need to be organized to succeed in my career and for my own peace of mind.**
- **Exercise will make me feel better.**
- **I need to go to bed by ten o'clock.**

Since I can't personally help you develop truths specific to your destructive thinking about each situation in your life, I've put together the following worksheet. Use this Constructing Truths worksheet to customize truths to support yourself right now.

THOUGHTS

Constructing Truths Worksheet

Destructive Thoughts	Possible Truths

Truth Bundle:

Here's how to use the worksheet.

Step 1. Write down all your destructive thoughts about a specific event or situation. Keep going until you run out.

Step 2. Create several possible truths that contradict each destructive thought. Step back and ask yourself, "What do I know when I feel clear? What would I tell a friend who was in this situation?" Ask yourself these questions about each destructive thought that tries to sidetrack you. Write possible answers on the right side of your worksheet. (If you feel blocked, shiver to relax your fear of not getting the right answer, then take a stab at it.)

Step 3. After you've generated a few options for a destructive thought, say each one out loud a few times. Keep saying and modifying the different statements until you hit one that fully contradicts your destructive thinking and feels intuitively correct. Double-check by asking, "Does this neutralize my old thinking?" or "Would an impartial person agree?" If it feels spot on, circle it. If not, try a different one. Repeat this strategy for each destructive thought until you find an effective contradiction for each.

It's as easy to remember a short truth as it is to forget a long one. When constructing a truth, remember the more succinct the statement, the more effective it will be. The words you use are important, because certain ones dilute a truth's impact. Refrain from using the following:

- Qualifiers (really, just, might, maybe, sometimes, sort of)
- Expectations (should, ought, must)
- Comparisons (better, stronger)
- Superlatives (greatest, best)
- Value judgments (terrible, weird, stupid)
- Negatives (can't, won't, don't, not)
- Disclaimers (but, but, but)
- Overgeneralizations (always, never, forever)

Step 4. From these truths, pick the statements that most succinctly contradict your old thinking and create a "truth bundle."

Constructing a Truth Bundle

A truth bundle is usually two to four truths strung together to counter a particular insidious thought pattern. You know, to offset the niggling refrain that you hear in your head a hundred times a day, such as, "I can't get it all done. There's no way I'm going to make it in time."

To create your own bundle, select a few constructive statements that resonate strongly with you. Then power on the bundle to test it out. With some refining, you'll find that your truth bundle has the same nurturing ring to it as a verse from a favorite song or poem.

To get a feel for what a powerful bundle looks like, read the following examples. These were possible truth bundles a client and I came up with to help her deal with her fear and move to peace:

Stop.
Breathe.
Slow down.
Be here now.

Everything is all right.
I'll do what I can, and the rest is out of my hands.
One thing at a time.

I'll handle the future in the future.
Everything will be all right.
The future is a figment of my imagination.

Ellen Does Some Spring Cleaning

When Ellen's design firm offered her an ambitious new project, she found herself torn. The assignment offered the recognition she'd been hoping for, but somehow she wasn't excited. She was considering passing on the offer. I was curious what she was telling herself.

As Ellen verbalized her mental chatter, I wrote it:

- *Maybe I don't have enough experience.*
- *Why bother?*
- *I might fail.*
- *I'm not good enough.*

Ellen was genuinely surprised. "Boy, I didn't realize what I'd been saying to myself."

I explained these thoughts had a long history. They'd originated a long time ago, but she could change them without exploring her past directly by entertaining their contradictions. I read the first statement — "Maybe I don't have enough experience" — aloud, and Ellen squirmed. "Is that true?" I asked.

*Without a second's hesitation, she said, "No, **I have plenty of experience**. I've been at this job for seven years."*

Bingo. She had just voiced the reality. That was easy. I read the next statement: "Why bother?"

*"**I owe it to myself**," she answered almost immediately. "**I've been waiting for a chance like this for years**." This is often how it happens. Reality just springs forth. "I don't know," she added. "This feels strange. What I'm saying now sounds so unlike me!"*

"Again, 'Why bother?'" I lightly prodded.

*"**Because I owe it to myself**." Ellen laughed. (Through the years I've observed that when people speak their truths, they can't help but laugh.) She repeated this truth a few more times. "I like that one," she said. "I feel good when I say it. It's powerful and grounding at the same time!"*

"And what's true about 'I might fail and that it's too much responsibility?"

I inquired.

*"Everyone is excited about my heading this project up. Some colleagues have already offered help. There's no way I'll fail. "**I can ask for help when I need it. Plus, my boss picked me because he knew I'd do a good job. It's true. I know I'm up for the task.**"*

"Okay, last crummy old message. 'I'm not good enough.' What is the reality?"

Ellen grinned. "I am good enough. I'm good at what I do. I know I can do this."

This whole process took us about ten minutes. I handed her the list of truths she had said so she could make a tidy truth bundle.

Ellen picked: I've been waiting for a chance like this for a long time. I can do this. I'm good at what I do.

Ellen decided to shiver and power for two minutes before going into her office each morning. It was her morning invocation. And she carried her truths around with her on a three-by-five-inch card everywhere she went.

Ellen was so tired of her old thinking, she went on a powering binge and relentlessly contradicted all her old thoughts the second they crept in. When I saw her the following week, she seemed like a different person. She was facing the exciting challenges of each new day with an upbeat attitude and level head. "I can't believe what I've been telling myself all these years," she said. "Guess it's time to say good-bye to the old and say hello to the new me."

Finding What Works

Identifying effective truths may take a little time. Just as most people need to write several drafts of a speech before they capture exactly what they want to say, you'll have to make adjustments to your truths here and there as you zero in on what's most effective. Just be patient with it, and use your creative imagination. Find words that resonate with you, and play around with the order. Experiment until they completely contradict your old thinking, are in language you would use, and resonate deeply when you say them.

Start with a statement that you think might work. Power on it a few times, and if it doesn't ring true, take another truth for a test drive. Continue until something really hits the spot.

When you find ones that work, stick with them. Don't choose too many truths; you won't remember any when you need them. When you feel satisfied, infuse your bundle with energy by powering on it for several minutes so they're ready to use when needed.

If you have trouble making up truths, shiver and power on something like, **"I can do this,"** or **"I'll give this my best shot,"** since you're probably telling yourself the opposite. Getting some input from a friend can help you nail down your destructive chatter and find statements that contradict it. Remember someone can offer suggestions, but only you will know the truth that will be the most liberating.

Say you've had an ugly fight with your partner and one of your neighbors calls the police. After the dust settles, you find yourself excruciatingly embarrassed, unable to imagine ever looking your fellow apartment dwellers in the eyes. Instead of judging yourself so harshly, find some constructive thoughts to negate your barrage of self-berating chatter:

- **I'm human.**
- **I forgive myself.**
- **We all make mistakes.**

Soften your tone as you repeat the phrases. Really take in what you're saying. You'll connect with some truths more than others. Powering on this bundle might spark a memory that your entire family tends to harshly criticize everyone, and that tendency has been handed down through the generations. **"I forgive myself"** might be the only truth you need right now.

Or you might create a forgiveness bundle:

- **Give yourself a break.**
- **It's okay to forgive myself.**
- **It's okay to forgive others.**
- **It's okay to forgive.**

Additional Time-Tested Truths

There are an infinite number of truths. Simple and profound, the following phrases are co-creations with my clients and students. They're powerful statements to unclench the jaws of limited living, and move you into the positive future of your choosing.

THOUGHTS

Encouraging Truths

Grab one or more of these truths when fear is electrocuting your heart, blinding your mind, and wrecking your body. You will steady yourself and stay on track. Hear, think, and say these words as if they're a wise coach, calming everyone down and putting things into perspective:

- **I can do it.**
- **Look for the good.**
- **Breathe.**
- **Relax.**
- **Speak your truth.**
- **Slow down.**
- **Come from love.**
- **Enjoy the ride.**
- **Keep perspective.**
- **Be patient.**
- **Say it again.**
- **Listen**
- **Don't doubt yourself.**
- **Trust your gut.**

Motivational Truths

Your intentions will waiver like waves rising, swelling and falling in the center of the ocean. So when you feel yourself crashing back into the flatness of old patterns, gain momentum by grabbing one of these:

- **I can do it.**
- **I can handle this.**
- **Little by little.**
- **The goal is greater than the moment.**
- **Life is not a straight line.**
- **Nobody said it would be easy.**
- **I know.**
- **I have what it takes.**
- **I'll do what I can today.**
- **I am worth it.**
- **I am responsible for my life.**
- **I'm the only person who knows what's best for me.**
- **I am doing better than I think I am.**

Cosmic Truths

Certain truths connect us with our inner selves — the part of us that exists independently of our accomplishments, possessions, thoughts, or feelings. These are life-affirming reminders that we're far more than our actions, characteristics or bodies. Select what resonates and repeat them often throughout the day.

- **I am not what I do.**
- **I am free.**
- **I am existence.**
- **I am consciousness.**
- **I am ageless.**
- **I am pure.**
- **I am knowledge.**
- **I am bliss.**
- **I am truth.**
- **I am.**
- **I am joy. I am love. I am peace.**

God Truths

Mention the word God and almost everyone will conjure up a meaning. If the word doesn't fit your framework, replace it with what best describes your unifying energy of the universe: higher power, nature, universal order or whatever. Or substitute a meaningful spiritual figure such as Jesus, Krishna, Buddha, Mother Mary, Mohammed, etc. to feel the joy, love, and peace they infuse. "God truths" remind us a force larger than ourselves is truly in charge, and everything — people, things, events, and especially you — embodies the same perfection. Say them slowly; feel their power.

- **God is love.**
- **God is great.**
- **God is everywhere.**
- **All this is God.**
- **I am divine.**
- **God dwells within me.**
- **You are God.**
- **God's plan, not mine.**

- **Thy will, not my will.**
- **Thy will be done.**
- **It's in God's hands.**

Got the troops ready for a full-tilt assault? That's what it's going to take to change your thinking, but with each repetition, you get stronger and more prepared. Every time those nagging thoughts rear their ugly heads, repeatedly beat them back with the truth. Views of yourself, others, and time shift from sadness, anger, and fear into what you want more of: joy, love and peace. The rewiring is happening as you're reading these pages! It just gets better and better.

Hey, Jude!

1. *Will contemplating the meaning of a truth help me internalize it faster?*

    Definitely. Thinking about ways a truth might apply to your life helps you really get its meaning. First do some concentrated blocks of powering then consider the implications of what you're saying. For example, what's the truth **"One thing at a time"** mean to your current situation? If you're moving to a new apartment and freaking out about how much there is to do, focus on just one thing at a time. When you're packing kitchen items, don't jump ahead and worry about what you have to do next. Stay in the present and just pack the kitchen.

2. *I'm continually comparing myself and my accomplishments to others.*

    Comparisons are a no-win situation. You fuel unhappiness, anger, and sadness every time you think someone else has something you don't. The antidote? Shift your focus from out there, to in here — yourself. Make a truth bundle along the lines of: **"What I'm seeking is with me."** or **"My job is to do the best I can."**

3. *Do you have a truth bundle that can stop me from snapping at my partner when she's focusing on the negative?*

    Try something along the lines of: **"That's the way she is. My job is not to fix her. If I find myself trying to prove her wrong, I need to refocus on how I can stay loving."**

4. *How can I use my breathing to help internalize what I'm powering on?*

Take full, slow, measured breaths. Try standing up or sitting erect so your lungs have optimal space to expand and your entire body can take in the meaning of what you're repeating. Short truths usually work best. Experiment. Silently repeat one statement as your inhale, and another as you exhale. Some good truths to breathe with are:

- **I love me.**
- **I love you.**
- **I am complete.**
- **I am joy. I am love. I am peace.**
- **I let go.**
- **Everything is okay.**

5. *How can I use rewiring to tap into my spiritual side?*

You're already tapping into your spiritual side just by stating reliable truths; it's inherent. They embody self-love, acceptance, and present-time awareness. But you can also power on a saying from your own religious tradition or a line from a favorite prayer. A Christian might power on a phrase like "Jesus Christ, have mercy on me"; a Buddhist, "Om mani padme hum," (the jewel in the lotus); a Muslim, "Allahu akbar" (God is the greatest); and a Jew, "Baruch hashem" (blessed is the name [of God]).

6. *Can you say something about crying when you power?*

Unleash some of what I call "power crying". I use it to swiftly shift sadness' embrace to the truth about myself. "Power crying" is a trifecta of body, heart, and mind in unison. Most of the time, I don't know exactly why I'm crying, so I just let the tears flow and remind myself of who I really am: **"I just need to cry. I love me."** You can also power while shivering ("power shivering") with **"Here I am. I am here,"** or while pounding ("power pounding") as you power on **"I love you"** or **"We are the same."**

7. Can I use specific thoughts to help heal a physical illness?

The causes behind an illness or disease are often mysterious. What is important is that you don't blame yourself for your physical condition, because negative thoughts definitely won't make you feel any better. When dealing with an illness, align yourself with what's constructive. For starters, power on an acceptance statement about your physical condition: "I have stage two breast cancer" or "I've been diagnosed with diabetes." Truly claiming the reality allows the associated emotions and destructive thoughts to arise so you can accept your current situation and then more clearly evaluate your treatment options.

3

Intuition: Firing Up the Power Source

Stop and get quiet.
Ask.
Listen.

Intuition is the invisible link between our personal inner world of emotions and thoughts and our outer world connection point through speech and action.

Think of it as the infinity sign lying on its side. What's on the inside, is always communicated to the outside. Intuition reveals what is really true for us deep down. It illuminates the high road, the graceful path of least resistance, and the route to living in the flow. The word intuition stems from the Latin intuire, which means "knowing from within." It's known by many names: inner voice, instinct, gut feeling, sixth sense. Regardless of what we call it, we recognize our heart's wisdom by the settled "yes" that permeates our being.

We all know when something is absolutely true. In those pristine moments, we are free of doubt. Moments of clarity happen whether it's a decision over an investment or how to help a friend. Our intuition guides us to what is indisputably true for us.

INTUITION

When making decisions, we tend to rely on social convention, logic, or impulse. Social convention produces outcomes more likely to please others (and our image of what we think is "right"). Relying on reason bypasses the heart and pushes us to conclusions that sound sensible, but may feel hollow. Impulse simply justifies why it's okay to do what we want right now regardless of the consequences.

When we get an intuitive hit, we know it. The feeling differs markedly from other ways of making decisions because we're settled and in sync with ourselves and the world. I jokingly tell clients the way to tell the difference between intuition and mind is that they reside about a foot apart. One comes from the heart, the other from the head.

Intuition sometimes doesn't have 'reason'. In fact, it frequently contradicts what we think we want or think we should want. Sometimes it's a wordless knowing. Other times, it's known clearly through words. Intuition taps into universal energy that pervades everything and is greater than ourselves, whether we call it nature, flow, force, or God as a direct line from this wordless, unchanging source. Our inner voice is a dependable compass amid changing circumstances. It is authentic and kind, promoting harmony and unity, never harm. It advocates connection over separation; love over selfishness.

It's unlikely we were taught to value, contact, or listen to our intuition. We're used to going about our lives in uncertainty, out of touch with our hearts, and at the whim of our fickle minds. Our clogged up sadness, anger, and fear causes an inability to hear our intuition. When that happens, it's hard to listen, much less heed, our inner compass. We're got thick mud in places we didn't know existed. Caught in the gunk of unrealistic expectations and unfounded projections, what we know deep down is obscured. We then operate from destructive feelings, such as insecurity, impatience, and the need to control.

If we hold fast to what we know is true in our quiet moments, we can stay safe and strong amidst any storm. So often clients say to me, "I don't know what I want," or "I don't know what to do." My years as a psychotherapist have shown me people find it difficult to hear their inner voices in the grip of unexpressed emotions. More often than not, they really do know what's true for them but are afraid to say it or act on it.

Intuition is not a momentary whim or a vague metaphysical concept. It is sage advice that urges us in the direction of what is good for us in the long-term. It is always constructive, automatically factoring in all possible outcomes. When we speak or act in a way we later regret, we know we aren't heeding our intuition.

Following intuition means letting go of "my way" ego thinking, "shoulds," and what seems fair or unfair. It means obeying what we hear within. When we do, confusion, doubt, and indecision evaporate. Your actions — taking your child to soccer practice when you're exhausted, or choosing not to run a marathon because of an injury — pave the way for more constructive things to follow. Obeying what we hear within, no matter what others think, ensures we'll be at peace and aligned with our inner selves. We're connected, grounded, self-assured.

But how do you know if the voice you're hearing really represents your deepest truth? It is possible to mistake impulse, whim, or mere self-interest for true intuitive wisdom. Any directive that disrespects or injures yourself, others, or things of value is not coming from your intuition. If what you hear promotes harm or selfish interests, you can conclude that it's motivated by unexpressed sadness, anger, and fear.

"But wait," you might say, "if my intuition is directed toward taking care of myself, why isn't it selfish?" Here's a clue: your intuition never going to ask, "What's in it for me?" That way of seeing the world comes out of unexpressed anger. Your intuition is bigger than that. It's always in line with what brings joy, love, and peace — with what is found on the right side of the Attitude Reconstruction Blueprint.

Use your inner barometer to find the answer to any type of question, even something as mundane as " Should I take a nap or mow the lawn?" It can be used for practical situations, such as deciding when to buy a new car, or critical decisions, such as deciding whether to leave your marriage. Or it can be used to get answers to one of the most profound questions of all: "What is the purpose of my life?"

INTUITION

Your Intuition is Your "I"

I call what's true for you, what your intuition reveals, your "I." Knowing your "I" creates strength to speak and act. It's an unshakable foundation from which you operate. Once you've found your "I," you clarify boundaries between yourself and others, set goals and priorities, and make decisions. You proceed with confidence, knowing you're honoring yourself (the first ultimate attitude).

Let me give you an example. Stan always wanted to be an actor, and he'd lay money on the fact his intuition was pointing him towards the stage. He pursued acting school and moved to Los Angeles, believing he'd be a super star.

But as time went on, Stan's success came in $10 dollar tips as a bar tender, not as recurring roles or steady acting gigs. He couldn't make ends meet, and wondered if his intuition was wrong.

Stan needed to check in periodically to see if his "I" had changed. Maybe he'd get an inner confirmation to persevere. Or he might realize he needed to express his acting passion as a hobby instead of a career.

Stan could still get his stage buzz by doing summer stock or helping his daughter with class plays. At some point, his intuition might help him reprioritize his dream of making it big time so that he could put food on his family's table.

Who doesn't want an experienced copilot or great caddy when you need some extra input? The gift of rock-solid advice to make decisions and get perspective is always within you. Aligning with your "I" brings peace. No more worries or second-guessing. It brings love, because you know you're doing what is constructive and good. It brings joy, because it feels so good to be centered and in your personal integrity.

Since you're busy stocking the toolkit, don't forget the power that intuition, tool number three, affords you. To get acquainted with this resource, pause, ask yourself a question, and then remain open to hear the answer. The more you listen to your inner voice, the more your choices align with the three ultimate attitudes: honor yourself, accept other people and situations, and reside in the present moment.

Thomas Makes a Monumental Decision

Thomas was struggling. After being with his high school sweetheart for seven years, he realized he either needed to propose marriage, or move on. "I just don't know what to do," he said. "Marie is such a wonderful woman. We've grown up together. She gave me a sense of being okay when I felt so estranged from my own family. But something's holding me back. I just can't convince myself that I'd be really happy married to her. I know I'd feel lonely without her and that she'd be crushed, so I talk myself out of breaking up. I seem to be an expert at talking myself out of what I feel."

"Are you sure it's not fear of the changes that a commitment would bring?" I asked. "What do you know in your quieter, centered moments?"

"I think you're talking about what I call my 'older, wiser me,'" he answered.

"Yep, that," I replied. "Neat name."

Thomas closed his eyes for a few seconds. "Well, it says that I love Marie but am not in love with her. It also tells me that we'll both be able to handle whatever comes if we split up."

"Let's put this together," I said. "Your older, wiser self says you love Marie as a best friend, but not in the way you would want to love a wife. It says that you can both handle whatever comes up. Your mind says, 'What if I'm making a mistake? Shouldn't I listen to what others are telling me?' What do you want to drive you? Your emotions and thoughts which often change, or your older, wiser self?"

"I've never thought of it like that," Thomas replied. "You're suggesting that I don't discredit my older, wiser self."

"Precisely," I said. "Keep your connection to your intuition. It's scary to put yourself into the unfamiliar, but following what you know deep down will free you from ambivalence. You can feel the difference."

"Again, what does your 'older, wiser me' say?" I asked.

"It tells me it's time to split up and move on," he answered.

To test his conviction, I asked, "How about postponing your decision until the new year?"

Without missing a beat, Thomas said, "Nope. I really know that now's the time for action."

When I saw Thomas again, he told me that breaking up with Marie had been the hardest thing he'd ever had to do. Since then, he had done a lot of soul-searching, was enjoying his solitary life, and was consulting his older, wiser self more and more.

Using Your Intuition is a Skill

You can tap into your inner knowledge any moment you want to. Whether you're debating revving up on a third cup of coffee, dating an unavailable man (for say, the tenth time now), or fudging your income taxes, if you chose to listen within you will get some really helpful information. You really do know the answer. Intuition is always at the ready.

Like any other skill, contacting your inner voice gets better and easier with practice. Consulting your intuition becomes second nature, and as your point of reference changes, you'll no longer waste time justifying your position to others. When your intuition illuminates what's true for you and you've learned to trust it, the need for validation from others lessens. Your life ceases to be driven by wouldas, couldas, or shouldas. As you give credence to what you hear, self-confidence grows. You slowly develop the faith that no matter what transpires or what emotions arise, you'll be all right if you stay true to what you know in your heart.

Learning to hear your intuition requires a one hundred and eighty degree turn from "out there" to "in here." The process is straightforward but takes practice. Here's how to start:

1. Stop and be quiet.
Your inner voice resides in silence so you have to slow yourself down. First, calm your body so your mind becomes more settled. Shivering vigorously for a minute will remove emotional static, as will shedding a few tears or pushing against a doorjamb. Taking several deep breaths also temporarily quiets your mind and body so you can be fully present. Accompany your soothing, centering activity by repeating truths: **"Everything will be all right. One thing at a time. I know what I know."**

2. Ask your question.

If you've never consciously called on your intuition, start with something small and immediate, such as whether you should call in sick at work. Pose your question. You might try one of these:

- **What's true for me about this specific topic?**
- **What do I want?**
- **What do I need?**
- **What do I feel?**
- **What do I need to do?**

Or try a more specific question, such as:

- **Do I need to talk to my husband about what I'm feeling?**
- **What do I need to do about my bad knee?**
- **Should I work out after work tonight?**

3. Be open and listen for the answer.

It doesn't have to be profound; it's simply what you know beneath the mental chatter and opinions of others. One of the biggest clues that you're hearing intuition is that it feels right in your body. Hearing your heart's truth brings a peaceful inner sensation, a relaxing, freeing, "yes" feeling. How does it sound to you when you say it out loud? The wisdom of your inner voice rings pure and truthful. There's no mind noise. It brings an expansive, tranquil feeling. Messages from your heart don't begin with "I guess…" or "I think I should…" or "I'd better…" That's your mind talking. If the answer is complicated, you can be sure you aren't hearing your intuition. Likewise, if what you hear sounds flat or empty, or has a negative edge or tone, you still haven't contacted your inner voice.

If you're having trouble accessing your intuition, shiver, then gently ask your question again. More likely than not, you already do know the answer. Just stop telling yourself that you don't. Ask, "What's true for me about this specific topic?" If you doubt the answer, you can subject it to the scrutiny by asking again. If you've heard your intuition, you'll get the same answer. If not, you'll hear rationalizations or justifications.

INTUITION

Do the same if you aren't getting a clear communication: ask yourself after expressing your emotions. Or set a specific time in the future to ask again. Some people recommend asking once a day and then giving it a rest. Be diligent in your inner inquiry, and something will emerge even if it is that it's not time to know yet.

You can also rid yourself of emotional interference by using your thoughts. If, for example, you're bombarded by negative self-talk "I can't decide," "It doesn't matter," or "I don't care," power on truths such as:

- **I can find the answer.**
- **This is important.**
- **I care.**

As you repeat these statements, be sure to nod your head up and down, not side to side. You can also gently but persistently ask yourself:

- What do I know when I'm clear?
- What does the best of me say to do about this?
- What's true for me about this?

Using Your Intuition as an Anchor

Your inner voice functions as an anchor, keeping you steady through the ups and downs of events and emotions. Emotional turbulence, especially fear, impels you to move so quickly that it doesn't even cross your mind to stop and check within. The consequence is you lose touch with what you know. For example, if a man remembers that his wife and children are his number-one priority, it's easier for him to turn down an invitation to join a softball team with three practices a week. Similarly, remembering what you know deep down will prevent you from making that late-night telephone call to restart a relationship you know is over.

To combat doubt about your intuition's messages, repeat:

- **This is what is true for me.**
- **This feels right.**
- **Everything will be all right.**

Your intuition will keep you centered and connected during emotional moments if you write down what your inner voice tells you.

During an emotional deluge when losing track of your convictions, you can check out what you wrote. Compile a list of what you tend to forget and what's true for you, and refer to it often. If you need to end a long-term relationship, such as Thomas did, your list might read:

- **There are people more suitable for me out there.**
- **I deserve to be treated well.**
- **I deserve to feel happy.**
- **It is better to be alone than in an unfulfilling relationship.**

Jenny Follows Her True Calling

Jenny had just graduated from college and was planning to attend law school in the fall. She'd always intended to become a lawyer, and had worked very hard to get into a top-rated school. The only problem was a nagging feeling it was the wrong move. Jenny was actually more drawn to journalism. She had a good chance to get a job with the town newspaper, but her logical mind rejected this as a foolish dream. It was impractical. Journalism was too competitive; what if she wasn't good enough? She'd convinced herself she wanted to be an attorney, and it certainly was what everyone else wanted her to do.

Jenny decided to go ahead, despite her misgivings. "My grandfather was a lawyer, my dad and brother are lawyers — it's a family tradition," she told herself. In the end, Jenny barely lasted a semester before dropping out. When I saw her, she told me she could have saved herself the turmoil (and a huge bundle of cash) if she had just listened within.

Testing Options

Sometimes we just can't get clear about which constructive action to take. Maybe we've tried emoting or powering on a truth, but we're just not hitting the mark. If a definitive answer is elusive when consulting your intuition, test the options.

Testing options asks for a tag-team approach of your head, heart, and body to evaluate alternatives and find a satisfying solution. With your thoughts, you gather multiple possible options. (There are always more than two choices, just as there are many roads to Rome.) Generate a variety of options, and expose yourself to the full range of possibilities. Tune into your body's reaction as you say each option, preferably out loud, and your answer will become unmistakably clear.

How to Test Options

1. Specify the topic or issue you seek to clarify.

2. Create as many alternatives as you can think of. Don't limit your imagination. Write out all the possibilities clearly and succinctly. Be specific.

3. Say the first option out loud with conviction and enthusiasm a few times, as if it were the perfect solution.

4. Check to see the feeling this option produces in your body.

5. Then say the second option aloud and see what physical reaction it generates.

6. Continue to repeat all your alternatives successively, or make up new variations until one fully resonates in your body, not just in your head.

If your topic is complex, write down all the choices. (Obviously this step won't be necessary if you're deciding on something as simple as evening plans.) Repeat each option four or five times aloud with levity and sincerity. State the alternative as if it were an indisputable fact and experience how it feels in your body. If you speak your options aloud, your body will tell you whether to accept that dinner invitation, decline it, or arrange to drop by for just an hour.

Keep repeating and modifying the option that resonates the most. Pose more alternatives until you come up with one that hits the nail on the head. Here are some possible options for the question, "Do I need to talk to my husband about what I'm feeling?"

- I'm going to talk with Jim tonight.
- I don't need to talk with Jim about this.
- I'm going to wait a week and then decide whether to talk with Jim about this.
- I'm going to talk with Jim about this after the holidays.

How does each feel when you say it out loud a few times? If all your options feel the same, do whatever it takes — emote, shiver, rewire, etc. — to move the stuck emotional energy and ask again. Sometimes an answer isn't apparent right away. In those cases, keep asking gently over time. It can be helpful, for example, to ask, "Am I ready to decide?" If the answer is no, put it on the shelf and don't keep analyzing it in your mind. After whatever time frame feels appropriate (a day, a week, a few months), ask again until you get an answer.

If you can't get a clear signal but need to act now, the best thing to do is emote. Then ask again and take your best option. Commit to it fully, and look for an internal signal to confirm or refute its accuracy. Remember that fear is natural when doing something outside your comfort range. Deciding to audition for a play might feel right — but it can also feel scary. Feeling fear doesn't mean you should discredit your intuition.

Why We Don't Listen to Our Intuition

Tapping into our intuition is one thing. Obeying it is another. Our habitual drive to control events or seize momentary pleasure makes listening a bit tough. Being true to our intuition may be inconvenient or uncomfortable. It may not jibe with other people's desires. That's why all too often the mind undermines faith in your inner voice. Moving out of your parents' house and getting an apartment or taking a job that pays considerably less could feel daunting but be intuitively correct.

When you ask within, "Is this relationship over?" and hear a resounding yes, the part of you that resists change and wants to avoid pain laments, "I don't want to break up. Not right before the holidays. I can't bear the thought of him becoming involved with someone else."

Your mind is seductive! It can convince you of almost anything, including settling for the status quo. You start doubting yourself. "Maybe my standards are too high. Maybe he'll change. At least he's not violent. Maybe I'll never find anyone any better." Six months later, there you are in the same unfulfilling relationship. Why? Because you ignored your intuition to avoid the temporary pain of breaking up.

Larry's Familiar Dilemma

Larry's appointment came just in time. "I can't stop thinking about this girl I met at the beach," he said, "but I'm happy in my committed relationship with Pam."

"What's the story?" I asked.

"Since I met Ginger at the beach a couple of months ago, we seem to run into each other everywhere. Yesterday, we exchanged phone numbers and agreed to meet later today. I haven't felt like this in years, and I love it. I know if I acted on this feeling, it would be the beginning of the end of my relationship with Pam...but Ginger's really gorgeous."

It was obvious that before Larry could proceed, he needed to shake and shiver to come back to present time. After he did so for a couple of minutes, with plenty of nervous laughter, I said, "It's helpful to remind ourselves what we know when we're feeling clear. What's the deal with you and Pam?"

"I'd been looking for someone like her all my life," Larry blurted out.

"That's worth remembering!" I said. "But since your physical desire is so strong, let's try testing options."

Larry hadn't made much progress sorting this out for himself, so he was game and rattled off a few options:

1. I'm not going to call or see Ginger again.

2. I'll just go for it. It will be intense and fun, and it's not a big deal.

3. I love Pam and want to honor our commitment, so I'm not going to act on this.

"You can sort these alternatives out by using your intuition," I said. "Say your first option aloud a few times and see how it feels inside."

"I'm not going to call or see Ginger. I'm not going to call or see Ginger," he solemnly stated.

"How does that feel?" I asked.

Larry instantly knew. "That doesn't feel right."

"Okay. Try saying the second option a few times," I continued.

Larry started in. "I'm just going to go for it. Life is short. Pam will never know. I'm going to see Ginger this afternoon and let whatever happens happen. I'm just going to go for it. It will be intense and fun, and it's not a big deal."

"How does that feel?" I probed.

Larry paused. "Exciting, but mostly bad. I feel really uneasy and guilty already. I wish I didn't, but I do."

"Now, try the third possibility."

"I'm not going to act on this feeling," he said. "I'm not going to act on this. I love Pam and want to honor my commitment."

"And how does that one sit with you?" I asked.

"That feels difficult, but true. What a drag! A big part of me really wants to go for it. But in my heart, I know better. I'm not going to act on my attraction. In fact, this option makes me feel sane."

"That's neat," I said. "You know what's true, and you can feel it's the right thing."

Obeying Your Intuition Can Bring Up Emotions

Aligning with your gut feeling can cause unexpected emotions to arise. The trick is to handle them constructively so you don't get derailed. That means being ready to experience your sadness, anger, and fear so you don't question your decisions. When you're considering leaving a less-than-satisfactory relationship, the alternative of being alone can feel scary and painful. Take some time alone to emote and rewire so you can confidently follow through with what you hear.

There's extra insight in finding out what your real thoughts are concerning any big decision. Are you reluctant to leave the relationship because you feel too inadequate to attract someone else? That kind of thinking perpetuates sadness. Are you concerned what your married friends will say about your still being single? Focusing on what others might think indicates anger. Are you holding on because you're afraid of what might happen in the future? Trying to control is driven by fear.

Speaking and acting in keeping with your intuition, naturally creates more joy, love, and peace in your world. Your true intuition will never fail you. It's ready, open, and available whenever you get quiet enough to connect and ask.

Hey, Jude!

1. Until now, I've never given my intuition any attention. Are you really suggesting that I run all my decisions by it?

Yes. Your intuition is not some abstract force. It's a faculty we all possess, whether we use it or not. I'm not saying we can predict the future. But listening within gives us a sense for what will keep us in the flow. Our intuition often sends us clear messages, but we ignore it. Here's an everyday example: you go out to dinner, and instead of ordering the usual hamburger, you scan the menu until you realize a salad feels like it would satisfy your body best. Messages from the heart are not accompanied by flashing lights. They simply reflect what is true and authentic for you.

2. What if I've tried everything but still can't hear my intuition?

You might be trying too hard. Your intuition's messages are usually fairly obvious. But if you've asked a question repeatedly and still can't hear an answer, emote, power for a couple of minutes, or do both, and then ask again. Or pose your question in a different way. Trying on some different wording may be just the thing. If that's still a no-go, take a more rational, logical approach. Expand your perspective by browsing through books, crunching numbers, or seeking opinions from experts and people you respect. Put a reasonable time frame on your data collection. Then pose your question again. Your answer will emerge in due time.

3. I hear my heart easiest when I'm hiking in the hills, but when I get back to my "real life," I forget what made so much sense and revert back to doubting.

Hiking in nature is a perfect way to quiet the mind. However, fear-based thinking will try to override your inner wisdom. Take a small notebook on your hikes and record the messages of your heart, then power on what you wrote down. When emotions come up, feel them and then remind yourself of what you knew when you were clear.

4. *My intuition tells me to quit my job, but my mother thinks I want to leave because I'm incapable of making a long-term commitment. How do I know if I'm leaving for the right reasons?*

Test your options. Start with "I'm going to stay at my job." Then try "I'm going to send out my resume," "I am going to give this job my all and then reconsider in six months," and "I am going to give notice at the end of the month." Keep modifying your options until one feels peacefully correct. Your mom can offer her opinion, but you're the one who needs to go to work every day. Only you know, so consult your intuition to find your answer.

5. *I'm afraid that if I ask my intuition, I won't like the answer.*

Messages from your intuition are sometimes not what you really want to hear. Asking within means relinquishing control over what you think you want. Frequently, intuition's answers take you out of your comfort zone and you feel fear as a result. Follow through on what you hear, however, and this dependable resource will always serve you over the long-haul.

6. *When I followed my intuition and dropped out of school, I got a lot of flak from my friends and family. I find myself withdrawing so people will stop guilt-tripping me.*

You won't always get support from others for following your intuition. Humans like their world to be predictable and they get uncomfortable when others rock the boat. Since dropping out of school came from your inner knowing and not from a desire to shirk responsibilities, hold onto it. Sounds like what you need are some skills to handle other people's reactions.

INTUITION

7. *My intuition has always been strong, but I routinely discount it because I want to please everybody.*

Easily accessing your intuition is a special gift, so good work there. Feeling pressure to be logical and conform to what we think others want is fairly common. Pleasing others is a tough habit to break. Remind yourself that your inner knowing is your most trusted friend. Practice giving it the right of way, and you'll see your choices will yield a life — now and over the long run.

4

Speech: Framing Doors, Windows, and Walls

"I"s
Specifics
Kindness
Listen

Communication, in all forms, allows you to engage and connect with the world around you. It can inspire you, expose you, infuse you, or deflate you. You can't escape interacting with it, receiving it, or broadcasting it in some way unless you lock yourself away in a room somewhere. But even then, the communication you have with yourself is alive and well and sooner or later, the messages come through.

Communication allows us to exchange information, to listen and to understand each other. When we don't handle sadness, anger, and fear constructively, our destructive core attitudes interfere with effective communication. Words turn into weapons, misinterpretations run rampant, and speaking escalates into argument. Whether we pull away or strike out, freeze or spin out of control, the result is a loss of love.

You're about to learn four rules of constructive communication that will assist you in every aspect of your dealings with other humans and animals, too! These rules and their opposing communication violations (which we've unfortunately cozied up to many a time) will help you skillfully navigate any social interaction. You'll get practical steps to speak up for yourself; handle communication violations; deal with people operating from sadness, anger, or fear; and resolve any conflict.

An Overview of the Four Rules and Their Opposites

Communicating should be easy, correct? I mean, we do it almost every minute of the day. Talking to people, talking to ourselves, making gestures vocally or physically to signal our likes and dislikes. But even though we do it all day long, we often don't do it well. We can thank our parents for that (sorry mom and dad). Most of us didn't learn very constructive techniques from them, because no one taught them how to communicate effectively either, especially at emotional moments.

Not surprisingly, unresolved sadness, anger, and fear create some really sticky communication situations. Unexpressed sadness makes us feel small and to give up when we meet resistance. Suppressed anger will push us to stonewall, lash out, or demand attention. Bottled-up fear digs its petrified claws into our skin, stopping us from saying anything or getting us so agitated we prattle on and on, grafting countless unrelated topics to the issue at hand.

Poker has rules. Music has rules. Grammar has rules. Similarly, communication has rules. The rules of communication evolved from the core attitudes associated with joy, love, and peace. When we're feeling centered and clear, we effortlessly abide by these rules, but we tend to violate them when we're under the spell of unexpressed sadness, anger, and fear.

The Communication Rules and Their Violations

The Four Rules	The Four Violations
1. "I"s	1. "you"s
2. specifics	2. overgeneralize
3. kindness	3. unkindness
4. listen	4. don't listen

These four rules apply to how we talk to ourselves and others. They work regardless of the nature of the relationship, how long we've been in it, how many people are in a conversation, or how painful the topic is. The rules are suitable for any setting, provided that they're accompanied by matching facial expressions, body language, and tone of voice.

The first rule — "I"s — means you only speak about yourself and what is true for you. You know you're in the right territory when you're talking about what you feel, want, need, and believe. All you can speak to with any certainty is your own experience.

By sharing your "I" with others, you experience the freedom, contact, and contentment that come from being honest and honoring yourself.

Violating this rule — "you"s — is the trademark of anger. Instead of looking inward when you're angry, you focus outward on others, blaming them for what's not working and telling them how they should be.

The second rule — specifics — instructs you to stay concrete and stick to one topic at a time. Specifics provide concrete information and clarify particulars. They invite peace because being vague triggers fear. With specifics what was once unknown becomes crystal clear.

Using words like always and never and overgeneralizing is the violation of this rule. It distorts what is real, dragging the future and past into the present, and painting global abstractions. That just creates even more fear, confusion, and uncertainty.

The third rule — kindness — and the fourth rule — listen — kindle love and feelings of connection. Their violations produce anger and feelings of alienation. Rule three accentuates the positive. In any communication, you can look for what you and the other person have in common. Unkind words arise when you attend to the negative: what you don't like or what won't work for you. They produce hurt and resentment. Rule four allows you to truly understand the other person's position. Not listening delivers the message "I count but you don't."

As you absorb and practice the four rules, you'll notice a huge difference in how your messages are received and might be surprised by others' reactions. Even if others don't jump on the communicating constructively bandwagon, you can significantly improve the quality of your personal relationships by changing how you speak and listen. When a client laments, "My partner won't come in for counseling," I remind her that it takes two to tango. If you stop dancing with the other person's communication violations, the dynamic will shift for the better.

Rule One: "I"s

It's more comfortable to stay outwardly focused. That's because it's what you've been conditioned to do for years. Keeping attention on others keeps it off of you so you feel less exposed. Perhaps you believe voicing your own feelings, beliefs, needs, or wants — your "I" — is self-centered, demanding, or too sensitive. Here's something important to note: the opposite is true. Turning inward and speaking up about yourself brings you back to honoring yourself. The way to keep communications balanced is to give half time speaking your "I" — what's true for you — with listening well the other half.

The distinction between "I"s and "you"s cannot be overestimated. It can literally make or break any communication. You'll get what I'm saying by looking at these illustrations of "I-ing" and "you-ing."

You: You never help with the dishes.
I: I need some help washing the dishes right now.

You: Are you ready to go home?
I: I'm ready to go home now.

You: You're monopolizing the conversation.
I: I have something I want to say.

You: We always do what you want to do.

I: I don't want to spend the weekend with your parents.

You: You make me feel so angry.

I: I'm feeling angry right now.

You: Don't be mean.

I: I feel hurt.

Couples laugh when I mention that most of us have earned an honorary Ph.D. in "you-ing." Somehow we think we're entitled to give others unsolicited advice, but telling people about themselves is presumptuous unless we've asked for feedback or are giving a compliment. "You-ing" creates ugly confrontations and hurt feelings, even when we believe our intentions are good.

Blaming, judging, and demanding are all forms of "you-ing" that can inflict painful wounds upon the receiver's self-esteem. Bullying, ridiculing, and gossiping can be equally destructive. There are more passive but equally unattractive forms of "you-ing" you probably wouldn't want to fess up to such as moaning, nagging, and complaining. Even when these aren't aimed directly at another person, they're negative and shift attention away from your legitimate territory: yourself. Talking unkindly about him, her, it, them, and even us are all forms of "you-ing" because they shift responsibility and attention from you, the only place it belongs.

Okay, I'm not saying you have to be the next Mother Theresa. It's not like the word "you" has to be stricken from your vocabulary and put to rest, only visited on anniversaries. It's just that you should use it with care; to clarify a request or identify a specific event. And the subject of your communications needs to be yourself. Always. Well, almost. There is only one exception to the rule: "you-ing" is okay as long as it's praise and appreciation.

Asking leading questions can skin a few knees and pour salt in a few wounds. Seemingly innocent questions usually hide an unstated "I." "Do you want an appointment with our therapist?" is a leading question.

What you really want to say is, "I want us to see our counselor, because I need a third party present to help figure this issue out." Rather than asking, "What are you up to?" it might be more honest to say, "I'd like to hear about your day, but first I need ten minutes by myself to unwind."

Maybe you just don't know what is true for you, but you still have the urge to speak something out. Reverse that metaphoric mirror one hundred and eighty degrees from "out there" to "in here." Gaze within and see what gems are waiting, even if they're painful to express. It may be hard to speak up at first, but with practice it gets easier. You'll feel truly connected in an authentic way. When you aren't sure of your "I," ask yourself the questions suggested in the last chapter:

- What's true for me right now about this specific topic?
- What am I feeling?
- What do I want?
- What do I need to say?

Carla Communicates

Carla wanted to work on how she and her boyfriend Tony, who wasn't open to counseling, communicated. "I'm so tired of the same old me," she said. "I do extremely well in mediation at work, but I'm not so good at it at home. I blow up when Tony pushes my buttons. He gets mad, and things escalate from there. Maybe we should just break up."

"Hold on," I said. "Let me translate what I just heard you say. Making him the problem is how you avoid dealing with your anger. When you threaten to leave the relationship, your fear is talking. Taking the giant leap from being upset with Tony to contemplating a breakup leads you to feel overwhelmed in a heartbeat. Tony isn't the root cause of your problem. When you blast him, there's something you're afraid to say about yourself."

"He just drives me nuts," she grumbled. Tony asked a lot of questions, gave advice about how she should run her life, and used the royal "we."

"In order not to feel so angry, you need to accept the things that drive you crazy," I said. "You have to accept that Tony is the way he is. He asks questions rather than being direct and talking about himself. He gives

unsolicited advice. He uses 'we' when he really should say his 'I.' That's the way he communicates right now. When you truly accept this reality, rather than getting mad, you'll feel lovingly amused."

Carla mulled over what I had said: *"Tony asks questions, gives advice, and uses the royal 'we.' Tony asks questions, gives advice, and uses the royal 'we.'"* After just a few minutes of repeating these facts, Carla commented that she felt lighter, as if a burden had been lifted.

"But how do I handle his habits that drive me batty? Like asking me questions rather than directly saying what he wants. When we were out of town last weekend, he asked if I wanted to stop and eat. When I told him I wasn't hungry, he got huffy. I felt set up and really let him have it. You're saying that I don't need to get stuck on Tony's delivery style or take it personally. I could have said, 'I'm not hungry, but if you are, I don't mind stopping.'"

"Yes. And?"

She made a face, sighed, then went on. "Instead of exploding, I'd be better off if I accepted that he was going to say things like that and remembered that all his comments come from his concern for me. All I can do is stick to my 'I' when he gives me advice about my job. I could say, 'I can't hear your suggestions about my work right now.'"

Then she broke off. "Why do I have to be the saint here? Is that something I signed up for?"

"Well," I said, "you want to become a better communicator in your relationship, right? You're learning to talk in 'I's, specifics, and kindness so you'll feel better. And you know what? It can't help but have a positive effect on both of you."

Carla worked on her communication and much to her surprise, started to get compliments from friends about losing her "edge." She even speculated that Tony was making his annoying comments less. One day, Carla showed up to her session with Tony so we could meet in person. She was wearing an emerald-cut engagement ring. "She's awesome," he told me immediately. "We're really happy. We're doing great."

Rule Two: Specifics

It's no surprise that good communication is built on a foundation of specificity. When you talk details, it's easy for everyone to be on the same page or at least attempt to be. Specifics allow us peace, because they remove ambiguity and make the unknown known. There's just one little hiccup: when we experience fear, physical agitation in our bodies is reflected in our thoughts. You leap out of the present moment and start to overgeneralize. You hurtle through time and space, making global pronouncements and coming to sweeping conclusions. Dragging in tangential topics, exaggerating dramatically, and resurrecting long-dead events from personal histories just become exhausting for anyone that has to endure it. You'll either be blowing things out of proportion or fueling the flames of fear, whether you're mowing down a partner or yelling at yourself in your head.

This will help you: read these examples aloud and feel the difference between overgeneralizing and being specific:

Overgeneral: My parents are so mean.
Specific: I'm upset that my parents wouldn't give me the car tonight.

Overgeneral: You always say stuff like that.
Specific: I got hurt when you called me a "gold digger."

Overgeneral: Men only want sex.
Specific: I didn't want to make love last night, but was too afraid to say so.

Overgeneral: Women just can't be trusted.
Specific: I felt awful when you told me that you shared our problems with your book group.

Overgeneral: I messed everything up.
Specific: I'm sorry I was late. I need to pay more attention to being on time.

Overgeneral: No one likes me.
Specific: I feel a little insecure right now.

Overgeneral: Nothing ever works out.
Specific: I'm disappointed that you needed to change our weekend plans.

Life gets simpler when you're concrete. Thinking and talking in specifics keeps issues contained and contributes to better mutual understanding. No matter what area of your life, the more precise you are, the more peaceful you feel.

So how does one become specific, or better yet, how can you tell when you're not being specific? I call the two ways we obscure specifics: "jumping" and "lumping."

Jumping into the future happens when we speculate, worry, and obsess about imagined what-ifs. Of course you already know a fraction ever come to pass, but that doesn't end the temptation to let our imaginations go wild. Jumping into the past, we drag old, unfinished business into the discussion at hand. At the end of an argument, we've brought in so many topics that we can't remember where we started, much less come to any resolution.

Lumping is a visual word that tells you a lot: it means you use sweeping generalizations about time ("always," "never," "forever"), people and things, ("everyone," "nothing," "they"), putting everything under a decisive law as if it was one of the Ten Commandments. Drama-makers of all kinds love this strategy, making specific events seem bigger by adding global implications, turning them into political, philosophical, or moral issues, all of which are irrelevant to the point under discussion.

Another way to lump is to put a big, fat negative label on what you don't accept (a sign of anger). Name-calling and making blanket statements — neither are beneficial. For instance, you see something you don't like and say, "You're so inconsiderate," or "He only thinks about himself." And it goes further. Labeling also take the form of all-or-nothing thinking as when you conclude, "That's good," "That's bad," or "You're wrong, I'm right."

You're in danger of getting derailed if you catch yourself lumping or jumping. Stop the potential negative sprint off yourself and into other people's business. Focus on returning to the present, your lifeline, and locate the specific topic at hand. Ask yourself:

- What are the specifics?
- Where is my "I" in all of this?
- What specifically do I really want to say about that?
- What information do I need to stay grounded in reality?
- Are the conclusions I'm making based on what actually happened?

So let's say you're upset with your partner about something that happened the night before. What do you do? Let's talk it through: don't bombard him or her with accusations such as, "You're so selfish. This relationship isn't going anywhere. You don't love me anymore. All we do is fight." Don't stay in a huff for the rest of the day. Simply state the specific topic, share why you feel the way you do and what you'd like to be different next time. "I'd like to talk about what happened at the party last night. I felt shy because I didn't know any of your friends. Next time we go out like that, I'd like you to introduce me to people and hang out with me for a little while." Now you've saved yourself from an argument and set the stage for a positive exchange, because your partner understands why you feel upset. As a result, you can have a ten-minute conversation instead of arguing about this once again on your tenth anniversary wedding party.

Everything Calls For Specifics

By now, you've grasped the concept that identifying specific emotions, topics, and events bring what you want to say into focus. Being specific is the essential ingredient when differences arise or you need to assert yourself. At those times, be sure to give definite information so other people can make clear and conscious choices. Your job is to state specific intentions, boundaries, requests, consequences, and possible solutions.

- **Clear intentions** squeeze out room for second-guessing or misinterpretations and let others know exactly what you intend to do. "I'm not going to decide who I'm hiring until I interview all the applicants. My assistant will get back to you by the end of next week."

- **Healthy boundaries** honor yourself and affirm your limits. They give others crucial information about what's okay and not okay for you right now. "I don't want to discuss this further until tomorrow morning so I have a chance to cool down and think it through."

- **Reasonable requests** state exactly what you'd like to happen in a given situation without accusations or insults. "Please let me know in the next half hour if you don't think you can finish this project today, so I can assign someone to help you if needed."

- **Reasonable consequences** allow others to make decisions based on the ramifications of an action or inaction. They must be fair and enforceable. If you don't follow through when you set a consequence, you lose your authority, because others will learn you don't mean what you say. "If you don't fill my gas tank after borrowing my car, I'm not going to lend it to you next week."

- **Concrete solutions** clarify each person's responsibilities and reduce potential conflicts. "Since you need to work late tonight, I'd be glad to pick up the kids and fix dinner."

How About Them Apples?

Here's an account from Susan, a mom who attended a communication workshop:

Last week I returned home from the market with six beautiful apples. When I got back from work the next afternoon, I found all the apples gone, with two in the garbage, one bite out of each. My son Sam and his friends unexpectedly come home for lunch and helped themselves to the apples. I felt taken advantage of, angry at not having my apples, guilty for not accepting my son unconditionally, and petty for being upset about six apples.

During my yo-yo shifts from anger to letting go, I realized I was thinking in generalities: "He never considers other people. This is just like him, leaving lights on and wet towels on the floor, not doing his chores..."

Remembering what I learned in Jude's workshop, I restricted my
reaction to the specific event and threw my fit privately. I gave the sofa
in the playroom a beating it won't forget anytime soon.

I wanted to communicate with my son about the apples in a loving
but assertive way. I made a plan to talk to him after school, and he'd had
a few minutes to unwind. I'd found my "I" and rehearsed it carefully.
Sam found me in the kitchen and I carefully delivered my speech. "When
I saw that all the apples I bought yesterday were gone today, I felt angry,
because I bought them for everyone in our family, and I wanted some for
me. Please don't eat all of anything without making sure that it's okay."

My son's reaction was genuine. "Oh, I'm sorry, Mom. I thought they
were for me. I didn't realize that we ate them all. I'll be sure to leave
some next time."' Then he gave me a heartfelt hug.

It was over. I had spoken up, and he had heard me. The exchange was
complete. I didn't get caught up in accusations and generalizations. The
exchange was not about our relationship; it was about a specific — shar-
ing the apples.

Rule Three: Kindness

Constructive communication is positive, not negative; helpful, not
hindering; unifying, not antagonizing. If you feel angry, pessimistic, or
ambivalent, chances are high you'll carry those feelings into interactions
with others. Keeping your sights set on kindness, you focus on staying
connected, because speaking and hearing kind words increases love.

Kindness is a multipurpose lubricant in any conversation. Voicing
the good elevates any conversation or communication. But it shouldn't
be confused with manipulative flattery. If your words are honest, true,
and useful — and the timing is right — they'll be constructive. To help
yourself be kind, ask yourself:

- What's most loving?
- What's most compassionate?
- What's most kind?
- Will what I'm about to say move me towards my goal?

There are several types of kindness. The first is being positive. You know the mom that shows up every weekend at practice and complains about everything from the away games to the cost of the uniforms to her teenage daughter's Facebook status updates? It's a real drag to be around someone who has something negative to say about almost everything. Accentuating the positive can make a noticeable difference. For example, you can declare the latest party you went to was a total bust because not many friends showed up or you could be delighted over the company of those who graced you with their presence. Looking at the glass as half-full is like giving water to a thirsty plant. By leaving out the negative observations and focusing on what you liked instead, you'll elevate your inner state as well as others around you. As you go through your day, replace the "no" with "yes, yes, yes."

A second form of kindness is praise. Who doesn't just love being told what they're doing right for a change? In his book *The Power of Positive Parenting*, Dr. Glenn Latham, suggests that the ratio between praise and corrective feedback should be about twenty to two. And this concept doesn't just apply to children. Across the board, it's infinitely more effective to praise actions that you want to encourage than to punish those you disapprove of. People can't get enough genuine praise, so keep it coming, especially when someone is going through a difficult time. Some examples of praise are:

- **I'm glad you brought that up.**
- **You did a good job on that.**
- **I like what you just said.**

The third type of kindness is appreciations. (I use "appreciations" and "gratitudes" in plural because it's often helpful to give more than one at a time.) A simple thank you or gesture of appreciation can be all that's needed to bring love into the room. Expressing appreciations for others doesn't negate the differences we might have with them, but it super charges the good we see in each other. Instead of criticizing and judging, we set our focus on characteristics or actions that we admire. Appreciations can be general or specific. And they can't be attached to qualifiers, superlatives, comparisons, or backhanded compliments, otherwise they're not effective. Examples of weak appreciations are:

- **You're the best friend anyone could ever have.**
- **You could have done worse.**
- **At least you finished the race.**
- **Sometimes you're a good father.**
- **You sure look better than last time I saw you.**

If appreciations are genuine, they won't be considered empty or excessively lavish. Here are some examples of strong appreciations:

- **I appreciate how you helped me on this.**
- **I appreciate your sense of integrity.**
- **I like how thoughtful you are.**
- **I appreciate that you cleaned your room this morning.**
- **I'm glad you understand how I feel about this.**

The fourth category of kindness is gratitudes. Being thankful for what you usually take for granted, you become aware of how fortunate and blessed you are. Gratitudes remind us of our bounty and thus offset complaints and feelings of entitlement. Specific gratitudes may be:

- **I'm grateful for my good health.**
- **I'm grateful for my friends and family.**
- **I'm grateful for this meal.**
- **Thank you for your help today.**

Rule Four: Listen

At the end of my communication workshops, I ask students to share what they will take away from the day. I'm continually surprised at the number of people who say, "The importance of listening." A huge burden is lifted when people realize they're not responsible for keeping conversations going by talking continually. People with a fear constitution often tell stories or engage in idle commentary to avoid silence. But they soon learn that lapses of silence give others the opportunity to speak up and time to integrate what has been said.

Ideally, listening and talking should be in balance. But listening isn't the passive experience you might be used to. Listening well is a skill that usually requires the most practice. Being a good listener skyrockets the quality of your relationships, and it's also one of the easiest ways you can promote intimacy, understanding, closeness, and love. If you can't listen to someone else with empathy, consider emoting and/or powering on a truth such as **"Your viewpoints and needs are as important as mine."** Virtually no one feels sufficiently heard. Half-listening, multitasking, or daydreaming while others are speaking is a no-no so you should get out of the habit as soon as possible. How many times have you asked, "How are you?" without pausing to listen to the other person's response? Hmmm. You're not the only one who probably can't remember.

The best way to show you're listening is to close your mouth, shut out background noise, and give the other person undivided attention. It's definitely not the 'normal' thing to do in this age where it's considered good to do ten things at once: speaking, while texting, while shopping for groceries, while picking gum out of your five-year-old's braid. Full attention when someone else is speaking also means you're not already gearing up for an opportunity to counter with your own opinions. You may think you're demonstrating empathy when you interrupt another person's story to chime in about your own experience. But you may be surprised to find the other person doesn't really care about a "bigger fish" story; they just wore their heart on their sleeves and you're trying to one up them! Communication has turned into competition.

If you tend to interrupt or dominate every conversation, slap some imaginary duct tape on your mouth when someone else is speaking. Hogging the airtime or not paying attention to another person who's speaking will produce anger in others. When you don't listen to someone, you're failing to acknowledge that person as an equal. And that's never going to inspire good feelings. The other person perceives it as a violation and responds accordingly. Listening well, on the other hand, promotes love. It's a form of selfless giving and an invitation to connect.

Just because you understand a person's position doesn't automatically mean you agree with it. For love to flourish, you must fully accept that other people's viewpoints and needs are as valid as yours. This seems to be challenging for many who have developed strong opinions about everything from politics to mothering techniques. Earnestly listening to people makes them feel comfortable and safe.

The following are listening "dos":

1. Be quiet (think duct tape!). Step back, observe, and see what's going on. Put yourself in someone else's shoes to get empathy for her position.

2. Smile and nod a lot. These are nonverbal gestures that express an open and compassionate stance of listening.

3. Support yourself mentally when listening by repeating such phrases as:

   - **Your viewpoints and needs are as valid as mine.**
   - **We are the same.**
   - **They are "you-ing" me and what they are saying says nothing about me.**

4. If a topic fills you with big doses of sadness, anger, or fear, take a short time-out to deal with your emotions. Then listen more.

5. Encourage people to talk more by saying things like, "Tell me more" and "I want to understand where you're coming from."

6. Ask questions sparingly to draw others out and further their thinking. Then listen some more.

   - What do you think?
   - How did that feel?
   - Is there anything you need to say or do about that?

7. Request a summary to make sure you understand the other person's point. "Could you tell me again what you want me to know?"

8. Show understanding by stating what you infer or observe. Listen further.

- I see you're sad about what happened.
- I bet you feel awful about that.
- I'd guess that must have been annoying.
- You're doing so well in this difficult situation.

9. Paraphrase what you've heard and ask for verification. Try to isolate the event and the emotions the speaker feels. You can show you were listening by repeating the contents and emotional component their message in your own words. "You're saying that when I spoke to you in that tone of voice yesterday, you felt angry, but you were caught too off guard to say anything."

Listening Don'ts

- Interrupting
- Leaping into problem solving
- Offering unsolicited advice or opinions
- Finishing others' sentences
- Changing the topic
- Matching stories
- Debating or challenging
- Cornering or interrogating

Eileen Uses the Rules

Eileen had a nasty habit of nagging her husband every time he left things randomly around the house. She had been calling him a slob for years, but this wasn't exactly creating marital harmony. Eileen was tired of both her own nagging and her husband's messiness. Since she put so much energy into harping at Greg, their relationship had become strained.

Eileen knew she had to focus on changing herself if she wanted to improve their relationship. She realized her reaction to Greg's clutter was under her control. Forcing Greg to change was not.

Telling other people what they should do is born of anger and not accepting reality. So before Eileen figured out what she wanted to say, she needed to accept what was. She repeated:

- **Greg is the way he is, not the way I want him to be.**
- **Greg's messiness is not a deal breaker for our marriage.**
- **I'm changing so I'll feel better about myself.**
- **I love Greg.**

Focusing on these truths for a few minutes, she felt a shift when she remembered that his whole family was like that and he wasn't being messy to spite her. She realized nagging was "you-ing" and that she really had an "I" to say each time she felt impelled to nag. Now she was ready to figure out how to talk about something specific that had happened earlier that day. Here's what she came up with:

"I got mad this morning when I saw your clothes on the floor, because I like to live in a neat house. I realize I've got to deal with my nagging, because that's not helping our relationship. I'm going to work on my part, and I'd also like to figure out what I can do with any of your things that I find on the floor so I don't have to look at them. Do you have any suggestions about what I should do with your stuff, so it will be out of harm's way and you'll be able to find it? I appreciate you putting up with my nagging all these years."

Greg couldn't resist Eileen's amazing admission and clear communication. He proposed getting a big box in which to dump the items she found lying around, including his favorite mug and water bottle. They joked as they hammered out the details. She'd decorate a cardboard box and they'd put it in the hallway downstairs. For her part, she agreed to genuinely appreciate Greg for his efforts at keeping the house clean.

For the first little while Greg didn't leave a single item on the floor. Then one day, Eileen walked into the bedroom and saw Greg's workout clothes strewn all over. This time, her anger didn't surge, and the impulse to draw sweeping conclusions didn't arise. She felt prepared.

*She repeated a few times: "**Greg's messiness is not a deal breaker for our marriage**," then put the clothes in the big box. Eileen could hardly wait to see Greg's reaction. He didn't say a word, but retrieved his possessions. She didn't say anything either.*

Their plan worked well for a few more days. But when Eileen saw Greg's racquetball gear and shopping bags in the den, her desire to blast him was so intense she immediately did a little "hinge anger." She grabbed the door and vigorously shoved it back and forth on its hinge. Eileen was surprised at how much anger she was carrying. In only five minutes, Eileen felt better. In fact, she felt great! She realized that her overreaction was due to a combination of many things. Part of it was Greg's transgression, but even more of her reaction was related to the dent she had put in her car that afternoon.

Eileen realized that she didn't have an "I" to say and didn't need to have a conversation with Greg about it. She put Greg's clutter in the box.

Over the following weeks, Eileen noticed a difference in the atmosphere around the house. Without the constant tug-of-war, there was more ease, affection, and openness between them that extended to the whole family. She also discovered how fun it was to make a concerted effort to catch Greg being neat.

Hey, Jude!

1. *Once in a while, it feels good to put people in their place with a righteous jab. They deserve it.*

   Satisfaction from "you-ing" lasts a few seconds as angry comments dart from your mouth and wound your intended victim. But that temporary pleasure of inflicting damage is short-lived, and quickly turns hollow as you carve deep grooves of hurt, anger, fear, and separation. People don't recover very easily. Taking your anger out on telephone books leaves no bitter aftertaste.

2. *I sometimes tell little white lies.*

People lie when they don't feel safe telling the truth. Sometimes lying is more convenient, helping things go our way or making us come across as more appealing. It also saves an emotional reaction that we don't want to deal with. However, expect those lies and half-truths to come back and bite you. The task of being honest requires courage. If you stick to "I"s and specifics, you only have to endure the moment of delivery and resolve not to take other peoples' reactions personally. Oftentimes, deception is harder than truth. For most of us, it's easier to handle the brief shock of honesty than the extended suffering of a half-truth.

3. *My partner and I often have our ugliest, least productive arguments late at night.*

The four rules are essential, all the time, but especially when it's late and you're tired, in a hurry, or preoccupied. Emotionally laden conversations are demanding, so you need the best conditions to handle them successfully. When you don't feel you're making headway, lovingly but firmly stop the conversation. Together, set a specific time to resume talking when you'll both be fresh, or agree on exactly how much longer you'll talk before giving it a rest. Don't succumb to pressure to continue past your personal limit.

4. *How can my husband and I help each other improve our communication with these new rules?*

For starters, give each other plenty of praise for following the rules. Change takes effort, and no one can ever be genuinely acknowledged too much. Since you're both learning something new, expect some transgressions. Lovingly help each other to locate the specifics, and your "I"s. Agree on a loving signal that indicates a rule is being broken. Point out your own lapses by saying, "Oops. Sorry. I need to rephrase what I just said." To avoid unnecessary fallout, I suggest that you use a nonverbal signal and agree to do something like throw a Kleenex on the floor as a penalty flag or give the time-out sign when there is a violation. These non-inflammatory signs automatically stop miscommunication and give you and your husband a playful opening to try again.

5. *The last time my fiancé and I fought, it got really nasty. When I told him that my parents agree with me about how self-absorbed he is, he really flipped.*

You know how a grill's flame goes sky-high when you throw lighter fluid on it? That's about what bringing in a third party to justify your position does. And the ends of your hair might even sizzle from the heat. Your fiancé can't help but feel angry, because bringing in your parents leads him to feel as if you're ganging up on him with people not even present in the room. Whenever you unilaterally make your private relationship problems public, you introduce an additional issue to resolve. In this case, you have the original topic that you were trying to discuss and your decision to involve your parents. I suggest that you apologize for your communication mistakes and then do some more listening so that he feels truly understood.

6. *I enjoy teasing and kidding. It's my humor. Are you suggesting that I give it up?*

You're asking for trouble with this kind of communication style. You are "you-ing" other people, and your fun is at their expense. What you call humor has an angry edge and hurts other people, causing them to become cautious around you. Stick to the "I"s and specifics, and I promise that you and others will feel more comfortable. If you continue with your present style, expect major resistance or lukewarm reception.

7. *I say such terrible things when I'm angry. The words just fly out of my mouth. How can I change this?*

Right out of the gate, become aware of the physical warning signs of an impending outburst. Physical signals — heat rising on the back of your neck, a pounding heart, breaking into a sweat — immediately mean you need to take a break, saying something along the lines of, "I don't want to blow up and say something I'll regret, so I'm going to take a few minutes." Express your anger physically and/or power on accepting what is. When you feel more centered, locate the specific thing that set you off and find your "I" about the topic. Return, deliver what you have to say with kindness and a smile and watch possibilities unfold before your eyes.

Reconstructing Relationships

These communication rules are like a root system that will ground you in support, love, truth, and integrity with every interaction you encounter. They may feel a little awkward at first, but you'll get it with practice. Now that you understand the rules, I'm going to show you how they apply to everyday life. The quality of your relations will improve dramatically, and you'll be grateful you learned these strategies.

Trading Time

Some of us talk too much, while others rarely say a word. Fix this imbalance by using your talking and listening skills to "trade time." The situation could involve a family around the dinner table, a gathering of friends, or a meeting of coworkers; trading time gives each person the opportunity to both give and receive undivided attention. When a couple has gotten into the habit of not talking, for example, this framework allows each partner to say what he/she has to say, while the other simply listens. The simple opportunity to express your "I" without interruption helps you come into your personal power, be in the present, and increase your empathy for someone else's position. You enjoy connection, understanding, and a venue for satisfying sharing.

Everybody gets the same amount of uninterrupted time to talk about themselves on a specific topic, which could be as mundane as how their day went, or as significant as views on what to do with an unplanned pregnancy. It's not a dialogue. While one person is speaking, everyone else gives full attention and only listens. Exchanges are free of name-calling, finger-pointing, debating, or rebuttals. When the next person speaks, he doesn't respond to what the preceding person said. Rather, he says what is true for him about the topic at hand. Use a kitchen timer to impartially keep track of time. If it goes off mid-sentence, allow the person talking to finish his immediate thought before the next person begins taking her time. In a group setting, participants can pass a "talking piece," such as a stick, so it's undeniably clear who has the floor.

Take one or two minutes for brief check-ins. Expressing important personal viewpoints might require a bit more time, perhaps three to five minutes. Try to avoid repeated lengthy monologues. Agree on the duration and stay flexible within those parameters. Although the time allotted might be short, those few minutes may be the longest interval of undivided attention and uninterrupted talking you've ever experienced. And don't underestimate the difficulty of just listening. (It might be the first occasion when you agree to use some duct tape!)

Talking about What You Feel

Verbalizing what you really feel is crucial to improving communication. Talk about your feelings, stay specific, and stick to the emotions you're experiencing right now. Saying, "I feel as if you..." or "I feel that you..." might seem like expressing feelings but those veiled forms of "you-ing," aren't going to illicit open responses. Rather than "I feel as if you don't like me," say "I felt hurt when you called me a slob."

Be careful about using words that imply that something has been done to you. Such words as manipulated, neglected, judged, and abandoned are basically disguised forms of "you"s. When you say, "I feel ignored," you're really proclaiming, "You're ignoring me," or "I feel ignored by you," which immediately puts the other person on the defensive. Pushing against the defense works in a football games, but not so much in communication.

Check out the two columns below to get a better idea of the difference between the two. Then start a campaign to eliminate the disguised "you"s. Why? Because it's "I" time to focus on what's real! This list is based on the work of Dr. Marshall Rosenberg's Nonviolent Communication model.

Feeling Words

Disguised "You"s	"I"s
used	insecure
put down	jealous
cheated	foolish
discounted	resentful
manipulated	impatient
abandoned	envious
abused	worried
attacked	bored
betrayed	lonely
bullied	blue
unwanted	embarrassed
cornered	tired
devalued	upset
diminished	hurt
interrupted	melancholy
intimidated	frustrated
judged	ashamed
let down	guilty
mistreated	separate
neglected	inadequate
overworked	selfish
patronized	helpless
pressured	overwhelmed
trapped	panicky
taken for granted	confused
threatened	depressed
unappreciated	anxious
unheard	nervous
unsupported	uneasy
rejected	stubborn
ignored	fearful

Handling Communication Violations

Just when you think you've got it, I'm going to add one more other piece to the communication puzzle: you can't control other people's reactions. Even if you abide by the four rules, for sure you'll have to deal with other people's communication violations. They'll speak in "you"s, overgeneralize, and focus on the negative. They won't listen. It's annoying, frustrating, and disheartening, but that's reality. By stonewalling or striking back, you only further escalate sadness, anger, and fear.

Adopt the role of a matador. You don't want to get gored! So instead of preparing yourself to be mortally wounded each time the bull charges, pull out your cape, step back, and let the bull's horns go speeding by. Charging back only antagonizes the bull further, so with each attack, pirouette and prepare to deflect the next assault. Remember: when someone is coming at you with a raised voice, guilt trip, or over-the-top drama, you have a choice. You can engage and give what you think they deserve (which gets you no where), or you can intentionally avoid the collision by sticking to the communication rules. Remain steadfast and don't act on the impulse to lunge back by defending yourself or responding to allegations with violations of your own. The dynamic will shift. Without your resistance, there won't be anything to fight against.

Another thing to keep in mind is those people are floundering as much as you have been. But they don't have the tools you do right now. They're still sinking in a river of sadness, anger, or fear. If you remember that, you won't get as offended or take their communication violations personally. Don't look for the germ of truth in their violations. Keep being the matador. Those horns are deadly. Dodge violations while repeating a truth or two about the other person and yourself, such as:

- This isn't about me.
- She is upset right now.
- She doesn't know any other way to communicate.
- He's feeling emotions and targeting them at me.
- He is feeling afraid and overgeneralizing.
- I'm fine.
- My job is to stick to the specific and take care of myself.

Take a break if you can't stick to the rules. A little distance never hurt anyone and will give you the opportunity to get re-centered. Then you'll be clear about what you need to say or do when you come back. If you take a break, the other person might get even angrier in the short term, but that's better than the damage you'll cause by staying in a conversation that's too heated to be a constructive interchange.

Before you leave the situation, offer a reasonable concrete time when you'd be willing to resume the conversation. This way it won't be confused with avoiding the situation or punishing the other person. Speak up so it will be seen for what it is: taking care of yourself. Leaving and not checking in for an update after more than an hour or two will usually be unproductive and generate even more emotions.

Sometimes, when you muster up the courage to say what's true for you, all you can do is sidestep the "you-ing," overgeneralizations, and negativity that comes at you. Refrain from justifying your point of view or responding to accusations, because this distracts you from delivering your message. It's not the time to draw a final conclusion or make an important decision.

Avoid labeling yourself the victim and retreating. Gently but firmly repeat your message. Don't give up or get sidetracked by people's reactions. Be like a broken record. Most of us cave in after one heroic effort. Often, three repetitions aren't even enough. Say the same thing lovingly, over and over again, up to eight times. Repetitions are not necessarily combative, but they do express how important it is that your "I" is understood. For instance: "I'm too tired to go to the concert, honey. I'm very tired, and that's why I'm not going. I checked in with myself several times and feel really clear that I'm just too exhausted to go out tonight."

No one is completely perfect, and it's normal you'll slip into communication violations from time-to-time. Don't beat yourself up. Just be aware when you're "you-ing," lumping, jumping, or saying unkind things, and recover by owning up to your mistake and saying what you really meant. Then listen to the impact that your violation had on the other person. Once you really understand the damage your words created, you can resume the original conversation.

How to Speak Up about Anything: The I-5

Asserting yourself may not come as naturally to you as it does to others. Perhaps you're a bit timid. Or you worry your viewpoint won't be accepted. Not knowing what's true for you, or knowing but not being able to speak up in a non-combative way can be big hurdles to communicating your needs. The four communication rules make it easier. First, figure out specifically what's true for you about the situation you're stuck in (rules one and two), then express your truth kindly (rule three), and finally, listen with openness to the recipient's response (rule four).

I know, I know. You're saying it's not that simple to do, especially when emotions are maxed out, the topic is super-sensitive, and you're strung out beyond belief. I integrated Attitude Reconstruction's four rules with the Nonviolent Communication model of Marshall Rosenberg, and came up with what I call the "I-5." The I-5 gives you a reliable way to say what's true for you about any topic in a non-threatening way.

The I-5

Steps	Use These Words
1. Identify a specific event or topic.	1. When this happened
2. Name your emotions and feelings.	2. I feel/felt
3. Give information about yourself: your needs, wants, vices, expectations, thoughts, values, past experiences.	3. because I…
4. Define specific boundaries, intentions, requests, consequences, and solutions.	4. and I…
5. Finish with some kindness.	5. and I appreciate…

Let's go over each of the steps.

1. When this happened... Identify one specific situation or topic at a time. It's not "You're so inconsiderate," but "I was upset when you were forty-five minutes late yesterday."

2. I feel/felt... This part is about you! Talk about the feelings and emotions you experienced around the event. Sticking to sadness, anger, or fear, you'll stay focused on giving information about yourself, rather than resorting to accusing "you"s or indulging in inaccurate generalities. Be careful about those "-ed" feeling words I mentioned a few pages earlier; go back and check them frequently. It's tricky at first to get the difference. Many are veiled "you"s, which make it hard for the other person to remain receptive

3. because I... Give information about yourself. Explain why you feel the way you do. This step is usually the hardest for people, because you have to look within and take responsibility for your feelings and emotions. Giving details about your needs, wants, thoughts, and values let's someone know where you're coming from. Instead of saying, "I'm angry because you're always late and only think about yourself," say, "I feel angry because I said I had a three o'clock appointment, and I understood that you would be home by 2:45 to watch the kids. I hate to be late."

4. and I... This step clarifies your specific position on the topic: your requests, what you'd like to see happen in the future, what actions you're planning to take, and when, and what you'll do to take care of yourself. In this step, you're setting specific boundaries, intentions, requests, consequences, and solutions. Get detailed. The more detail, the better. Make sure that what you say is doable, suitable for the current situation, and within your control. If you don't follow through with what you say, you'll lose credibility and gain heartache.

5. I appreciate... Finish with kindness. A positive comment or appreciation sets the tone for the ensuing dialogue. "Thanks for listening," or "I'm glad we're talking about this." Make sure you mean what you say. (Lovingly say it more than once if the other party doesn't seem to hear you the first time.)

Practicing the I-5

If you already know someone is going to get offended, reactive, or angry, it really takes forethought, boldness, and timing to speak up effectively. It may be scary to tackle sensitive topics (shaking beforehand helps), but you just have to do it if you want to honor yourself. The key is to use a warm and loving tone. Here are some situations and possible I-5s.

What's your "I" when...

- **you learn a friend has been talking about your divorce at work?**

   When I heard that you told Jane about my divorce, I felt angry, because I want my personal life to be private. I want you to stop discussing my affairs with other people in the office. I appreciate our longstanding friendship and enjoy being able to confide in you.

- **your daughter cooked lunch for her friends but didn't clean up?**

   When I went into the kitchen this afternoon and there were pots in the sink, I felt angry, because I had spent an hour cleaning the kitchen this morning. I would like you to clean up after you cook for your friends. All that being said, thanks for leaving me that plate of delicious pasta. I enjoyed every last bite.

- **your husband leaves the house without saying when he'll return?**

   When you said you wanted some alone time, I felt afraid, because when I was young, my dad used to disappear for days at a time. In the future, if you need to get out of the house, please tell me when you'll return so I won't feel so apprehensive. Thanks for hanging in there with me.

Below are some familiar situations that call for an I-5. Try writing out all five steps for each. To better develop this skill, share your ideas with a friend and refine them together until you both agree they're clear. Remember to make the topic and your request specific.

- **You finally return a friend's call two weeks later**
- **Your boss asks you to take on a project at 5:15 p.m.**
- **The bill from the mechanic is twice what you expected**
- **You don't want to take a class with your partner**

Here are some possible solutions to the I-5 practice scenarios laid out above. The information isn't in exact sequence, but they cover all the I-5 components in a way that promotes clear communication. See if it gives you some ideas:

- **You finally return a friend's call two weeks later**

    When you called me a couple of weeks ago and asked for the name of my personal trainer, I freaked out because I didn't know what to say. I know I said I'd call him and see if he was taking new clients, but I realized I think of him as a confidant and felt uncomfortable with sharing him. If you're still looking for someone to work with, I'd be glad to ask him to recommend someone else. I'm sorry I took so long to get back to you. I value our relationship and enjoy the time when we get together.

- **Your boss asks you to take on a project at 5:15 p.m.**

    When you asked me to type those letters at 5:15, I felt really torn. I really want to help you with this project because I'm committed to my job, but I promised my son I would go to his ball game tonight because his dad is out of town. I'll be glad to type the letters first thing in the morning or if you need them today, I'll see if anyone else is available before I go. In the future, if you suspect there will be work for me after hours, I'd appreciate it if you'd let me know a day or two beforehand.

- **The bill from the mechanic is twice what you expected**

  I'm in shock! This morning, you told me that the bill was going to be about three hundred dollars, and it's six hundred and change. I'm on a tight budget and can't possibly pay you that much. I'm willing to pay four hundred, but that's tops. In the future, if the work is going to be more than your estimate, I need to okay it before you start work. I like coming here and love the excellent service you've always provided.

- **You don't want to take a class with your partner**

  When you asked me to take that cooking class with you, I started to panic. I love to please you, but I don't want to spend my Saturday indoors. I'd be happy to do an outdoor activity with you, or if you want to go with a friend, I'll look forward to hearing all the details when you return. I love that you like to learn new things, especially around food.

A client of mine took home a list of practice examples to learn how to speak up assertively and lovingly. She reported back her biggest learning: it was okay to be honest. Next I asked her to create fifteen of her own scenarios, and come up with ways she could communicate what was true for her. After going over that list together, she realized how down on herself she had felt for not mastering this new way of communicating right away (especially step three, giving information about herself). Her reaction is a great example of how we interpret our experience.

It may take practice, just like any new skills does. But over time, you'll be able to quickly identify what you really want to say and sound casual and non-confrontational when you say it. Your words may sound stilted to you at first, but you'll still find the benefits far outweigh any temporary discomfort.

Bob Boldly Speaks Up

My brother, Bob, generously volunteered to help a friend with a new web site, thinking it was going to be a little slam-dunk project. As the scope exponentially escalated, he lost his enthusiasm and started to feel taken advantage of. As a laid-back guy, he rarely ever called foul, but with each passing day, realized if he didn't say something, his tolerance would be severely tested. Without knowing it, Bob sent Roger an e-mail that was a perfect example of an I-5.

Hey Roger,

I'm feeling a bit confused and frustrated at this stage working on the web site. It would be really helpful to me if we first settled upon and finalized the general structure and overall look of the site. We can make changes later, but the firmer we have it now, the easier it will be to build it and the fewer revisions we'll have to make in the future.

It would also be really helpful if we drew up a checklist of things we need to get the job done: which pieces you've already sent me, which pieces replace earlier pieces, and which pieces you are going to be sending. Then, when I have most of the tasks laid out, we can go through them together, clarify any questions, do some last-minute editing, and then declare them "done, finished, and ready."

At that point, I can build the entire site and get it up and running. Then we can spend some time going over it and getting some feedback. After that, we'll do a final "spiffication" and voilà, we'll have the coolest web site on the Net!

Love,

Bob the Taskmaster

Bob was so pleased when he heard back from Roger immediately, thanking him profusely for taking charge. Roger was relieved to have someone set a direction for their project. He included his list and vowed to add new topics to the roster before immediately diving into them.

Bob's boldness in writing his e-mail totally shifted the quality of his interactions with Roger. They were now on the same team. They worked well together with light-heartedness and focus. At launch, both of them were ecstatic with their end result.

The Three Bridges: Communicating with People in the Grip of Emotions

Seeing and hearing are natural gifts for us. Look at the way animals use their senses to their advantage. They can sense safety, danger, play, and even food from them! You can use your senses to determine if someone is swept up in sadness, anger, or fear and then know how you can best help. With just a little practice, you'll recognize the emotions underneath other people's destructive demeanors, words, and actions. More than likely you were once where they are now. Then, rather than reacting to what they say or do, extend a communication "bridge" to help shift their emotional state. You can say what they truly long to hear but don't know how to ask for.

The Three Communication Bridges

Sadness	→	appreciation	→	Joy
Anger	→	understanding	→	Love
Fear	→	reassurances	→	Peace

Where is their attention focused? That's the first question to ask your observation skills. People feeling sadness but not crying are most likely thinking poorly of themselves. They yearn for appreciations. In your interactions with them, convey the idea, "I love you. You're great." Remind them of their strengths and contributions.

Bitter folks striking out in anger and spewing "you"s all over the place really just feel isolated and are in desperate need of understanding — not debates, lectures, or reprimands. The chances they'll hear what you have to say are slim to none unless you can genuinely connect with them first. You need to sincerely hear them out without taking what they say personally. Try silently repeating or saying, "I want to hear what you have to say." Focus on what's going on with them behind their angry words.

If one of your friends is easily overwhelmed, chances are she's got some unexpressed fear stocked up. She needs honest reassurances. Comfort, soothe, and repeatedly remind her that everything is and will be all right. Other reassuring comments are "I'm here," "We'll make our way through this together," "I'm not leaving," or "I'll take care of it." Or offer reassurances by reminding her of the objective reality: "Your boss really likes the work you do," or "You've done this successfully before."

If you're unable or unwilling to offer a communication bridge, it's probably because your own unexpressed emotions are getting in the way. It's okay. You're human. Contemplate what's going on for you. To quickly reignite your compassion, take a brief time-out to do some emoting, rewiring, and/or looking within. Then you will be able to meaningfully extend a bridge.

Give yourself the support of asking others to extend a bridge to you when you're in the grip of sadness, anger, or fear. Even better, do it for yourself. Sadness, for instance, is a cue to give yourself some extra self-appreciation. Anger indicates your need for some gentleness, compassion, and understanding. And fear is a sign to reassure yourself that everything is indeed okay and unfolding in its own time — because it is!

You'll deepen your personal relationships when you become adept at recognizing the emotions that people struggle with. And you can use this knowledge to communicate in the ways most helpful to them. What an amazing talent you'll be cultivating. For example, if you know that your husband has an anger constitution, you can consciously listen silently and understand his position, especially at times when he is upset or under stress. If a workmate clearly has a sadness constitution, you can choose to validate her gifts and skills a little more often.

How to Resolve Differences

When couples differ, they usually refuse to listen. And that's the beginning (or the continuation) of the downfall. They resort to "you"s, overgeneralizations, and negative comments. The inability to reconcile differences harmoniously extinguishes love that once burned brightly. It's not just intimate partnerships that are destroyed by differences.

Business associates, neighbors, friends, and colleagues are affected as well. In each case we have a choice when conflicts arise. We can fight, give in, deny, and avoid, or we can cooperate, collaborate, negotiate, and accommodate.

Reconciling differences can happen with commitment to teamwork and by abiding by the four communication rules. Adversarial confrontations just amplify original differences and polarize parties. Regardless of the situation, the goal is to create a solution that's workable for everyone and connects, not separates. Expressing and hearing each person's position takes time. Depending on the complexity of the issue and the number of people involved, the process can take from ten minutes to several lengthy meetings. Don't be deterred by the time it takes to thoroughly resolve an issue. In the long run, your time investment will pay off, and you will have contributed to positive, effective communication that teaches others connectivity in the diversity.

The Two-Step

Small details or big issues, no matter! Two steps are all you need to resolve any difference. If you do the first step well, the second will be easy — even fun. This model works for any number of participants. Keep it handy especially when tempers flare and discussions stall.

The Two Steps to Resolve Any Difference

1. Exchange views about a specific issue until all feel understood by alternately talking and listening.

2. Together, find a workable solution that honors all parties.

Step One: Exchange views about a specific issue until all feel understood by alternately talking and listening

You're not looking for a solution here, just saying everything you need to say on one specific topic. This initial step is identical to the "trading time" format discussed earlier in the chapter. (A kitchen timer is very helpful.) Say everything you need to now because once you go to step two, talking about why you believe what you do is off topic.

This can be a bit of a time-consuming process. It's a challenge to articulate thoughts, especially if they need to be truly understood by another person. Keep alternating until neither person has anything more to say. That might mean ten rounds! Although you don't have to agree when you listen, you must recognize that all positions are equally valid. If communication violations occur (e.g., "you"s, overgeneralizations, unkindness), get our your matador cape. Gently remind the person you're communicating with to speak about himself or herself so you can understand.

In this process a prolonged emotional outburst might occur. If it does, take an agreed-upon amount of time for a breather — a few minutes or even a few days. When you get back together, just begin by addressing the specific event that triggered the outburst by trading time on that topic. Once the specific event is handled, go back to the original issue.

Understanding each other can be a bit of an issue-maze: as you talk and listen, new topics may emerge. Note them so they can be discussed at a later time, but resist the urge to throw out new issues on the table and complicate matters unless you both consider the shift helpful. When each person feels his or her position on the chosen topic is understood by the other, step one is done.

Step Two: Together, find a workable solution that honors all parties.

Integration. Seems like a very synergistic word to use when talking about compromise, but that's exactly what I'm suggesting. You have to be able to integrate all points of view in this step two in order to make it work. Your attention stays exclusively on seeking a suitable agreement. Step two is not the time to revert to espousing your grievances or challenging others, proclaiming who's right and wrong, or using threats and intimidation. It's not about rehashing your opinion of what happened in the past or interpreting the other person's behavior. Relish in this creative dialogue about finding sound solutions that are acceptable to all, right now and for the future.

As for what a good agreement looks like, it should combine the ideas of everyone concerned. It does not mean "your way" or "my way," but some way in the middle. Using the goal of connection as a guide, ask yourself these questions:

- How can we find a middle ground between our differences?
- What is a workable solution?
- Is the position I am proposing, or agreeing to, coming from self-ishness or love?

If there are bumps in the road, try adding in trading time to step two. You'll be surprised by how many alternatives you come up with. Collect every idea and extract the merits and liabilities of each. After listening to all suggestions, brainstorm to find the best blend of positions. Remain open, stay specific, build on each other's suggestions, and trade time when the discussion gets lopsided. Break big problems down into manageable pieces. Keep talking, and keep listening.

Clamming up like a shell or becoming the loud bully isn't going to win you any merit points nor compel others to find a happy solution. Focus on teamwork, putting the "we" first and personal desires second. Sometimes surrendering your own wants and needs is necessary for the good of the whole. If you normally give in, consult your intuition before acquiescing to another person's suggestion. Persist until you arrive at a win-win solution. Workable solutions that honor everyone are possible. If you can't find one, shelve the topic temporarily and set a specific time to resume the discussion, or bring in a neutral third party.

Once everyone's come to an agreement, it is imperative you honestly accept it, and not back out whenever emotions arise. Be careful not to consent to a solution that doesn't feel right, or you'll definitely experience a backlash. If the solution feels correct, you'll be able to let go of what you sacrificed and deal with your emotions about not getting your way. Avoid keeping score or bringing up your concessions later, either out loud or to yourself, in an insincere attempt at humor. Comments make hair on the back of the neck stand up and don't reflect acceptance.

They indicate you haven't truly handled your anger about your difference and the solution. If you constructively express your emotions physically, you can accept the best fit for all involved.

Armando and Angela Get on the Same Page

The couple's conflict seemed irreconcilable. Angela wanted a child and Armando did not. A part-time baby was not a possible compromise, so the question remained: what amicable solution could they both live with? They agreed their goal was to find a solution they both could accept.

First, they talked and listened to one another, voicing thoughts and feelings, for what seemed like the thousandth time (step one). After half an hour, in which they alternated talking in blocks of two minutes, they both felt understood and had nothing more to say.

Now they were ready to try to find a solution (step two). They brainstormed and came up with these options:

- *Doing therapy weekly*
- *Postponing the decision for one year and having fun together in the meantime*
- *Engaging more in the care of nieces and nephews*
- *Taking in a foster child*
- *Becoming a Big Brother or Sister*
- *Buying a dog*
- *Revisiting the issue using the "trading time" format once a month for no more than an hour at a time*
- *Splitting up in a year if they couldn't eventually reach an agreement, as painful as this would be*

During this step, there was no more talk about why one wanted a baby and the other didn't. In this excruciating example, since the couple did not want to break up, they had no choice but to fully accept their differences and reach a solution based on that reality.

After discussing each option, they realized participating in ongoing counseling sessions and taking a more active role in raising their nephew felt like appropriate first steps. They'd spend time with their nephew at least twice a week and not talk about the baby issue for three months, except in therapy sessions.

Armando and Angela ended their exchange with appreciations, to reconnect, honor their cooperation, and put their differences to a compassionate rest. Now they were free to focus on everything that existed outside their conflict, which included the deep love they had for each other. They had paved the way for unencumbered time together and agreed to patiently give each other a hug or a reminder of their agreement if one couldn't resist bringing up the topic during the hiatus.

This couple knew after three months that taking on a secondary parental role wasn't a satisfactory solution for either of them. Therapy, however, had helped them improve their communication and the resolving-differences format actually yielded the possibility of adoption for the first time.

Making Specific Agreements

No one gets lost or mixes up signals when specific solutions and agreements are clearly defined. Those vital life-robbers called unexpressed sadness, anger, and fear cause us to forget what we knew to be true when we made an agreement. That's why it's helpful to write down the details of a mutually agreed-upon solution. As needed, decide who is responsible for what, when, and how. Be definite about time schedules. Set suitable consequences for fulfillment and non-fulfillment of designated responsibilities. Be sure the consequences are clear, just, and understood, so everyone knows exactly what he or she is agreeing to.

Include a predetermined check-in time for reevaluation. If you need to change an agreement, renegotiate it with all parties before the agreed-upon deadline so everyone stays on the same page. Broken agreements are violations that evoke anger and erode trust. Keep in mind a new adversarial situation is created if someone doesn't keep his word, and that's counterproductive to all the time you just put in. Each unmet agreement must be addressed in a timely manner to prevent derailing the solution altogether.

Whoever doesn't keep her end of the "bargain" should apologize and give information as to why she broke the agreement. More importantly, she should listen to the offended party to understand the effect of her actions. Self-justification needs to take a backseat to listening. After everyone feels heard about what happened (step one), they must together fashion a new workable arrangement (step two).

Guidelines for Resolving Conflict with Groups of People

You can successfully navigate conflicts in groups of people with widely differing points of view. From religions to politics to sexual preferences, it is possible to respect other point of views and to even have peaceful dialog as long as you're committed to following the communication rules and using the two-step solution. Here's a summary to successfully reconcile more complex differences. These guidelines apply to two people, multiple countries, and everything in between.

1. Establish an agreed-upon meeting time and length with all participants beforehand. Expect to meet many times if the topic to be discussed is complex or many people are involved.

2. Before coming to the meeting, each participant should identify specific topics to discuss and determine what is true for him or her about each. Preparation could involve emoting, rewiring, and/or consulting one's intuition. Participants might power on truths that affirm their commitment to reaching a collaborative solution.

3. When the meeting convenes, have each person declare an intention to follow these guidelines. Designate a facilitator, recorder, and timekeeper to ensure that the meeting is well run and documented. For couples, the facilitator might be a therapist, but any objective third party will work. The

facilitator keeps the discussion focused and steers it away from communication violations. The recorder writes down the details, agreements, and responsibilities. The timekeeper ensures that everyone abides by agreed-upon time limits. It is imperative that the timer intervene when a person's interval has expired. One person can fulfill one or more of these roles.

4. Begin the discussion by trading time for a minute or two on how everyone is doing in general, apart from the specific issue at hand.

5. Together, have the group formulate a joint goal and common positive vision of how they want to resolve the conflict. Make sure that it includes a commitment to finding the best solution that honors every position.

6. Collect all the topics that participants want to cover. Sometimes, there will be only one; other times, there may be a dozen. If there are several, write them down. Resist the impulse to start discussing a given issue before finishing the list. Prioritize the topics for discussion. If you can't agree where to start, trade time until you reach consensus. Alternatively, you can write down all items, put them in a hat, and pick one.

7. Follow the two-step conflict resolution process. Exchange views by talking and listening, and together find a workable solution for each topic. If an tissue becomes complex, reaches a stalemate, or extends beyond an agreed time, shelve it temporarily and agree when you'll return to it. It's normal that new topics will arise and require airtime, so don't set yourself up for trouble by expecting a quick fix.

8. Before any meeting ends, review agreements you've made and set a follow-up meeting time. Each person then offers some appreciation about what has transpired. Discussions that finish on a positive note reinforce the goal of resolving differences and reconnecting, or at least of peacefully coexisting.

9. Begin each subsequent meeting with a review of the agreed-upon goal, then add new agenda items if needed. Tie up loose ends from the previous meeting, reviewing one item at a time. Then select a new topic for discussion. Ignore laments about how much time the process is taking and keep meeting until your slate is clean. Schedule regular check-ins to follow up on each meeting, as appropriate.

10. If you need assistance to keep the discussion flowing smoothly and stay on task, call in an impartial mediator, whether a professional or a friend. I suggest choosing a loving, wise, and experienced third party who can remain neutral in emotionally charged situations.

Hey, Jude!

1. *I don't want to try the I-5 with my family because I'm afraid they'll consider it too staged.*

If they do, ignore their snide comments and "you"s. Most likely, however, they will breathe a sigh of relief at the change in your communication style. If you feel overwhelmed or lost with the entire sequence of the I-5, just remember what's most important: "I"s and specifics.

2. *How can I know if what I'm about to say is constructive?*

It will be, if you stick to the rules of communication and double-check with your intuition. Or ask yourself four simple questions (the gateways to peaceful speech in Buddhist philosophy): Is it true? Is it kind? Is it useful? Is the timing right?

3. *I give my sister great advice, but she rarely takes it. It's so frustrating — I'm just trying to help.*

Your well-meaning, unsolicited advice is still "you-ing." If your sister isn't ready for or doesn't want feedback, it's counterproductive to offer it. Don't share your insights unless you ask and receive permission first. If your sister declines, let your pearls of wisdom go and accept that she is responsible for her own happiness. Refocus on being happy yourself and take time to appreciate what you like about her. Power on truths such as **"My focus is myself," "We're all on our own paths,"** and **"I wish you well."**

4. *My partner gets so jealous when I spend time with other people that she insists I talk with her before I make any plans. I'm starting to get resentful.*

It sounds as if it's time to discuss this sensitive issue. At some point, all couples need to determine what issues are a "me" and what are a "we" — that is, what's okay to decide unilaterally and what's not. Follow the resolving-differences format and trade time until you agree which issues and decisions are individual and which are joint. Stay specific to clarify what is and isn't appropriate. Relationships are not about giving in or doing solely what you want, but about compromising and accommodating each other.

5. *Do you have any tips for what to do when my partner and I start bickering?*

Any kind of "you-ing" is a hot bed of negativity and exponentially increases the chances of saying something hurtful and damaging. Halt that process immediately by switching to the trading time format. The other strategy is to stop talking, take a time-out, and agree on when you will discuss the issue again at a calmer moment. In the interim, re-center yourself by pounding out your anger energy, accepting your differences, locating the specifics, and/or finding your "I" about each topic.

6. *When my husband and I were talking about which bills we need to pay this week, I couldn't help but bring up all his extravagances over the last years. I knew I shouldn't, but I did.*

The new golf clubs or the restaurant receipts for lunch — all of the unfinished business that comes flooding into your mind — should be noted, but addressed at a different time. Right now, stick to the topic of bills that need to be paid this week and how much money is in the account right now. Just stay with that task and celebrate your team effort. If you lump more than one issue together, your communication will inevitably get out of hand, and little will get resolved.

7. *How can I call it quits with my partner in a constructive way?*

First, end a relationship because you are following your inner knowing, not because you're in the midst of an argument, emotional meltdown, or have specific topics that need resolution. At the end of a relationship, it's difficult enough to mourn the good, so don't make matters harder by adding accusations and ambivalence to the mix. Targeting the other person, being uncivil, or engaging in endless hours of circular conversation will only create additional hurt, anger, and fear.

Communicate what is true for you with kindness, and listen to your partner's reaction. You might have to repeat the news several times. Lovingly sidestep any "you" communication. Talk with two or three friends for support and feedback, rather than trying to enlist everyone that you meet to "take your side." Breakups are endings that inevitably bring up emotions for both of you. Focus on expressing yours constructively so you can move on.

8. *What is the key to having good communication in a relationship?*

Focus on your half, abide by the four rules, extend the three communication bridges, and seek win-win solutions to resolve differences.

5

Actions: Hammering and Nailing

State your goal.
Create small doable steps.
Emote as you go.

When you're building a dream house, you pour over plans, ask for opinions, draft dozens of possibilities, and contemplate, sometimes months at a time. It's a rich, fertile playground for the mind, as you take daily tours through your imaginary future home, trying on all kinds of designs, locations of rooms, feelings of what it would be like to have tall ceilings or arched hallways, a nursery for a future little one, wooden floors or energy efficient tile. There's a lot of work involved in thinking things through. You're committing to manifesting your dream, but first you have to know what it looks like.

Building your inner dream home requires the same clarity, the same thorough deliberations. First make a solid plan to actualize your goal. Then grab the last tool — action — because you know a dream is nothing more than a figment of imagination (no matter how great it feels) until the contractors are hired and the house is under construction.

The word action gives sensation, doesn't it? Something dynamic. Pushing and moving; designing and creating; expanding and evolving. All of your tools are finally together in one place, ready to harmoniously take you from concept to reality. You've put on the hard hat, and understand that action is the most direct path to change. But where to start?

Contradicting old feelings, thoughts, words, and actions involves movement of some sort, which means using the tools you've acquired. But if it were that easy, why hasn't everyone created the magnificent life they want? Because we're creatures of habit, and we're stuck in acting out ingrained patterns without even realizing it.

It's hard to take action, when you're "stuck in the mud", a phrase created because we've all "been there, done that", and are still doing that. Maybe you've tried to make changes in the past, but your feet, body, heart, and head don't cooperative.

Behaving in compromising ways or turning your back on what needs attention because you just can't seem to change, is nothing more than succumbing to the byproducts of unexpressed sadness, anger, and fear. You probably understand that point by now. And you also get that years of not expressing those emotions have added up. Like sun damage, causing lots of funky-looking dark spots on your skin years after you were a sun goddess, those destructive habits are cumulative. They show up in all sorts of shady ways throughout your life, and interfere when you try to act in new ways.

Stuck Situations

Stuck situations challenge us all, and they can last for a few minutes or a lifetime. They are events that we have unprocessed emotions about. Stuck situations can be an ordinary event in the present, such as feeling misinterpreted by a friend or losing a client you've been pursuing for months. Maybe you're haunted by events in the past. Traumatic events happened to everyone in childhood, to varying degrees. Maybe you were bullied or lost a parent. Events that are in our future, such as getting married or filing a restraining order, are stuck situations, too, if you have unexpressed emotions about them.

I think of them as different splatters on a mirror. Each blob contains unexpressed emotions and all the sensations a particular event triggers. Overtime, there are so many splatters covering the surface, we can't see ourselves in the mirror anymore. Our ability to act constructively is diminished, and our choice of words is limited. And accessing joy, love, and peace, thinking clearly and flexibly, or hearing intuition is nearly impossible.

Suppose you get into an argument with your girlfriend today and you're in a standoff. That's a stuck situation. You react like she's committed the biggest love crime in the world because the exchange reactivates unexpressed emotions about your parents' volatile arguments when you were young. Rather than talk it out today, you revert to what you learned then: you shut down in order to avoid friction.

You actually have two stuck situations — your childhood wounds and the current argument. Often, if you dig deeply enough, you'll find the root of a current stuck situation in the past. Emotions from both the past and present swirl in at warp speed, making you dizzy and creating a dust storm of confusion. It's doubly hard to remain centered and clear. Because you haven't dealt with the emotions you felt as a child, it's hard to act in a different way today. It's as if you've constructed a big roadblock to feel joy, love, or peace. Sign says, 'Unstable conditions ahead: detour now.'

What emotions are interfering with you taking constructive action? What emotional footprints are influencing today's choices? If you aren't interested in exploring the emotional component of a past, present, or future stuck situation and prefer to get right to making a plan to handle the issue, skip the next few pages.

Defusing the Emotional Charge of a Stuck Situation

Recently, a new client came into my office. "I'm so angry at my ex-husband for having an affair," she said.

"That's painful," I replied. "When did that happen?"

"Fifteen years ago."

Whoa! What a perfect example of how holding on to past traumatic events colors our present experience. This is an extreme example, so it's easy to spot in her case. Is it as easy to pinpoint what emotions you are holding on to? Sometimes we need to return to the emotional component of an event and face what we aren't, didn't, or couldn't at the time before we can take action today.

Letting go doesn't mean saying you're over it. It means you no longer ruminate about what happened or cringe when you hear someone speak your ex's name. Letting go allows you to think about a situation, and come from a place of authentic neutrality, with a strong sense of compassion (for yourself and them) in your heart.

You can dismantle a stuck situation by yourself, with someone you trust, or in a group where constructively expressing emotions physically is truly okay. With a particularly traumatic event, it is advisable to have the assistance of a trained, licensed health-care professional who has been down the path many times before. She or he can lend a hand and provide a nurturing space for your exploration.

Choose a safe time and place to tell your story (you can either speak it out loud or write it down). Allow your mind to do a little investigating. Focus on what you suspect are benchmark events, and describe what happened.

Say you have a fear of abandonment that manifests as being clingy with your friends, desperate that they might exclude you from their gatherings. Get a sense of what was going on when you first felt needy. Maybe it was when your younger brother was born or when you had to change schools midyear.

Describe what you remember. Recount the specific event again several times, adding more details with each repetition, until you start feeling the emotions that you suppressed at the time. Keep talking until you've hit the pain and then keep your attention there. Suppressed emotions will explode on the surface, allowing you freedom to do what you didn't do then: constructively express your emotions physically without indulging your destructive thinking.

When you feel a calming resolution sink into your bones, move on to another incident and describe it in detail, emoting as you go. If calm remains elusive, there's something about that super sticky situation you're not fully accepting. Dealing with a layer of anger is often the solution. Accepting doesn't let other people off the hook; they're still responsible for their actions. But acceptance brings new insight about what you need to do today.

Forgiveness is also necessary if you've cried buckets and still feel hurt. Tell yourself people did the best they could at the time, given their own circumstances, limitations, and histories. Forgiving them doesn't mean you have to be best friends, but you do need to view them in a genuinely compassionate light. Here are some possible truths:

- **Mom learned to lie to cope when she was growing up.**
- **Mom couldn't handle raising a family by herself.**
- **People and things were the way they were.**
- **We all did the best we could at the time.**
- **I forgive you.**

The gift of forgiveness must also be given to yourself. It's fairly common to believe you were somehow to blame for traumatic events in your childhood. The reality is that you were little and did the best you could at the time. Stop beating yourself up or clinging to regrets. Power on truths such as:

- **If I knew then what I know now, I would have done things differently.**
- **That little girl sure was in pain.**
- **It was a difficult time.**
- **I did the best I could in order to survive.**
- **My job is to take care of myself now.**
- **I'm doing fine.**

After you emote and rewire, you will find yourself able to consult your intuition and determine what needs to be said and done to feel resolved. Sometimes, feeling complete is entirely an internal process. Other times, speaking up and taking action is imperative. If action is required and you follow through, the future opens its doors, and the present welcomes you with open arms.

The Roles of Fear and Peace in Taking Action

Why are you avoiding your friend? Your taxes? A mammogram? There is one answer: fear. Fear of feeling sadness, anger, and more fear about specific situations. You're living the life of a fear gal or guy! Fear of other people's emotions, the future, the new, rejection, failure — it goes on and on. You can justify it all you want, but somewhere underneath your reasons for not acting is a layer of fear that's stopping you dead in your tracks.

Acting in any sort of a 'new' way, propels you into the vast unknown. It's a scary prospect when you're losing control and traversing out of your safety zone. But you've experienced the other option: when you don't deal with your fear, you mind reverts to being in the future or past, overgeneralizing, forgetting what is true and real, and attempting to control.

The solution to taking action: (1) stick to the present and what's on your plate right now (including your emotions), (2) stay specific, (3) keep reminding yourself of what you know to be true in your clear moments, and (4) take small doable steps toward your goal, giving it your all and enjoying the ride. You'll recognize these as the core attitudes associated with peace.

Get specific and determine what you need to do in order to feel peace. Shiver beforehand and then just do it. Avoidance clearly hasn't been working and certainly hasn't brought you joy, love, or peace. So don't let old habits and destructive thoughts temp you back into complacency. It doesn't help you feel good about yourself, others, or life in general.

Do what you're avoiding. Set a reasonable deadline and take the plunge, emoting along the way. If you need to get a realistic picture of your credit card debt so you can decrease monthly payments, make a list of who to contact, pick up the phone, and start making calls. You'll have more information to determine your next reasonable step.

Deciding What To Do To Handle a Stuck Situation

Constructive action is the fastest way to resolve any stuck situation. But what if you're uncertain about what to do? I have three quick ways to determine your best action. First, take a brief time-out and tap into your intuition. From a quiet space, ask yourself, "What's needed here? What is the best course of action?" If the answer is clear, take time to translate it into doable action steps.

Let's say you've consulted with your intuition and you're still not sure. Number two: go back to the Attitude Reconstruction Blueprint. Often, constructive action is the opposite of what the "old you" would have done. Suppose your teenage son went ballistic after you said he couldn't use your car tonight. He did exactly what you were afraid of, screamed at the top of his lungs that you were mean, selfish, the worst mother in the world. And then just for effect, he stormed into his room and slammed the door.

Now what? If you check the Blueprint under the action column, you'll find "you-ing" and unrealistic expectations of others. That's what you've done in the past, what he's just done with you, and what you don't want to do again. So instead of striking back, genuinely accept what he said, and then say what's true for you.

Repeat to yourself, "Don't take the bait. He's feeling angry and taking it out on me." Follow him down the hall, lovingly acknowledge his frustration, and repeat your "I" about not using the car this evening. "As I told you last Sunday, until I hear from your teachers that you are getting Cs or better in all your classes, I'm only willing to give you the car one night during the week."

If it's impossible to get clear direction from your intuition, and the Blueprint isn't specific enough to get you into gear, go with the third choice. Set your goal and make a plan. Identify and use logical thinking to draft a sequence of small doable steps to get to your destination. I'll lay out how to do this, but first, let's look at how Martha's story illustrates the point.

Martha's Stuck Situation

Martha felt very close to her sister-in-law ever since Sally had married Martha's brother. They lived in neighboring states, and she cherished being able to visit often. But something had changed. Recently their phone conversations felt superficial and strained. Martha was devastated, having considered Sally her closest confidante.

Martha asked herself, "What have I done? Maybe I shared too many details about my marriage woes with her. Maybe I gave her too much advice." This rift was clearly eating at her. Martha needed more information from Sally, figuring out how her sister-in-law felt before she could decide what to do, but she was paralyzed with fear. She knew she had to talk to Sally, but the idea of being emotionally vulnerable on the phone made her uncomfortable.

Okay, now let's take a break from this story. What do you think is going on here? Why is Martha so afraid? Well, she fears her sister-in-law will reject her if she puts her feelings on the line. What would you do at this point? That's right: remember "My job is to honor myself" and remind yourself that you know in your heart you need to talk with Sally.

Now back to Martha. After rehearsing her speech dozens of times, Martha courageously picked up the phone and dialed Sally's number. "I've been feeling like our friendship is strained recently and wanted to check in with you to see if I've said or done something to put you off..." Before she could even finish, Sally interrupted. "One hundred percent of what's been happening between us is me! I didn't want to burden you. I've felt totally overwhelmed. My stepfather's been really ill, our business is not doing well, and someone filed a lawsuit against us. I'm so sorry I shut you out. I love you so much and feel so blessed to have you in my life."

By being so direct, Martha found her fears were unfounded. The rift wasn't about her at all, and her friendship with Sally was deeper and stronger than ever. She gulped, leapt, and took action. Martha ended months of self-inflicted torment and righted her sinking ship.

Not all stories have such a happy ending, so let's try on the opposite scenario. What if Martha poured her out her heart and Sally coldly claimed that nothing was wrong, shutting her out. Martha is a smart gal. She had a strategy: rather than giving a laundry list of ways Sally had pulled away and expressed displeasure, Martha would simply restate how much she missed their chats and ask Sally to let her know if she'd offended her. In the meantime, she would do her own inner work so she could genuinely feel good about herself, remain friendly, and give her sister-in-law some space for now.

Making a Plan

Wouldn't it be great if life just kind of worked out on it's own, without much thought on our parts? Magic does happen sometimes. But often, reaching our goal requires a bit of planning and fortitude. A student learns to take notes and outline a term paper before writing it. A painter sands the surface and tapes the trim before applying the color. A salesperson has a strategy before making calls.

Taking action, regardless of whether you're trying to get out of a stuck situation or change an old habit requires planning. I'm not saying you have to orchestrate every aspect of your life or you can't leave some situations up to the universe. It just means taking the time to plan, increases the likelihood of attaining the desired results. Planning is easy if you keep one eye on your goal. You can look at planning like a jigsaw puzzle. Visualize and actualize. All you have to do is put the pieces together to see the whole.

Sometimes extra information is needed in order to choose the best route to reaching your target. Get input from many sources: experts in the field, friends, books, or the Internet. You'll be a lot less fearful by getting data from outside sources. It will bring a little objectivity to the situation. But don't get lost in the details. Know when enough is enough. Being obsessed to gather tons of data can just be another way to put things off, especially if you have a fear constitution.

With a little practice, planning will become second nature. You won't be so overwhelmed or afraid when you need to step out into the unknown. And you'll move out of the passive and into actively building a better life.

The Steps to Unstick a Stuck Situation

If you feel like you're caught in a stuck situation, it's easier than you think to set yourself free. We're not talking rocket science here, but there's definitely a formula. I've made it as painless as possible. The following worksheet was created to get you 'unstuck' from whatever situation you're facing right now. You'll be surprised at how easy the process can be, once you put the wheels in motion. They key is to break your goal down into small, doable steps. I promise you'll find big breakthroughs if you're simply willing, open, and ready to drive.

Action Worksheet for Stuck Situations

1. Identify the specific situation.

2. Define your goal and select helpful truths.

3. Translate your goal into a series of small, doable steps.
   A. Write a list of possible actions and test each one against your intuition until you identify the option that rings true.

   B. Determine the actual steps to achieve that goal.

4. Anticipate possible scenarios that could arise, and figure out what you'd do.

5. "Gulp and leap." Emote as you go.

Let's go through the steps one at a time.

1. Identify the specific situation.

Nail down exactly what event or events need attention. Examples of stuck situations:

- **I haven't told my parents I'm gay.**
- **I need to find a new place to live.**
- **I don't like to be around my mother lately.**

Read the last one again. See how it is a little too general? Break it down to something more specific. Is it her complaints about how no one planned her birthday dinner? Is it what she said to your daughter last Sunday? If you discover more than one topic, deal with each one at a time to get resolution.

2. Define your goal and select helpful truths.

The stuck situation is in focus. Now, set your goal. Athletes, students, musicians, and executives all set goals to keep them going. To handle a stuck situation, you need a goal, too. The question is "What will bring me more joy, love, and peace?" A selfish goal that depends on others doing something, or does harm is not constructive and won't produce the results you want.

It's possible your goal might spur emotions in others such as breaking up with a boyfriend who is very dependent on you. But you understand feeling joy, love, and peace requires staying true to what you know in your heart, whatever that needs to look like.

Goals serve several functions. They are your "I" and connect you directly with your centered self. They're like a flood light on the correct path to getting you where you want to go in the dead of night. They also boost your momentum when you're lagging. That's why it's best to write down your goal. Write it and keep it with you at all time. The value of writing it down will become obvious when you "forget."

- **What's my goal?**
- **What's true for me about this situation?**
- **Why do I want to do this?**

State your goal. How does it feel in your body? If it's not a feel good proposition, tweak it until it is. Possible goals for the three situations listed in step one are:

- **I want to be honest with my folks.**
- **I want to live in a clean place.**
- **I want to feel loving when I'm around Mom.**

Find a couple of truths to contradict your sabotaging thoughts hanging in the wings, ready to pounce in a weak moment. The lists of truths in Part II, Chapter 2 will offer many possibilities to dissolve those spooky ghosts into thin air. Here's one bundle that helped Paula, an artist who was looking for work.

- **It's going to take as long as it's going to take.**
- **Just take the next step.**
- **I can do this.**

To acknowledge all the small victories, say to yourself, "**Good for me. I'm doing good.**"

3. Translate your goal into a plan of small, doable steps.

Once you have a goal, you're well on your way. Now you need to visualize and determine the actual steps to reach it. Doable steps are the specifics that keep you in the present moment, engaged in actions toward your goal. There are two parts to building an effective strategy.

A. Write a list of possible actions and test each one against your intuition until you identify the option that rings true.

Does figuring out what you'll do sound intimidating? It's really quite straightforward. Begin formulating your general plan by writing a list of actions that could possibly take you to your goal. Be creative. Ask yourself:

- What will take me to my goal?
- What is the most loving thing to do?

Write down all the options. Then close your eyes, test each one by repeating it earnestly (preferably out loud), and listen to your body's cues. What's it saying? Repeat the most promising possibility a few times. When you're flooded with a peaceful, centered feeling — that's the best option.

Finesse your strategy until it resonates fully. In the above example about having a conversation with your mother, maybe what feels right is, "I'm going to talk with my mom about what she said to my daughter last Sunday."

You might decide your mother is getting more burdensome to spend time with. You may decide to accept who she is, but limit time around her. Or maybe what feels right is to continue to spend time with her and work on feeling less hooked into the negative things she says.

B. Determine the actual steps to achieve that goal.

Tasks can seem like scaling the Empire State Building. Just envisioning the goal can be a daunting prospect. Start by breaking big steps down into little units. Map out how to get to your goal from where you are right now. Make sure each step is realistic and so easy that you simply can't help but succeed.

If your plan requires you talk to someone, think through and write out the key points that you'll be addressing to keep on target. Continuing with our example, say you decide to talk with your mother about last Sunday. Get specific. Ask yourself concrete questions: "What do I need to say?", "What topics am I not willing to discuss tonight?", and "How long am I willing to listen or discuss this today?"

Planning takes time and a little massaging. Continue to refine and adjust your plan, setting smaller goals that advance you toward your ultimate goal. Set realistic time frames. In the above example, you may have to double-check with your daughter about what happened, decide exactly what you want to say to your mother, figure out when to talk to her, think about how you'll respond to her reactions, and clarify how you'll follow up.

4. Anticipate possible scenarios that could arise and figure out what you'd do.

When your game plan is set, and strategizing seems finished, step back and take a look. Go on a mental journey, seeing yourself walking through, fleshing out details in full color, full frequency, full sensation. Whatever feels vague, make adjustments and get more specific. The final draft should make so much sense that anyone could understand it. Ask a friend to look at your plan and give you a reality check. He or she can help dial in the details and identify potential pitfalls.

Now take a guess at what might happen. Let your mind wander to the positive or negative reactions you may encounter when you speak your truth. Imagining worst-case scenarios will prevent you from being caught off guard. A few minutes to role-play a confrontation will give a sense of what might transpire and how you might handle it. You can actually practice the way you'd like to respond beforehand. That doesn't guarantee you will, but your chances are better if you've gone through the steps in your head.

To continue our example, you'll need to choose a specific time to speak with your mother when she won't be distracted. Avoid the times of her favorite television programs or in the evening when she might be drinking. Steer clear of other subjects, such as what your brother told you or what you think about her alcohol consumption. Lovingly stick to the points you've decided are important and repeat them until you feel heard.

You might say, "Christie came home in tears on Sunday, and I want to check with you about what happened so I can help her sort out her feelings. I want to figure out what might help her to talk with you in person about it."

Then put on the invisible duct tape, and listen to your mother's side of the story so you understand what is true for her. Your role isn't to agree, but you do have to sincerely understand her position. This can be challenging. You need a discriminating ear and a desire to hear what she says, which could involve digging through some mud slinging.

She may try to blame your daughter or deny anything happened. But you're prepared because you've thought through possibilities.

Just remember to be the matador so her "you"s, overgeneralizations, and negativity don't distract you or tempt you to respond in kind or take what she says personally. After listening, restate what is true for you, ask a doable request and/or define a clear consequence for the future. "I hear that you don't think anything is wrong, but I'll give you a call tomorrow to see if you have any suggestions about what I can tell Christie." Before your exchange ends, thank mom for talking with you. Then listen to your inner applause.

5. Gulp and leap. Emote as you go.

Timing is everything, like picking lush, juicy berries straight from the vine — not too green and not too ripe. If you wait too long to take a certain step, it may do nothing. If you act too hastily, you may miss the mark entirely.

You've made great strides and have a doable plan in place. At some point you just have to "gulp and leap" which means just do it. I've always loved the book title *Feel the Fear and Do It Anyway* (by Dr. Susan Jeffers), because it conveys this notion perfectly. Courage is being scared but plunging ahead anyway. The good news is that you'll plug back in to the universal flow, and back into your authentic self.

Sure, you'll have some fear and be tempted to melt down. When you're traversing new territory, after all, uncertainty is going to trip you just a bit. Just shake and shiver and quiver all you need to. Ignore those sabotaging thoughts (born of unexpressed emotions). Power for a minute or two on a helpful truth, such as I'll do what I can, and the rest is out of my hands. Then gulp and leap.

If you're scared to tell your parents you're gay, decide when and what to say. Moving the emotional energy through your body will leave you more peaceful no matter what truth you've got to share with the world. If you keep putting it off, double-check within to see if it's still the correct thing to do and the right time to do it.

Keep those warm, fuzzy praises coming, too, even if you don't achieve every step. Praise and self-appreciations work really well especially if you have a sadness/anger constitution, because you tend to be particularly hard on yourself. All humans stumble, make mistakes, and suffer setbacks. Don't use those little growth opportunities as an excuse to give up or get down on yourself. Like parents who naturally praise the first step an infant takes and see his falls as part of the learning process, concentrate on all the little things you are doing well.

If you follow the instructions offered in this chapter but still don't reach your goal, rethink the plan. Maybe you have to deal with some emotions embedded in the stuck situation. Maybe you need to break the steps into even smaller units. Maybe you need to check in with a friend about your progress at regular intervals; accountability from outside pushes you to follow through on your good intentions.

Don't forget, you're making positive changes in yourself and in your world. You've got some spectacular surprises and delights awaiting you. Expect to experience some divine shifts as you instantaneously go from stuck to free; restricted to expansive; sadness, anger, and fear to joy, love, and peace.

Paul Sets a Strategy

"I've lost my sense of direction," Paul told me. "So many things have happened since I last saw you. I'm two months behind on my mortgage and don't have any money coming in. I'm on the verge of bankruptcy."

Paul had owned his own graphic-design business for over ten years, but business had been worse than lean. His savings were gone, and bills were piling up. "I just can't decide what to do next. I feel hopeless and down on myself for letting things get to this point."

"The most important thing is not to trash yourself," I said gently, "because that won't help. You need to get clear on what you want to do. Then it's just a matter of setting out the little tasks that need to be done."

Although Paul's business hadn't been doing well, he wasn't ready to abandon it. He had invested so much energy in it and enjoyed being his own boss. After some discussion, he decided that he had a couple of viable choices for boosting his cash flow.

Paul had strengths and talents other than graphic design. He realized he could look for a part-time job giving sailing lessons, or check out the possibility of putting together an architectural tour of Santa Barbara for tourists. Saying each option aloud a few times, he settle on, "I can see myself offering tourists and locals a high-end architectural tour," he said.

To explore the viability of this option, we got specific and laid out a plan. In the next month, one task at a time, he'd identify houses and landmarks of interest, make a tentative walking route, create a brochure (his specialty), talk with concierges at a half dozen high-end hotels about potential referrals, and set up a couple of tours for friends to see how leading tours felt.

Paul found that well-established hotels were wary of offering new services with someone they didn't know. It would take time and energy to get the word out. Since the tourist season was just about over, architectural tours didn't seem worth pursuing right now. Paul went back to his drawing board and concluded that, humbling as it might be, his next step was to contact other design firms to see if any of them were looking for an energetic employee.

In session Paul dealt with his emotions, especially disappointment as his lack of ability to market himself, saying good-bye to being a financially successful entrepreneur, and facing his loss of pride admitting that his business had failed.

Now with confidence and determination, he got ready to tackle the daunting task of reaching out to his colleagues. He generated a list of potential firms to contact, polished up his resume, and practiced his pitch outloud. That brought up anger about not wanting to beg. Paul dealt with his emotions by hitting a telephone book. By the end of the session, he felt more optimistic and raring to go.

Procrastination and Resistance

Hmmm… it's going to be sunny this weekend, so maybe I should wait to start my plan next week. I mean, the kids are out of school, and the holidays are coming up, so really, it might be impossible to start… uh — program break, please! I can hear all the excuses (and pretty much already have) as to why it's not the right time, how it will be easier when you're skinnier, when you're not so busy, and how later you'll be ready. Procrastination is your enemy. There will always be an excuse to not create change. For starters, it's uncomfortable. If it were fun, everybody would be doing it.

Doing something new sparks resistance. Fear pulls you like a magnet towards the familiar and away from the unknown. When you act in a timely manner, you feel happy, clear, and energetic. Putting something you need to do off for days, weeks, or longer, just makes you feel crummy, lazy, and disconnected.

Procrastinating is a just a label for avoiding emotions and succumbing to destructive thoughts. Maybe you are worried about the implications of your actions in the future (fear). Maybe you put things off because it feels as if some outside force is making you do it (anger). Or perhaps your perfectionist mentality believes that if you can't do it perfectly, you won't do it at all (sadness).

Dissolving those excuses and shelving resistance is as easy as emoting and rewiring your thinking. Physically move the emotional energy out of your body in whatever way works for you. As you emote, you might discover some surprising reasons you feel the way you do. And they may even be quite different than you'd thought. When you find your resolve waning, pause and find out what it is you're trying so hard not to feel. Is it sadness, anger, or fear? When in doubt, start with some pounding or shivering. During and after emoting, keep repeating your goal and powering on your truths.

If pounding and shivering or any kind of physicality isn't your thing (or you're telling yourself that), you can move through procrastination just by countering your destructive thinking with its constructive opposite. But wait — there's more to it. You have to do it tenaciously and rigorously, I mean full-on, no holds-barred style. Don't stop until you experience a shift back to your centered self and can do what is called for. You might power on **"I'm doing this for me. I'll feel better when I handle this."** You can also find someone to support your efforts and check in with on a regular basis.

If you can't seem to move beyond the procrastination point, double-check within to confirm you've chosen the correct course of action. Maybe you need more information, or the steps you've laid out are a little too big. Handle what needs attention so you can achieve your goal and experience more joy, love, and peace.

Hey, Jude!

1. *I want to go to college, but I find the application process overwhelming. Do you have any suggestions to make it less intimidating?*

College applications can seem overwhelming, but completing them is all about breaking big tasks down into small, doable pieces and keeping your eyes on today's actions. Find a buddy who also needs support and help each other. Decide how often you'll check to keep motivated.

Now identify potential schools. Assemble a list by going to the library, meeting with school counselors, or tapping into other resources, such as college guides. Do research in small blocks of time. For example, make an appointment to talk with someone one day, visit a campus, or gather information by surfing the Internet for a half hour (or even less).

Next, request applications. Make a checklist to keep track of each school's submission deadlines and requirements. The checklist should include all applications, essays, recommendations, transcripts, etc. Fill out one application at a time, one question at a time, using pre-established work blocks.

Attend to what's in front of you to avoid becoming overwhelmed. Whenever you start to feel anxious, stop and shiver, then repeat a couple of personal truths like "**I can do this**" or "**I'm doing this for me.**" Praise yourself regularly. Do little steps each day. Then just know you've done your best and see what tomorrow brings.

2. *I don't feel like writing down a plan to cope with being left by my partner. I'm too crushed and can't think straight.*

That's natural. Before jumping back into the world of action, give yourself room to feel your pain. It takes time to mend injuries, whether physical or emotional. Start with whatever emotion is in the foreground. Pound if you can't believe what he said or did. Cry buckets because it's a loss, but don't indulge in blaming him, freaking out about the future, or feeling sorry for yourself. Just mourn and say good-bye. Interrupt destructive thoughts, particularly worries about an imagined future, even if they come up a hundred times a day. Shiver instead and remind yourself, "**These feelings will pass. This situation is temporary.**"

After the shock has worn off, you'll feel less buried by your emotions. I promise it won't take as long as you imagine if you deal with your emotions. Now you can make a plan to restore your self-esteem, reflect on what you've learned, and engage in any necessary communications. If your emotions are intense, be extra mindful to eat, sleep, and exercise regularly, because throwing off your physiology hinders the healing process and your quality of life.

3. *I'd like to be more outgoing, but I'm extremely shy. What can I do?*

After retreating to the safety of your room or hiding behind the computer screen for years, reaching out to others can appear monumental. Like any new behavior, you've got to confront your fear if you want to overcome shyness. Shiver, cry, and contradict your outdated thinking. "This probably won't kill me. I am and will be okay. I want a social life. Step out, just for today."

Identify some interests and find other people who share them. Explore volunteering, classes, clubs, or lectures. Start small. Planning and shivering before taking each little step will reduce fear and increase your comfort level. Then just gulp and leap! Smiling or saying hello doesn't entail much risk and comes across as a welcoming invitation. Try looking at others as if they were friends. You can also rehearse a short introduction beforehand. Think of some specific topics you feel confident discussing.

As you venture out, shake off the jitters. Remember your goal. Even if your attempts don't meet expectations right away, each step is significant. Keep at it, speak up a little more each time, and praise yourself for each effort.

4. *I've postponed taking my contractor's licensing exam for over two years. How can I finally take the plunge?*

If putting things off is a longstanding problem, it can be helpful to explore the roots of your struggle with time, exams, and deadlines. Shiver out the fear, give yourself permission for a big cry, or pound out your frustration. Then power on something along the lines of "I'll give it my best shot," or "If I don't pass my exam, I'll try again next spring."

Come up with a reasonable schedule based on how much time you need to prepare, when the exam is, and other responsibilities. List different topics that need to be studied, keep the work blocks short so you don't burnout. (You can always study extra if you so choose.) Give yourself plenty of praise each time you meet your daily goal. Ask a friend or, better yet, someone else who is taking the same test to get a boost of support.

5. *I think I'm going to quit my book group.*

If you've been contemplating that move for a while, maybe it's time to leave. If you're seized by sudden impulse, think back and see if something upsetting happened the last time you got together. If so, deal with the specific event and handle your emotions so that you're clear before you do something final. If it feels right to leave, find your "I" and communicate it. That way no one will be confused about why you're leaving and/or suspect you have ulterior motives.

6. *Why do the principles of Attitude Reconstruction seem easier for my children than for me?*

Kids intuitively understand Attitude Reconstruction! It just makes sense to them. Children yearn to have permission to express their emotions when upset. They love to talk about themselves. They naturally accept differences as normal. They respond well and can accomplish any task when it's broken down into small, doable steps. When children receive praise, they flourish!

7. *My partner and I fight and break up, only to get back together again. What's wrong with me?*

Big decisions such as whether to break up, get married, quit a job, or make a huge purchase, must be made from an emotionally clear space, otherwise you won't have the conviction to follow through. Rather than being rash and doing something impulsive like splitting up during a fight, get yourself back to a loving place first. Resolve the specific topic that started the fight. Then, when you feel centered again, look within and ask what's true for you about the relationship. Hold tight to what you know at those times of clarity, and align your behavior with your heart.

8. *Can you apply the Attitude Reconstruction model to making love?*

Contrary to what steamy romance novels and spicy scenes on the big screen portray, making love isn't just about physical pleasure and orgasms. It's about expressing love and creating experiences of intimacy and unity. To bring joy, love, and peace to your sexual relationships, try some of these suggestions:

1. Be here now. Keep your eyes open, stay out of your head, and enjoy the present.

2. Play and laugh. Have fun. You're not trying to win an Oscar with a demanding performance.

3. Make a place for emotions. You will genuinely feel joy, love, and peace. But being intimate can also stir up huge amounts of fear, sadness, and even anger. It's frightening to be so open and vulnerable, but acknowledging your emotions keeps you in the present.

4. Power on **"I love you," "Here I am," "I'm fine just the way I am,"** or **"It's okay to speak up."**

5. Communicate. Give appreciations. Talk. Your lover is not a mind reader. A partner can't possibly know what you want and need unless you give specific feedback like "This feels wonderful," or "That doesn't feel good."

6. Initiate. Don't wait. Like listening, give at least fifty percent of the time. The other fifty percent is for receiving fully. Soak in the attention and what is being offered, scary as that might sound.

Demolishing Old Habits

You're packing for a trip to Colorado for your niece's birthday party, and after trying on every pair of pants you own, you realize nothing fits. The scales are pushing almost 200 pounds for your petite frame. Looking into the mirror, disgusted by the muffin-top hanging over your jeans, you curse how much you hate what's staring back. It's not like you haven't tried. You've been on everything from the Atkins Diet to the Bible Diet but nothing worked more than a week. You've purchased wholesome foods to cook with your hubby, started walking, and are listening to podcasts from self-help gurus.

But that half-empty suitcase stares back you, "you're a failure!" it yells. "Just think about Joanna. Why can't you be like her? Look how skinny she is, and she just had a baby not long ago! Everyone thinks you're disgusting. No wonder Steve doesn't want to make love to you."

You feel pathetic as images of people laughing at you floods your head. No one's ever really liked you, you think, reaching for two candy bars from the secret drawer. Locking yourself in the bathroom, you're careful not to rattle the paper as you eat them as fast as you can.

This isn't an unfamiliar story. We're all riding on the roller coaster of life although the height and speed all differ. And whether we're on a thrill ride, floating on the easy river, or crashing on the nightmare express, depends on the individual story we're telling ourselves.

Our storylines have complex character development. We've spent decades perfecting the details of who we think we are, labeling ourselves based on how we think others see us or care for us, tattooing failures into our psyche so we never forget our shortcomings, carving out coping mechanisms so we don't lose balance, and directing events in a 'controlled' manner so no one catches us off guard.

Those old habits are insidious. They eat at us from the inside-out, whispering all kinds of lurid lies to keep us captive in cycles of sadness, anger, and fear. We hide from the true beautiful spirits we are, blinded by all the layers of our 'personas' on top.

The "you" I just described could easily refer to any of us. Her award-winning teary drama is familiar: as she struggles with obsessive eating, she never remembers her mother dying young, leaving her with a distant aunt who never touched her or said she loved her. She never pauses to reflect about the kid's cruel jokes at school about her freckles, short hair, or not having a boyfriend. Withdrawing in silence, she'd spend nights locked in her room with cinnamon rolls and cookies, setting the stage for a lifetime role as an obese woman, hiding her heart along with the candy bars in the secret drawer.

Not dealing with sadness when feeling minimized or rejected can destroy lives. When events go by without us expressing nary an emotion, we revert to destructive habits to distract ourselves from feeling our emotions. We all compensate in the same predictable ways. The default? Behaviors that don't honor ourselves, don't show acceptance of other people and situations, and don't allow us to enjoy the present moment (the three destructive ultimate attitudes). We invest in practices that don't produce joy, love, and peace, the qualities we truly long for.

Your old habits will fall into two categories. They'll either be destructive attitudes or addictions to substances and activities. Both are anesthetics. They are what you use to avoid feeling emotions. Old habits are driven by fear, evident by the knee-jerk way you default to them, and the frenzied agitation you feel when you don't. It's no surprise old habits are ruled by the fear-based core attitudes, especially the first one: the impulse to avoid the present. That fleeting shot of instant gratification is so addicting because it keeps us feeling in control. But are you really in control if you're high tailing as fast as you can away from your own emotions? Not so much.

What drives you to avoid your emotions? You don't believe you are and will be all right no matter what transpires. Being vulnerable feels scary. You can't resist destructive attitudes and addictions — even when you know rationally that they're not in your best interests — because you get immediate comfort, feel safe, and less vulnerable or at least reduce your feelings of emotional discomfort. Suppose you feel afraid that if you open your mouth, your partner will go ballistic. So you engage in superficial conversation or stay quiet because you don't want to hear her yelling and don't know how to say what you feel anyway. You sneak back into your old habit of retreating inside yourself as if you're being forced to act in the same old way to keep peace. But at what price to your personal integrity and happiness?

I think you've had enough of your own misery, and you're ready to change. Still, destructive behaviors that leave us feeling yucky or damage our relationships can feel impossible to give up. Haven't we all sincerely made New Year's resolutions that we couldn't sustain for even a week?

Betty's Neediness Scares Men Away

Here's what Betty told me after having the latest in a long line of second dates:

Every time I date a man, I scare him off by getting too intense right away. I leap in our future together, imagining our wedding day and what our babies will look like. I get this desperate feeling and become convinced that my whole survival depends on his loving me and that I'm nothing without him. Future thinking and fantasizing about having a husband have been my constant companions ever since I can remember.

Walking my dog the evening after a first date, I realized I was gripped with both fear and sadness because my new man hadn't called yet. I wasn't even enjoying a starlit autumn walk with my dog. Once I noticed how tense my body was, I checked in on my thoughts. I noticed the neon flashing lights of fear going off like a grand opening on Broadway. I was telling myself my future well-being depended on one man I barely knew. I was creating my condition by what I was doing with the emotional energy I was feeling in my body. I didn't want to stay in this all-consuming state and didn't want to succumb to the impulse to call him or drive by his house. I realized drastic measures were in order.

*Because I had waged this battle before, I knew what to do. I took deep breaths and said: "**Everything is all right. I'm complete without a man.**" I repeated this to myself as I shook the tension and fear from my body, from my shoulders and out my arms. I was doing a funky dance down the street as I shook it out of my legs. (I'm pretty sure it was too dark for the neighbors to see.)*

*The relief was almost immediate. My body felt more fluid, my mind and heart more trusting. As I trembled the last of the tension from my body I repeated, "**Everything is all right, I'm complete without a man,**" I began to smile as I continued walking and returned to regular breathing. I felt deeply connected to all that is and stopped looking for an excuse to call him. I was ready to get on with my evening.*

Destructive Attitudes

Beating yourself up whenever something goes wrong, getting quiet when you feel ridiculed, or, like Betty, putting all your hope for the future on one man you scarcely know are just a few examples of destructive attitudes. They're reflected in how we feel, think, speak, and act.

Betty's reaction shows how an anxious attitude manifests. Her anxiety was reflected mentally in her belief that a call from her dates was a matter of life or death. Her body took cue with tightness in her chest, shortness of breath, and a knotted sensation in her gut. Her speech relayed anxiety as she talked about her date's wonderful qualities to her girlfriends, even though she had little real-life evidence to back her admiration up. In terms of action, Betty often acted impulsively when she felt desperate for a man's love, creating additional angst as her neediness pushed her dates away.

Take a look at the list of destructive attitudes below. If you have a sadness constitution, you'll recognize some destructive attitudes about yourself in the first list. If your most dominant emotion is anger, you'll see your attitudes about other people and situations listed in the middle. If you have a fear constitution, you'll identify with the time-based attitudes in the third list. Most of us possess attitudes from all three. Which strategies do you use instead of actually dealing with your emotions?

Some Destructive Attitudes

Sadness (Self)	Anger (People and Situations)	Fear (Time)
intimidates	frustrated	worried
insecure	blaming	overwhelmed
lonely	cynical	doubting
rejected	judgmental	numb
perfectionists	grouchy	moody
guilty	jealous	serious
ashamed	arrogant	impatient
self-critical	rebellion	procrastinating
depressed	ungrateful	obsessive
passive	prejudiced	preoccupied
weak	aggressive	panicking
submissive	mean	anxious
helpless	resentful	exaggerating
devastated	complaining	compulsive
victimized	stubborn	manipulative
lacking	negative	speedy
inadequate	bossy	restless
unconfident	argumentative	antsy
dependent	righteous	spacey
needy	superior	careless
self-loathing	vengeful	rigid
unmotivated	defensive	unsatisfied
unlovable	competitive	dramatic
unanchored	envious	indecisive
self-pitying	disappointed	lazy
undeserving	critical	confused
small	selfish	lost

Addictions

Picking your fingernails, eating a quart of chocolate ice cream, or mandatory daily vigorous exercise. Or maybe it's an addition to cocaine or alcohol. Old habits can show up in addiction to any substance or activity that masks our emotions and provides an immediate but temporary dose of pleasure. If you've become physically and emotionally addicted to a substance so that you are a danger to yourself or others, being under the care of a physician and going through a rehab program are good options. But many of us have addictions to substances and activities that are under the radar. And they are equally hard to give up.

We live in a world of temptations. The thing is stopping when we know it's enough. Many potentially addictive behaviors and substances are benign and enjoyable as long as they remain recreational activities. But once we're excessively devoted to them, and they become our number-one priorities (so that we cancel all social plans to stay in so we can feed our habit) we've graduated into the addiction zone. You're addicted when you can't stop doing that 'something' for any length of time without becoming agitated. It's easy to point fingers at the poor souls struggling with drugs, alcohol, gambling, food, or even sex. But check out the chart on the next page. What do you do?

ACTIONS

Some Addictive Activities and Substances

cigarettes	talking
alcohol	television
food	pornography
chocolate	seeking people
sugar	gambling
coffee	religion
prescription drugs	fantasizing
recreational drugs	approval
romance	possessions
hair twirling	stock market
nail biting	web surfing
sex	hypochondria
exercise	travel
movies	working
reading	thrills or danger
money	video games
shopping	gum
shoplifting	excitement
music	hobbies and collections
clothes	computers
physically hurting yourself	inflicting injury on others
beard pulling	conflict
sports	list-making

The Steps to Remodel an Old Habit

Get out the armor and prepare for heading into battle. The war against old habits isn't for the faint of heart. You didn't get here overnight, and it's going to take some field combat to get the upper hand. You'll have to be strong and focused, otherwise your sneaky foe will come up behind and thwart your success.

As with stuck situations, this mind-bending combat requires perseverance, because at those critical choice points, every fiber of your being will push you towards the familiar. Know that change is made up of a series of defeats and victories. You will need a short- and a long-term battle plan so you can wage your war until the enemy retreats, and that takes time and patience.

The strategy to change an old habit is similar to handling a stuck situation. Both ask you to make a plan so you can take successfully take small, specific steps toward your goal. For old habits, the actual plan itself has three distinct elements:

A. **Pinpoint when and what triggers your old habit.**

B. **Decide what you will do instead at those moments.**

C. **Lay out an ongoing plan for a set amount of time.**

Determining some viable options ahead of time will help you resist temptation, because at those choice moments fear will play mind games with you. Good preparation is key, whether it's to stop being stubborn or gambling on the ponies. Plan each step, and you'll overcome any obstacle. Constantly remember your goal, make necessary adjustments to meet the demands of the day, and then just execute your plan.

ACTIONS

Action Worksheet for Changing Old Habits

1. Identify the destructive attitude or addiction.

2. Define your goal and select helpful truths.

3. Translate your goal into a series of small, doable steps.
   A. Pinpoint specifically what triggers your old habit and when.

   B. Decide specifically what you will do instead at those moments.

   C. Lay out specific time frames.

4. Anticipate possible scenarios and decide how to handle them in advance.
   • Praise yourself plenty.
   • Pick suitable rewards.
   • Track your progress.
   • Line up support and accountability.

Weeks of _____

New Actions	Su	M	T	W	Th	F	Sa	Su	M	T	W	Th	F	Sa

5. "Gulp and leap." Emote as you go.

1. Identify the destructive attitude or addiction.

Name your old habit as precisely as you can. Here are some examples:

- **I pick my cuticles.**
- **I'm sarcastic.**
- **I smoke cigarettes.**

2. Define your goal and select helpful truths.

Pick one old habit and get clear about why you want to change it. Your goal will be the shining light at the end of the tunnel, and give you a vision of your rosy future. Make sure it's oriented toward producing more joy, love, and peace. Possible goals could be:

- **I want to be relaxed.**
- **I want to feel closer to my family.**
- **I want to feel confident.**
- **I want to feel healthier.**

A few helpful truths will shut down that old chatter when it arises. Here are some effective possibilities.

- **I'm doing this because I want to feel better.**
- **The goal is more important than the moment.**
- **I'm breaking this habit now.**
- **I don't like what this is doing to my life.**
- **Feeling these emotions won't kill me.**
- **I can do this.**

3. Translate your goal into a series of small, doable steps.

A. Pinpoint specifically what triggers your old habit and when.

Take smoking, for example. Identify what situations and times during the day you want to light up a cigarette. What precedes the strong desire for a cigarette? Is it physical sensation such as a tightening in the jaw, or inner feeling such as nervousness or boredom? Maybe it's an activity like driving your car, or a stressor like sitting down to pay bills. Maybe you have thoughts: "I'll worry about quitting tomorrow," or "My father smoked for forty years and suffered no ill effects, so I'm genetically immune." There are as many rationales as there are personalities. Write them all down so you see them a bit more objectively.

B. Decide specifically what you will do instead at those moments.

The prescription is the same for both changing old attitudes and addictions: at those critical moments of choice, you've got to have a quick constructive reaction on the ready to counter the impulse. These choice-point replacements are called "constructive substitutes," or just "subs." To find a sub for the habit of interrupting other people, imagine the constructive opposite of the old behavior. If you draw a blank, consult the Attitude Reconstruction Blueprint. (Rolling your eyes is not a viable sub.) What does count as a viable sub? Staying silent and genuinely listening (keep plenty of duct tape close by) or telling yourself, **"Their viewpoints are as important as mine,"** or "This person talks slowly but is trying to communicate something."

It's going to be much easier to keep doing what you've been doing for decades than trying something new. But after you make it through those first agonizing moments, the physical urge will pass, and with it, the impetus to race back to your old habit for dear life. You'll feel the joy of victory and soak in the benefits.

Details about Constructive Subs

Your subs are like a big tablespoon of that pink stuff your mom made you take for an upset stomach after too much Halloween candy. They neutralize the emotional energy that drives the habit. Because don't forget, that's always the old habit's modus operandi: to avoid what emotions you're really feeling. Subs can be any of the five tools. It could be calling someone for support, or saying "yes" instead of saying "no".

Physically expressing your emotions, as always, works quickest, because not doing so is what created the habit in the first place. The reasons behind the emotion are secondary. Find an appropriate, safe setting, and emote without voicing your old destructive thoughts. A good shiver, pounding, or cry works wonders to shift your physiology so you can get back to what you were previously doing.

Rewiring your thinking is a great substitute, if you do it with gusto. When indulging the habit feels better than saying no, your self-defeating thinking will give thousands of justifications. "This moment is an exception." "I've been so good." "I deserve a break." Blast that devious chatter by rigorously repeating what's true (**Just for today. I'm breaking this habit now. I'm doing this so I feel better.**"). Say it as much as you need to, until the desire to give in goes away and calm is restored. If your truths aren't doing the job, try some new ones.

Because that pesky unexpressed fear puts you in a state of agitation and paralysis, you naturally lose perspective and forget what's true. As a sub, you can also power on what you know when centered or on your goal. Some examples are:

- **I want to feel closer to my partner.**
- **I want to be a nonsmoker.**
- **My boss is going to let me go if I don't get to work on time.**

And don't forget your closest confidant and friend, your intuition. It always has your back. When impulse to engage in old behavior bubbles up, take a mini time-out to pause and reconnect with your heart. Dialogue with your inner voice or ask for help from a higher power. You'll stop that urge in its tracks and put yourself in touch with what's really true for you. (If you can't hear your intuition, emote or do something constructive to improve reception.)

You're often triggered by social situations, so speaking up constructively is another excellent substitute. Listen or speak your "I" with kindness about the specific event that ignited your urge to do or say something destructive. For instance, if you have a habit of making jokes whenever your wife tells you what to do, don't shoot back something witty, speak your "I" about the specific. Be patient. It may take a few minutes to identify and figure out how to say what's true for you. "We've agreed the garden is my domain. I'd be open to hearing your suggestions, but I've thought about what I'd like to do here." The three communication bridges of appreciations, understanding, and reassurances are reliable subs, too, so go back and review them if needed so you can give them to yourself at those choice point moments.

Lastly, action is your power pusher to new behaviors that open your heart to freedom. If you consistently tailgate and curse when you drive, decide to slow down and say nothing whenever you're close to the car in front of you. If you always reach for cookies after dinner, eat a piece of fruit and feel the emotions that this change in routine brings up. If you stick to your plan, I guarantee that sooner or later, one of two things will happen: you'll either experience a divine shift in your inner state, or emotions will surface. Be sure that your sub is easy to do and constructive, so that it truly honors you!

Subs for Destructive Attitudes

The Attitude Reconstruction Blueprint can help you identify a destructive attitude and its constructive subs. For example, if you make negative comments, locate "critical" under the action column on the left side of the Blueprint. Then go to the right side to discover an opposite action: "Attend to the positive." The strategy is clear: commit to voicing only the good. Maybe it starts with a small appreciation each time you feel the impulse to be a downer. "I had no idea you felt that way," or "I'm glad you told me about what happened at school today."

If you've neglected your mail, work on your pile for ten minutes each day. If you always seem to volunteer when something needs to be done, let someone else step forward. If you freak out in the middle of the night, get out of bed and shiver for two minutes.

Subs for Addictions

To battle an addiction, your new action must be simple, doable, calming, and powerful enough to absorb your attention when the energy and impulse is heading for demolition. If you have addiction to sugar, using sugar-free gum, diet soda, and cigarettes to replace the habit isn't going to cut it. They also compromise your health and don't neutralize your emotions.

It's no secret that many people succeed in getting off drugs or alcohol only to grab onto another addictive substance or activity, such as coffee or exercise. That is because they haven't adequately dealt with what led to the addiction in the first place. Selecting another excessive behavior, such as biking at full speed for several hours, renting half a dozen movies, or shopping "until you drop" isn't constructive in the long run either. It's not helping you to honor yourself or deal with your emotions honestly.

You've got to find a good list of replacements that will smash that deep craving for sugar immediately: fixing a cup of herbal tea, visualizing a tranquil place, dispassionately observing the physical urge until it goes away, or talking to a supportive friend. Actions shift the agitated fear physiology of your emotional state and neutralize the situation. Leave the scene of the craving, play with your pet, dance, or run up a flight of stairs to redirect your focus until the emotion and impulse dissipate. All that said, emoting is the best substitute.

Detoxification and rehabilitation from severe or long-term substance addictions — especially to drugs or alcohol, which create extreme physical and psychological dependency — often require medical and psychological help, and sometimes a controlled environment. If that's your case, it's best to go through withdrawal in a safe, supportive space with others facing the same struggle. Do your diligence. Gather information about possible facilities, talk to people who have attended them, or if possible, visit them in advance.

Your intuition will tell you which program serves you best. You'll be swallowed in an intense need to escape what you're feeling so handle those emotions physically, especially those that arose when you initially took up your habit. Relapse is likely if you don't deal with your emotions constructively regardless of how good the treatment program is.

C. Lay out a plan with specific time frames.

Conjuring up grand expectations about what you'll do for the rest of your life sets you up for failure almost before you've even begun. Projecting into the future and resorting to abstractions will bring on fear, and fear takes you back to old habits. Your best strategy is to focus on the present and stay specific. A good battle plan makes confronting today possible, and that's where your focus should stay.

Making sweeping statements such as "no sweets ever again," has never worked before, and it's not going to work now. You'll get quickly overwhelmed and punt on any positive momentum you created. Baby steps: start by foregoing sugar for one or two evenings a week. Select a doable time frame, and when you reach it, celebrate wildly. Practice for your Oprah interview when you're nominated for "Biggest Positive Change-Maker," throw confetti, put on your tiara and dance the Macarena! Then reevaluate and set another short-term goal.

You need to have a plan in advance for what you'll do at moments of choice because rational thinking is nearly impossible. Locating an effective sub or two takes trial and error. Test each possibility out. You'll know shortly if your plan meets real life. Adjust accordingly. After three or four close calls, you'll know the exact recipe and action.

4. Anticipate possible scenarios and decide how to handle them in advance.

Be your own tour guide and walk through your plan in as great of detail as possible. Clarify the details. Visualize the party you're going to attend and what you'll do when offered a drink. Decide in advance how you'll react when your spouse forgets to run an errand yet again. Don't focus on the craving, reminisce about an idealized past, or repeat an old phrase like "A cigarette sure would hit the spot right now." If you let your enemy get one toe in your territory, you're asking for trouble. If you haven't already, write down your litany of destructive thoughts and find suitable contradictions for each.

Powering on a contradictory truth such as **"Just for this moment"** can be thrown in any time but especially when the destructive chatter begins. Remember, it's an ongoing battle! You've been under the enemy's control for a long time. Fight tooth and nail. Here are additional actions you can take to break the chains of old habits:

- **Praise yourself plenty.** Focus on the wins. Don't beat yourself up when you revert to your old habit. Be your own best cheerleader. Compliment yourself on accomplishments and celebrate every tiny victory. Remember: **We all make mistakes. It's never too late to begin again. Setbacks are part of the process. Change takes time. Just start again now.**

- **Pick suitable rewards.** Liberation from your old habit is the best reward — and you don't even have to pay for it! But extra "treats" to celebrate small victories are also helpful. When you're trying to establish a new workout routine, purchase new gym clothes after your tenth visit to the athletic club. Looking forward to a reasonable extravagance after a series of triumphs can make those first weeks much easier.

- **Track your progress.** Note the strides you're making and the times you revert to old habits. You'll be able to see what you're doing in concrete terms, and you'll be motivated to stick with the plan. Mark a calendar or use the simple tracking system provided on the worksheet. Begin with one or two specific target behaviors and record your daily progress. How many times did you resist (or not) your old habit each day? Look at what you actually did, not what you guess you did. Don't judge yourself. Just record. Keep your "pencil and paper" where you'll see it often. Sometimes just making yourself aware of how many times old habits or new behaviors show up is all you can do. Those check marks and numbers might just motivate you to make a change.

- **Line up support.** Don't underestimate the boost a support team can give you. Trying to change destructive attitudes and addictions can feel isolating and nearly impossible. Build a support or check-in system when you're in the planning stage or after you've deviated from your intention a certain number of times. Think through what would realistically work for you and make the necessary arrangements.

5. Gulp and leap. Emote as you go.

This is your jumping off the high dive moment. You have to feel the fear and do it anyway. The first time you deny the old habit and choose the new is significant. With that single success behind you, you'll know that you can do it again. You've experienced the sweet taste of triumph, and it wasn't as hard as you imagined, right?

If you aren't gulping and leaping, emote — shiver like crazy. Power to combat those insidious messages. Focus on the next step and take it, appreciating how courageous you are along the way. A lapse isn't an excuse to quit so don't give up. Turn it into a learning moment. What derailed you? What can you do differently next time? As you get a sense of what works and what doesn't, revise your plan.

The Dwindle Effect

Backsliding comes with almost every new habit you're trying to engrain. I call it the "dwindle effect" because the initial impetus to change an old habit wanes, and it's easy to lose sight of good intentions. It's common to rebel against the effort the new action requires, forgetting why you wanted to change in the first place. Your persistent mind chatter becomes the only voice you hear, and you just want to numb out the emotions of the moment with your familiar, safe (and yet oh-so-destructive) habits.

Like you did with procrastination and resistance, use the one-two punch of emoting and rewiring to battle the dwindle effect. When your momentum flags, check in with your emotions and destructive thoughts. What specific event happened? Deal with that. Did a violation or injustice occur? Are you feeling angry or stubborn because you don't want to be denied? There's no external force "making" you do something, so stop giving it power and remember you're changing for you.

Are you feeling fear, moving fast, or forgetting what you know when you are centered and clear? Did you get hurt or experience a loss? Are you feeling sad, small, or powerless? Whatever it is, emote, repeat your goal, or power on your truths until the perspective is restored. Then you'll be able to make a different choice.

The dwindle effect can either drain your resolve or provide a learning opportunity. With a little observation and introspection, you can identify some of the whens, whys, wheres, and whos that spark falling off your sterling intentions. Keep the warning signs in mind, and you'll be better prepared next time. Ask yourself, "What will I do next time this happens?" Develop a strategy, like choosing some truths for tough moments, selecting another substitute, or setting a shorter-range goal that's more achievable. If you relapse, don't abandon your goal. Just remember the dwindle effect. Deal with your emotions and then step back onto the battlefield of life.

Creating Accountability and Support

Accountability means committing to do something measurable within a given time frame. You can check in with someone else in person, by e-mail, or on the phone at a prearranged time to report your progress. This is a strong incentive because you'll be more likely follow through on your good intentions. Others will know if you're sliding, and you won't be able to deceive yourself as easily with a witness.

Make an arrangement for a few times a day, weekly, or anywhere in between. Agree on exactly when and how long your check-ins will be and discuss what the check-in will entail. A good check-in can take as little as one to five minutes. (Use a timer and stop at the agreed-upon time.)

When checking it, it's important you talk about and write down exactly what you'll do, when you'll do it, and the consequences of reaching or not reaching your goal. Regardless of the format, the emphasis is on talking about yourself and what will help you today and tomorrow. Support, no matter where you get it, makes your lonesome ride toward change feel less solitary.

Support from Another Person

It always feels good to have a personal cheerleader so I suggest you find one! Seeking support from another person might take a little courage. Maybe you'll feel vulnerable, embarrassed, or concerned about imposing. Do it anyway.

Generate a list of possible candidates and choose one. Write out your request first, then make your communication. Feel your fear and dare to ask. If someone declines, don't take it personally. Just try someone else. Ideally, the person you select will be working on making personal changes too, so you can cheer each other on.

Make contact at the appointed time. Watch out for the dwindle effect, e.g., making excuses not to check in. If you resist, shiver or pound, then make the call. Remember you're both responsible to initiate your check-in, so don't wait for the other person.

Check In

1. Review the steps you've taken and where you are in relation to your goal.

2. Identify the emotions that came up and how you handled them.

3. Talk about what you learned.

4. Review your goal and personal truths.

5. Determine what you need to do next.

6. Praise yourself.

7. Confirm your next check-in time.

8. Exchange appreciations.

The support person's not there to take charge and tell you what to do. If she has her own stake in your changing, she'll lose the ability to encourage you when you don't meet her expectations. You want your cheerleader primarily to listen, look for the positive, and, with your permission, kindly point out attitudes or actions that seem counterproductive. If they're upbeat, empathetic, congratulatory, and reliable, you've found the right person.

Support from a Group

For some, it's a good fit to come together with others trying to reach complimentary goals. Most communities offer all kinds of support groups for like-minded individuals. Visit several and pick one feels like the best fit. Commit to it and participate regularly, even if you find one hundred excuses not to attend (a sure sign that you need to deal with some emotions). Ideally, your group will be long on praise and short on "you-ing." If you don't feel safe, speak up and offer constructive suggestions to make the environment more supportive for all involved. Don't give up after just one request. If the atmosphere doesn't change, just look for a more suitable source of support.

Here's a radical suggestion: form your own group with a couple of friends who are also applying the Attitude Reconstruction principles to their lives. Experiment until you agree on a format and meeting time that works for everyone, and then follow through. Make sure each person receives a block of undivided attention and that appreciations are the order of the day.

Support from a Higher Power

When you can't do it on your own, many find strength in a power greater than themselves. Having God as a pinch hitter or captain of your team can be source of strength and foundation when striving for change. Reaching out to a higher power acknowledges that, ultimately, you aren't in control. A simple prayer or request into the ethers can elevate you from fear and into peace. Call on your "spirit guides" or "chosen power" to stand with you anytime you need support and especially in crucial moments when you're footing is failing and you can't go it alone. Consider asking your higher power for an assist, aloud or in silent prayer:

- **Help.**
- **Please give me strength.**
- **Please help me get through this moment.**

Support from Yourself

And don't overlook your best source of support — YOU! Particularly because you're available anytime and usually know exactly what you need (that is, if you pause and look within). Commit to a regular check-in at an appointed time, using the same points you would use with another person. It also helps the effort to take a moment to check in with yourself randomly, at any moment in the day.

Or dedicate a journal exclusively to Attitude Reconstruction and jot down your experiences. Warning: stay constructive with what you write! Don't wallow around in pity or do the blame game on these pages. They're there to keep track of your goals, plans, truths, insights, appreciations, communications, and observations. For example, if you want more intimacy in a personal relationship and decide to physically reach out each day, ask yourself, "What did I do to show my affection? How did it feel? What was his reaction? If I didn't do anything, why not? What will I do tomorrow?"

Ideally, spend a couple minutes every morning reminding yourself of your goal and setting intentions for the day. At night, spend a few minutes recording your behavior, reflecting on your accomplishments, praising yourself, and determining what needs to be done tomorrow. If you get hung up on unforeseen hurdles, modify your plan. You may realize, for example, the steps you've chosen are too big. Just keep breaking them down until they're realistic. Or you may discover that your next step is unsuitable for the present circumstances. Remember change emerges through a string of small victories.

Hey, Jude!

1. *Does giving up an addiction mean I have to give up my friends?*

Often giving up an addition means giving up some of the company you keep. Change means new choices. Your new routine should take you out of the vicinity of temptation. Just as it doesn't make any sense to have chocolate in the house if you're trying to break a sugar habit, it's not advisable to hang out with your pot-smoking pals when you want to quit getting high. Likewise, if you want to stop buying clothes, stay out of the shopping mall.

2. *I know I'm addicted to caffeine, but I can't fathom giving it up forever. That's why I don't even consider trying to stop drinking coffee.*

"Forever" sets you up for failure. Scale your lofty intentions down into small, doable steps. Try going without caffeine for just a day, or have one cup of coffee less each day, and you'll learn something. Maybe you'll deal with a headache, but you'll also receive the reward of breaking a longstanding habit. Repeatedly shiver when cravings arise, repeating, "**One minute at a time,**" or "**Just for today.**" With your short-term victory, notice the positive difference you feel, you'll know that you can do it again for another day.

3. *I get so impatient when my wife is late. How can I work on this?*

It's wonderful you're looking at your half of the relationship to break the cycle rather than insisting your wife is the problem. Your impatience is a destructive attitude. Observe how it usually plays out. When your reactions to your wife's tardiness have ruined evenings instead of making her punctual, determine a constructive opposite to your impatience. Accept that she's usually late. Try a substitute such as taking a deep breath or reminding yourself, "**This won't matter a year from now,**" or "**I don't like that she takes so much time to get ready, but I always enjoy the results.**"

Not getting impatient takes some time, so cut yourself some slack when you relapse. Tell your wife you're trying to change your negative reactions and genuinely thank her when she is on time. You'll experience copious personal rewards and maybe even inspire her to make some changes herself.

4. *I grew up being my mother's emotional confidant, and now I find it very hard to assert myself with my significant other. Can you give me some suggestions to work on this?*

Sometimes parents can't handle the cards life dealt them. Rather than finding an appropriate adult to talk to, they confide in their children to meet their emotional needs. Like you, these children generally grow up taking care of others at their own expense.

Next time you need to speak up, contradict the impulse to remain quiet and acquiescent. Lovingly assert yourself about the specific at hand and decide on a strategy to deal with the consequences if the other person gets upset. Rehearse a line such as "This is difficult for me, but I have something to say," so you can alert the other person that you are stepping out of your comfort zone. You might also want to find a safe setting, with an appropriate person, and talk about and express the emotions you had as a child taking care of your mother's emotional needs.

5. *How can I stop insisting on having my way?*

What I call "selfishness" is one of the four core attitudes associated with anger. Being egotistical, narcissistic, or stubborn indicates you believe your needs and views are more important than others'. Find a way to constructively channel your anger physically. Try on "**Your viewpoints and needs are as important as mine**" or "**How can I help?**" Or strap some duct tape (imaginary) on your lips and start to listen, understand, and acknowledge the other person's position. Work together to find solutions (Part II, Chapter 4 covers how to resolve differences). Or consciously practice surrendering your own desires for what's best for the other person.

6. *How I can stop driving like I'm at the Indy 500?*

Driving the speed limit is one way, as crazy as that might sound to you. For sure, your blood pressure will rise as you watch the cars go flying by while you keep your foot off the accelerator. You'll probably be angry at being denied a great source of pleasure: going fast. At some point, you'll also probably feel incredibly antsy, which indicates both fear and a lack of ease with what's happening in the moment. Sadness can also surface, as you feel hidden hurts and losses or realize just how far away you've been from yourself.

As you continue to wrestle the temptation to race, repeat your goal to yourself ("**I want to be more mellow**") and/or recognize the reality of the situation ("**I can't afford to get another ticket.**") Keep easing your foot off the pedal, shiver like crazy, and sooner or later, you'll rediscover the pleasure of the present. You'll actually feel peaceful, take in the scenery, prevent yourself from doing something potentially dangerous, and experience indisputable triumph of beating an old habit.

7. *How do I know if I'm addicted to sugar?*

Try giving up sugar for a month, and you'll know. If you can easily stop, you're not addicted. If it's "impossible," you're probably experiencing some level of addiction. It's okay to have a moderate helping of sugar occasionally. The difference is in the frequency. Have it once, fine. Eat it for two days in a row, and you're on shaky ground. Have some for three days running and odds are you are back in sugar's grip. Like water seeking its own level, our old habits are just waiting for an invitation to seep back in.

PART III

Quick Charts to Remodel 33 Attitudes

Changing Attitudes

Set your goal.
Take small steps.
Celebrate your victories.

Part III is your go-to section for quick information when you're strung out, pushed to the limits, or about to blow your lid and need help now! I've outlined 33 destructive attitudes and given you easy-to-read bullet points that will send you in the right direction to make the changes you desire.

On these pages, Attitude Reconstruction will put any destructive attitude to the test, and I guarantee you'll find success if you're courageous enough to try. You'll see this section is arranged around destructive attitudes. That's intentional. People are usually more aware of what's not working in their lives than what is.

Remember your toolkit? No master craftsman/woman leaves home without their tools. Here's where you have a chance to use any or all, to chip away at unstable foundations and build a life "that's meant to last" on joy, love, and peace. As you roll up your sleeves, you'll find yourself leaning towards the constructive ultimate attitudes — honor yourself, accept other people and situations, and stay present and specific.

This section may look simple, but don't let it fool you: the suggestions here are transformative. Discover how to handle such challenges as mourning a loss or forgiving someone you've been angry with for a long time. Learn how to shift a lingering dark mood and let go of guilt, worry, defensiveness, or low self-esteem. Practical paths to radical breakthroughs await you. But you must persevere. Overcoming a long-standing attitude takes persistence — today, tomorrow, and over the long haul. And every time you contradict your old ways of operating, an internal shift, a divine shift, will confirm you're on the right track.

Part III contains three chapters. Chapter 1 focuses and dissects attitudes about yourself that are rooted in the emotion of sadness. They will help you come into your personal power, take charge of your life, and feel more joy. Chapter 2 addresses attitudes based in anger and how they're affecting how you relate to other people and situations. You'll get straightforward advice on achieving true acceptance and acting from a place of love. Chapter 3 is all about fear and attitudes that come from that agitation. You'll explore how to peacefully live in the moment and responsibly enjoy whatever comes your way.

I've included a quick reference here of all the destructive attitudes and their solutions, so you can find the exact one you're struggling with and turn immediately to the chapter that deals with it. Be explorative and experiment. You can select a recommendation for a current situation that keeps you beating your head up against the wall. Or if you're ready for a radical life change, randomly pick one suggestion each day, to contemplate or practice. With over 30 to choose from, you can devote an entire month to honoring yourself, accepting other people and situations, and staying present and specific.

DESTRUCTIVE ATTITUDES   **SOLUTIONS**

Sadness	Joy	Page #
1. Unworthy	Connect with yourself.	222
2. Lonely	Befriend your aloneness.	224
3. Needy	Approve of yourself.	226
4. Self-critical	Appreciate yourself.	228
5. Guilty / Ashamed	Forgive yourself.	230
6. Lost	Find your purpose.	232
7. Undirected	Set some goals.	234
8. Indecisive	Shift your priorities.	236
9. Passive	Speak up and take action.	238
10. Heartbroken	Mourn and say "good-bye."	240
11. Helpless-hopeless	Deal with hurts and losses.	242

Anger	Love	Page #
1. Blaming	Come back to yourself.	246
2. Frustrated	Accept what is.	248
3. Resigned	Abandon unfounded hopes.	250
4. Pessimistic	Accentuate the positive.	252
5. Judgmental	See unity beyond differences.	254
6. Defensive	Apologize.	256
7. Betrayed	Forgive others.	258
8. Ungrateful	Offer "gratitudes."	260
9. Opinionated	Empathize.	262
10. Egocentric	Give selflessly.	264
11. Mean-spirited	Deal with injustices and violations.	266

Fear	Peace	Page #
1. Worried	Be here now.	270
2. Rushed / Impatient	Slow down.	272
3. Overwhelmed	Little steps.	274
4. Moody	Shift your mood.	276
5. Doubting	Reassure yourself.	278
6. Irresponsible	Remember that actions have consequences.	280
7. Dissatisfied	Find enough.	282
8. Out of sync	Be mindful of the timing.	284
9. Uncomfortable	Participate authentically.	286
10. Controlling	Let go.	288
11. Anxious	Deal with perceived threats to your survival.	290

Before you jump in, I want to point out that Part III doesn't go into depth about the possible origins of these destructive attitudes. You may find it helpful to explore when your attitude first began. Almost always, you can trace it back to a specific trauma or a series of events that triggered a destructive coping strategy. So if you've been trying a solution over and over but it's just not working, (or if you're simply curious about the root of a less-than-sterling attitude), flip back to Part II, Chapter 5 and review how to defuse the emotional charge of a stuck situation. If you need the assistance of a qualified mental health professional to deal with your unfinished business, interview several until you find a good match.

You're a stellar human being to want to make changes for the better! Don't forget to praise yourself for each effort and for each step that moves you out of your old rut and closer to the amazing life you're creating. Little by little, small victories add up. Over time, these powerful attitude adjustments will change your life forever.

You can grab the tool that feels most comfortable and give it your all. However, to turn your destructive attitude around the fastest, cycle through all five tools in sequence. Use the first two tools — your emotions and thoughts. Then consult your intuition (tool 3) to get clear on your goal and set your strategy. Then you'll be able to use your last two tools — speech and action — to unfailingly make the change you desire.

Whenever you stall or falter, you can move towards your goal by constructively emoting physically, and relentlessly interrupting your negative chatter with what is true.

Select one or two truths that resonate. If none of my suggestions feel like they hit the mark, make up your own.

1

Moving from Sadness to Joy

Feeling heavy and deflated in your body, and sinking easily into thinking, "I'm not okay." These are the hallmarks of destructive attitudes associated with sadness. In this chapter you'll find suggestions to decrease sadness and embody the core attitudes that go with joy: know your true worth, be self-reliant, appreciate and respect yourself, and speak up and take action in accordance with your intuition. These solutions are guaranteed to reinforce a healthy sense of who you are.

Crying constructively is the most fundamental way to transform negative attitudes about yourself. By befriending your tears and using your thinking to remind yourself what's really true about you, you'll gain more energy to take personal responsibility. You'll experience an inner lightness and realize you already possess whatever you are seeking. More joy, bliss, and ecstasy will be waiting for you.

Sadness Attitudes	Solutions
1. Unworthy	Connect with yourself.
2. Lonely	Befriend your aloneness.
3. Needy	Approve of yourself.
4. Self-critical	Appreciate yourself.
5. Guilty/Ashamed	Forgive yourself.
6. Lost	Find your purpose.
7. Undirected	Set some goals.
8. Indecisive	Shift your priorities.
9. Passive	Speak up and take action.
10. Heartbroken	Mourn and say "good-bye."
11. Helpless-hopeless	Resolve with hurts and losses.

1. Attitude: *Unworthy (unlovable, inadequate, incomplete)*

Solution: *Connect with yourself.*

What You're Experiencing

- Believe you are somehow not okay
- Equate who you are with how you look, what you do, what you own
- Identify yourself by traits, possessions, accomplishments, such as: "I'm a doctor" or "I drive a Range Rover"

The Price You Pay

- Feeling bad about yourself
- Echoing phrases and believe them such as "I'm ugly," "I'm a loser," "I'm undeserving," or "I'm missing something," "I'm not enough"
- Having low self-esteem and fading into the background

How to Change

- Embrace who you are, independent of labels: you are whole, complete, and worthy, no matter what
- Realize your true self exists from the first day of your life until the day you die and doesn't change

Power On

I love myself unconditionally.

I'm not perfect, but I'm good enough.

There is nothing wrong with me.

I am whole and complete.

I am lovable.

I am enough.

God (*or whatever creator you choose*) dwells within me.

Try an 'even if' statement:

I love myself even if the parent of one of my students complained about my teaching to the principal.

I'm worthy even if my son got busted for drugs.

I'm okay even if I'm unemployed.

Try powering on who you are NOT statements:

I am not what I do.

I am not what I have.

I am not what others think of me.

I am not my body.

I am not my actions.

I am not my emotions.

I am not my job description.

I am whole and complete.

Crying while powering is fastest and most dependable way to connect with your Self

Get a double boost by powering while looking in mirror

The Upside

- You fill the black hole of unworthiness yourself

- You hold an unshakable positive view of yourself

- You think well of yourself no matter what

- You assert yourself and step out by taking bold action in line with your intuition

2. Attitude: *Lonely (unloved, abandoned, forlorn)*
Solution: *Befriend your aloneness.*

What You're Experiencing

- Feel loneliness as if it is an endless and painful void
- Starved for attention, comfort, love
- Desperate to have people to say you're okay, and they'll always be there to protect and love you
- Deny other's love you and never contented with their affections

The Price You Pay

- Endlessly seeking fulfillment outside of yourself, maintaining the illusion something/someone can fill your inner emptiness
- Engaging in nonstop activities, pacifying substances, or having to be around others all the time
- Isolating yourself

How to Change

- Truly embrace your loneliness by recognizing feeling alone is a universal condition and must be befriended
- Understand whether single or married, you're born alone and die alone
- Socialize if you know you need more human contact
- Counter feeling isolated by lending a hand or volunteering time
- Plan and take small doable steps, join a group that shares your interests, take a class, reach out to a forgotten friend
- Cry out unreleased sadness cleanly when old feeling arises, with "I am alone"
- Shiver when fear and "what ifs" arise, with "I'll handle the future in the future"
- Pound out the anger, with "I'm on my own"

Power On

I am alone, and I am connected.
What I'm seeking is within me.
I am alone.
I love myself.
I am responsible for myself.
I will always be here for me

The Upside

- Your emotions will run their course and you replace loneliness with healthy sense of self-sufficiency

- You feel powerful and confident

- You understand that you and everything are all right no matter what

- You are free to do what brings you joy, love, and peace because you know what you are seeking inside you

- You realize you are the cake, and others are the icing

3. Attitude: *Needy (dependent, insecure, people-pleasing)*
Solution: *Approve of yourself.*

What You're Experiencing

- Stuck on seeking approval through achievement
- Sacrifice what's true for you just for others to stick around
- Enter into codependent relationships
- Put other people's desires and priorities ahead of your own
- Feel super sensitive and take random statements as exclusion or rejection
- Seek validation, praise, or signs others think you're attractive, smart, fun — "something"

The Price You Pay

- Turning into a chameleon, camouflaging your true colors to get approval
- Becoming a people pleaser and appeaser
- Becoming clingy
- Finding it difficult to make decisions

How to Change

- Realize we all want recognition, but only you can give yourself the approval you seek
- Tell yourself what you wanted to hear growing up
- Figure out what you yearn to hear from others today, genuinely recite that to yourself, anytime, anyplace, over and over
- Stay securely connected to your inherent worthiness when others blame you for their emotions and misery, don't take others' anger-based words and actions personally
- Take little steps on your own, try new independent activities
- Speak up what's true for you when your intuition tells you it's important

Power On

I'm a good person.
I'm okay no matter what.
I'm pleased with myself.
Good for me.
I love myself.
What I'm seeking is within me.
My job is to take care of myself.
What others think about me is none of my business.
What you say about me is just your opinion.
They are feeling emotions, and I'm fine.
I'm still a good person even if you don't approve of my actions.

The Upside

- You stop compromising yourself to keep others from feeling sadness, anger, or fear

- You are more self-reliant and confident

- You have strength to follow your heart, say what you have to say, do what you have to

- You lovingly speak up and act from a centered place, aligned with your personal integrity

- You fill your own needs and desires

- You realize your own approval is more important than the approval of others

- You know you are whole and complete, no matter what others think, say, or do

4. Attitude: *Self-Critical (self-deprecating, self-loathing, demanding perfection)*
Solution: *Appreciate yourself.*

What You're Experiencing

- Believe your caretaker's, parent's, or other's negative judgments and demeaning labels
- Trash yourself by calling yourself "stupid," "pathetic," "a loser"
- Turn anger inward and beat yourself up for not living up to your unreasonably high expectations with "I should have…" or "I shouldn't have…"
- Take one problem and turn it into two; add brutal self-loathing to the mistake itself — a social blunder, poor financial decision, or thoughtless comment

The Price You Pay

- Pressuring yourself to do and say everything perfectly, dread making mistakes and taking risks
- Hating yourself, making self-deprecating comments
- Punishing yourself, such as cutting or starving yourself
- Raising the bar to be perfect, believing your worth is determined by what you do
- Expecting unrealistic possibilities, judging yourself negatively
- Limiting your own potential

How to Change

- When you make mistakes praise what you did well, and look for the lesson
- Replace self-demeaning messages with self-appreciations either when berating yourself or being criticized by others
- Ignore discomfort in saying nice things about yourself, start with something small like a positive trait, talent, or quality
- Compliment your abilities, characteristics, qualities, efforts
- Recite self-appreciations and soak in their meaning, stand tall

and proud, nod your head up and down, and physically express any emotions that surface (laughing is good)

- Try writing one, two or three self-appreciations each day, and at the end of a week, read list out loud with enthusiasm, conviction, and a smile

Power On

Vigorously interrupt all the "Yes, buts" or discounting thoughts while appreciating self

I have a good sense of humor and can be funny.

I'm a dependable friend.

I exercise and eat healthy food.

I'm a loving mom.

I keep in touch with my grandfather.

Start small and appreciate little accomplishments.

I paid my rent on time.

I've resisted doughnuts for three days.

I didn't say something grumpy when the alarm went off this morning.

I helped my neighbor jumpstart his car's battery.

To make statements more powerful, begin sentences with "I appreciate that I...", "I like that I...", or "I love that I..."

The Upside

- You accept and respect yourself, are gentle with yourself, and become your biggest fan
- You feel proud of your accomplishments and yourself
- You are increasingly more confident

5. Attitude: *Guilty/Ashamed (regretful, self-reproachful, disgraced)*

Solution: *Forgive yourself.*

What You're Experiencing

- Shame yourself, disparage yourself, feel unworthy and embarrassed because of a personal trait, physical characteristic, belief, feeling, or deed

- Feel guilty because your thoughts, feelings, words, or actions don't conform to your own moral code or others

- Believe there's something wrong with you when others disapprove

- Fear that others are viewing you as harshly as you view yourself and reject you

The Price You Pay

- Taking on negative judgments from parents and authority figures; "You don't care about anyone but yourself," "You're a sinner," "Your mother would turn over in her grave," or "You humiliated me"

- Judging yourself harshly, "I'm a disgrace," "I'm nothing," and "I'm damaged goods"

- Shaming yourself in extreme cases says, "I don't deserve to live"

How to Change

- Let yourself cry as you wholeheartedly affirm your true worth when you make mistakes

- Express your anger over the judgments and labels from others

- Shiver out the embarrassment about what you think others might be saying or thinking

- In a safe setting, talk about your darkest secrets and/or recount your early memories of feeling shamed or guilty, over and over, with pride and loving tone. Express your emotions and contradict your negative self judgments until what you're saying actually registers and you at least get a glimmer of the possibility of self-forgiveness

- When others try to shame or guilt you, let their comments go flying by or speak up what is true for you to take care of yourself

- Consult your intuition to see if there's anything you need to say or do to get closure with others involved

- Genuinely apologize for a specific event you regret, then drop it

- If can't let go, talk with person involved, listen to their perspective, and speak your "I"

- Ask, "What can I learn? What's the gift? What do I need to do?"

Power On

My intentions were good.

I did the best I could at the time.

If I knew then what I know now, I would have done things differently.

No matter what you say, I'm still a good person.

I am not what I do.

I am whole and complete, no matter what I do.

I forgive myself.

Sandwich "**I forgive myself**" between each of your chosen truths

The Upside

- You grant yourself a full pardon and let go of your burden

- You are free to make more flexible day-to-day choices, less rigid

- You are at peace with all of your mistakes or shortcomings and enjoy life more

- You've created opportunities for healthier, more balanced relationships

- You believe you are whole and complete

6. Attitude: *Lost (disoriented, meaningless, unanchored)*

Solution: *Find your purpose.*

What You're Experiencing

- Feel lost in the question, 'Why am I here?'
- Wonder why you feel empty and what would bring you more joy, love, and peace
- Confuse your life purpose with material goals, such as being a wife and mother, or earning a lot of money

The Price You Pay

- Envying others who seem to know and are living their purpose
- Feeling lost in the world, like you don't belong anywhere
- Feeling something is missing, never quite happy with your life
- Bouncing from doing new thing to new thing, desperately trying to find meaning

How to Change

- Reflect on the following questions a few minutes daily and write down your answers

> Why am I here?
> What am I doing?
> Where am I going?
> What is my purpose?
> What do I truly want?
> What is truly important to me?

- Suspend judgment about responses
- Keep asking questions on regular basis and eventually something satisfying will emerge

- Repeat what feels right to confirm its validity
- Your purpose will get stronger and sweeter each time you affirm it, if not, go back and ask yourself these questions some more
- Be patient and persist in your inquiry

Power On

Whatever your purpose, remind yourself of it frequently.
I'm here to be happy.
I'm here to create joy, love, and peace.
I'm here to be loving.
I want to contribute to making the planet more peaceful.
I want to make the world a better place.

The Upside

- You keep on track in moments of doubt
- You can separate the important from the trivial
- You feel content, knowing the reason you are alive today, tomorrow, until you take your last breath
- You can put whatever happens in your life into perspective
- You know your life direction and what is fundamentally important
- You have a beacon to help make moment-to-moment choices today

7. Attitude: *Undirected (lazy, unmotivated, complacent)*

Solution: *Set some goals.*

What You're Experiencing

- Feel unmotivated or complacent
- Avoid setting goals because you're afraid you'll fail
- Know you're neglecting some aspects of your life
- Hard to prioritize

The Price You Pay

- Struggling with clearly defined direction
- Failing to take action to actualize your ideals

How to Change

- Fill out the goals worksheet that follows. Work rapidly, you don't need to fill out every box right away. Add new goals later, do the worksheet alone or with a friend
- Check and see if your daily and yearly goals align with your longer-range goals
- Set aside time to review your goals regularly, understanding they may change over time
- Try doing the worksheet at start of each year or on each birthday

Power On

I can do this.

I'm doing this for me.

I am responsible for my life.

The Upside

- You have a clear picture of your long-range objectives so you manage your actions accordingly
- Your long-term objectives make short-term choices easier
- You achieve your goals, improving personal satisfaction and boosting confidence
- You find continued joy in moving forward, taking charge of your destiny

Goals Worksheet

Area	Lifetime	Five Years	One Year	One Month
Health				
Career and Prosperity				
Family and Relationships				
Spirituality				
Community, Work, and Planet				
Recreation				

8. Attitude: *Indecisive (ambivalent, stuck, unclear)*

Solution: *Sift your priorities.*

What You're Experiencing

- Agonize endlessly over an issue, whether it's to break up with a partner, take a new job, or rent an apartment

- Dwell on just a few aspects of the decision instead of seeing whole picture

- Feel confused about what's really important to you

The Price You Pay

- Allowing someone/something else to determine your fate

- Losing time that could be spent on enjoying the present moment

- Feeling stuck and down on yourself for not being clear

- Staying in untenable situations long beyond what's sensible

How to Change

- Use the "priority sifter" to gain perspective about your dilemma

- To use the "sifter": Write out a list of ideal qualities you'd like if you could have it all. Come up with at least 30 items. Then rate the person(s) or situation(s) on each quality, assigning a "1" if they/it has that quality, "0" if they don't, and "1/2" if they have it somewhat. When you're finished, add up your total. Then divide your total by the number of ideal qualities to yield a percentage

- Determine what percentage you require. Remember, in school 90% is an A, 80% is a B, 70% a C, 60% a D, and below that an F. Assess your percentage

- Check your results with your intuition

- Realize and accept that they are just fine the way they are

Power On

Power on your conclusion and express the emotions that arise
Accept qualities he has that you don't like
In areas of differences, find workable solutions

The Upside

- You gain clarity and perspective about what is true for you

- You are able to make a firm decision

- You move forward and refocus on relishing the present and living life

- You can stop dwelling on what you don't like

Priority Sifter

Ideal Qualities	Rating #1	Rating #2	Rating #3
Total Items			

Divide the total number of items into your Ratings total to yield your percentage.

9. Attitude: *Passive (unimportant, victimized, shy)*

Solution: *Speak up and take action.*

What You're Experiencing

- Felt punished, discouraged from asserting yourself by bigger, older, stronger people
- Feel small, shy, and unimportant, and have learned to cope by being vanilla
- Play the helpless, submissive victim and don't feel you have the right to speak your needs or ask for what you want

The Price You Pay

- Failing to do what you know in your heart in true
- Feeling insignificant, becoming excessively polite to avoid rocking the boat
- Thinking things are too big, out-of-control, or beyond your ability to handle
- Remaining quiet, focusing too much on others and neglecting yourself, instead of taking charge and asserting yourself

How to Change

- Start with inner work by emoting and rewiring, so you start to believe that you are as entitled to be on the planet as much as anyone else and claim your personal power
- Obey your inner wisdom
- Align your behavior with your intuition and your convictions with your words
- Learn how to speak up about your point of view and take action on what's true for you
- Assert yourself with specific, reasonable, and enforceable boundaries and consequences
- Follow through on the limits you set

- When don't know what to do, imagine what someone you admire would do and do that
- Ignore diminishing messages from others and replace self-limiting beliefs (e.g., "I'm useless," "I can't do anything about this") with truths that reinforce your true worth

Power On

I am important. I matter.
I'm entitled to be here.
My job is to take care of myself.
What I'm seeking is within me.
I have choices.
I can do something about this.
I am responsible for my life.
Everything will be all right.

The Upside

- You feel your personal power, are more capable and strong
- You realize your own innate importance
- You realize honoring yourself is higher priority than someone else's emotional reaction
- You can lovingly stand firm even when you ruffle others' feathers with your truth
- You speak up and do what you need to do, boldly moving through fear, by aligning with your heart's directives
- You set goals and take small doable steps towards them
- You shiver when you find opposition to speaking up but do it anyway
- You reach out for help when needed — knowing that's just being human
- You're simply a lot happier and more connected to others and your world

10. Attitude: *Heartbroken (devastated, grief-stricken, miserable)*

Solution: *Mourn and say good-bye.*

What You're Experiencing

- Suffer great loss; people, places, or things you loved have ended or changed

- Feel heavy hearted and discouraged from talking about it or expressing yourself

- Deny or silently endure the profound loss, acting as if it's business as usual, but pain is not going away

- Fear pain will never end, fear to openly expressing the depth of your grief, not understanding the healing benefits of crying

The Price You Pay

- Feeling less joy, feeling flat and detached, day-to-day doesn't hold interest or meaning

- Fuming in anger when you come face-to-face with harsh reality you can't have what you want

- Feeling your sense of safety if compromised, if loss is unexpected, acutely aware of your own mortality

How to Change

- The operative word for befriending losses is good-bye so you acknowledge the ending

- Must face all material things have a beginning, middle, end, endings = loss = sadness

- Accept that life's not always fair, the cosmic plan is unfathomable

- Express anger (to help accept), as well as shiver fear about imagined uncertain future

- Cry and say good-bye until there are no more tears left

- Reach out to others for company and find support where you can safely cry

- If you can't cry, here are some ways to get the ball rolling:
- Look at pictures or mementos
- Visit shared places
- Reminisce about good memories
- Verbalize what you appreciated, loved, and liked about what you've lost
- Write about what you will miss
- Look at the good you experienced

Power On

I miss you.

I feel so sad. I just need to cry. My heart hurts.

We had good times.

I love you.

It's really over.

I wish you well.

Thank you.

Good-bye

Accept the ending and forgive yourself for regrets

Life is not always fair.

Some force larger than me is in control.

I did the best I could at the time.

The Upside

- You realize mourning is a normal human process
- Your sadness is gradually replaced by a sense of sweetness as you say good-bye
- You're ready to say hello to the present, re-engage, and open your heart again

11. Attitude: *Helpless-Hopeless (wounded, hurt, depressed)*

Solution: *Deal with hurts and losses.*

What You're Experiencing

- Feel the pain, hurt, grief, sorrow and it feels bottomless, you feel powerless against it
- View the world as big and cruel
- Lack interest in life, have no motivation, can't find meaning or sense of belonging
- Feel helpless-hopeless, neutralized, and depressed

The Price You Pay

- Feeling like you can't be open, safe, or vulnerable
- Pulling inward and withdrawing from daily life to buffer yourself against further pain
- Handling life's challenges feel like an impossible assignment
- Let go of daily responsibilities that need attention, hard time taking action
- Turning anger against yourself or blaming others
- Losing perspective, are deflated, overwhelmed, unable to enjoy much of anything

How to Change

- Confront your pain head-on, focus on and acknowledge the depths of each hurt and loss
- Crying will miraculously get you moving again
- When you're sinking, take few minutes to emote, relentlessly contradict bleak thoughts
- Express anger and fear physically
- If feeling hopeless-helpless for extended period of time — especially if you're entertaining suicidal thoughts — reach out to a physician or qualified mental health professional to help you climb out of the depths through a combination of counseling

and/or pharmacotherapy (often a powerful adjunct to psycho-
therapy)

- Create a plan to deal with each hurt or loss composed of small, doable steps
- Take a few tiny action steps that nourish you daily
- Reach out and help someone
- Sleep, eat, and exercise regularly to maintain balance
- Find a support person or group that fits your personality

Power On

Oooowww.

I'm in pain.

I feel sad.

It's okay to cry.

I'll feel better if I cry

Power often so thoughts about worst-case scenarios don't derail you

I can handle this.

Little steps.

I'm fine and I'm doing fine.

People and things are the way they are, not the way I want them to be.

The Upside

- Your enthusiasm, confidence, and energy return
- You feel empowered
- You realize hurts and losses are part of life
- You choose to turn hurts and losses into something constructive
- Your generous praise (for yourself) gives impetus to gracefully handle what's next
- You can speak up when you know you need to
- You can take action and enjoy life more

2

Moving from Anger to Love

Do you have a recurring image of punching someone in the face? Do you see your family/friends/co-workers as plotting against you and trying to make your life miserable? If any of that resonates, you're having the telltale signs of anger-based attitudes.

Physically wanting to strike out or viewing other people, things, or situations as enemies isn't going to get you where you want to go. In fact, it could land you up in prison or equally worse, locked up in an emotional prison of being alone forever with biting anger as your only companion. The following solutions cause anger impulses to melt. They're love boosters, associated with love's four core attitudes: obey what you know to be true for you, accept people and situations, appreciate and respect what is, and give selflessly.

Anger Attitudes	Solutions
1. Blaming	Come back to yourself.
2. Frustrated	Accept what is.
3. Resigned	Abandon unfounded hopes.
4. Pessimistic	Accentuate the positive.
5. Judgmental	See unity beyond differences.
6. Defensive	Apologize.
7. Betrayed	Forgive others.
8. Ungrateful	Offer "gratitudes."
9. Opinionated	Empathize.
10. Egocentric	Give selflessly.
11. Mean-spirited	Deal with injustices and violations.

ANGER TO LOVE

> **1. Attitude:** *Blaming (accusing, condemning, jealous)*
>
> **Solution:** *Come back to yourself.*

What You're Experiencing

- Focus attention on others, accusing, condemning, gossiping, or envying them
- Don't look within and take responsibility for what's happening
- Find fault in other people and situations as a rule
- "Out there" instead of "in here" in your heart

The Price You Pay

- Attack and find fault out there
- Pointing fingers, deflect from taking responsibility for your part and yourself
- Feeling alienated, separate, different, disconnected from others

How to Change

- Refocus on yourself when you notice your attention is on making "them" the problem
- Ask yourself, "What's the specific issue? What's going on with me?" and investigate
- In conflict with others, remember all parties share equal responsibility for social discord so don't wait for others to make first move, look for how you can move closer and reach out, offering some appreciations or speaking up what's true for you
- When blaming, do some introspection, stick to incident at hand and ask yourself:
- What is the specific?
- What's my part?
- What's true for me about this?

- What do I need to say or do about this?
- What can I do?
- Ask yourself the same questions when you feel competitive, jealous, or envious

Power On

My focus is myself.
My job is to take care of myself.
We're all on our own paths.

When other people target their anger on you with teasing, accusing, competing, etc., don't retaliate, don't take it personally, or defend yourself, use truths such as:

What they're saying has little to do with me.
They're venting their emotions, and I am the target.
They are "you-ing" me.
They're upset and I'm okay.
It's not personal.
I'm fine.
My job is to take care of myself.

The Upside

- You feel more loving and connected to others
- You are more honest, authentic, and powerful
- You speak and act in line with your heart
- You're able to hear your intuition
- It's easier to cooperate and be on a team

2. Attitude: *Frustrated (resistant, annoyed, rebellious)*

  Solution: *Accept what is.*

What You're Experiencing

- Believe everything would be fine if only "they" shared your brilliant views and completely agreed

- Frequently feel disappointed, frustrated, annoyed, intolerant of others due to your expectations

- Feel entitled to give unsolicited advice and opinions

- Invalidate what you don't accept or like, disguising anger with indifference, caustic tones, demeaning looks, and impatience

- Focus on differences and feel separate

The Price You Pay

- Creating more frustration by not accepting people and things the way they are

- Making things difficult for yourself by resisting what you don't want, like, or believe

- Alienating others by speaking and acting cruelly and mean

- Complaining and whining, teasing and kidding

How to Change

- Acceptance is not "I don't believe it." It's **"I'd better believe it because that is what happened**." It's not "I accept her, but she's obnoxious." Acceptance is, **"I accept her because that's the way she is**."

- Accept reality: acceptance doesn't condone a given person or event, it connects you. You're not rolling over and giving up by accepting someone/something, rather it reframes your understanding so you respect another's view as valid as yours

- When annoyed, frustrated, or crabby, don't take out on others — know it's a sign you need to release anger and accept the reality about what is. Then you can look within and discover what is true for you, what you need to say or do, and set boundaries and define consequences for the future

- Make a list of everyone and everything you don't like, don't accept, or believe should be different. Then take the first item on list and personalize the generic statement "People and things are the way they are, not the way I think they should be," such as "My father is the way he is, not the way I think he should be." Release your anger and/or power on that statement until you shift, then go to next item and repeat this procedure

Power On

People and things are the way they are, not the way I want them to be.

We see things differently.

Your views and needs are as valid as mine.

This is the way it is.

For added benefit, throw in an appreciation with your acceptance statement:

"Maria sees things differently and she's always there for me when I'm down."

The Upside

- You feel more loving and lighthearted
- You appreciate the positive more
- You have more realistic expectations of others
- You enjoy the fact others feel warmer towards you
- You set the stage for meaningful conversations and connections
- You find ease in aversive tasks and face tough situations with a genuine smile

ANGER TO LOVE

3. Attitude: *Resigned (discouraged, disappointed, unrealistic)*

Solution: *Abandon unfounded hopes.*

What You're Experiencing

- Wait, always hoping someone or something will change
- Remain attached to someone's "potential" rather than the reality, don't accept they're unlikely to be any different
- Feel discouraged, hopeless, neutralized, at someone else's mercy
- Live in agony

The Price You Pay

- Clinging to false hope that people, organizations, or situations will be different in the future if you just hang on
- Failing to take the action you know in your heart is required, give up trying
- Sacrificing yourself and your needs
- Clinging to crumbs

How to Change

- Look reality in the face, give up hope that things and people will change OR that they need to change
- Accept that most likely, the future will be the same as the present
- Write down everything you wish were different, then take the first statement and put before it, "I give up all hope that…" such as "I give up all hope that Linda will ever understand me the way I want" or "I give up all hope that Bob will propose on Valentine's Day."
- Keep repeating the statement, express any anger or sadness that arises constructively, interrupt destructive thinking, and focus on what you are saying. When you "get it," repeat this procedure with the next item, and then the next

- After you are finished, look within to see what's true for you and what's in your control right now about each item. Get specific, make explicit requests, set specific, reasonable deadlines and boundaries, and announce well-thought-out consequences
- Speak up and take action with love and conviction as needed
- Follow through on what you say or your words will be empty

Power On

I give up all hope that xxx will ever change.
This is the way she/he/it is.
My job is to take care of myself.

The Upside

- You stop wishing and hoping, channeling your energy into what you want instead of feeling thwarted and disappointed
- You relinquish comfort of the familiar, put an end to waiting for something outside your control to change
- You truly honor yourself
- You step through your fear and create the life you are entitled to

4. Attitude: *Pessimistic (negative, bitchy, complaining)*

Solution: *Accentuate the positive.*

What You're Experiencing

- Find fault in everything, endlessly using words such as "no," "won't," "can't," and "shouldn't"
- Dwell on what's wrong
- Feel life is pretty bleak
- Focus on the half-empty glass, everything and everyone seem useless, pathetic, stupid
- Complain about things you don't like, repeat stories about how others did you wrong, or zoom in on worst-case scenarios

The Price You Pay

- Draining your life of anything positive or good
- Draining everyone else around you, you become a joy-kill
- Feeling life and everything in it is fundamentally flawed
- Failing to experience free-flowing dialogue, connection, and generosity
- Punishing others when they do things you don't like, generating aggression, insecurity, and alienation
- Injuring others' self-esteem, triggering fear, making others feel unsafe around you

How to Change

- Accentuate the positive, overlook what you don't like, praise what you do
- When you want to complain about something, just stop! Revert to silence, look hard until you find the silver lining and voice that, or just remain silent
- Recognize you have choice to frame situations as positive opportunities or negative roadblocks

- If you can't find anything good to say, physically release your anger energy, try again
- Roll out kindness, but be honest and have your tone match your words
- Voice appreciations daily, acknowledging the positive in others
- Give at least two appreciations a day to loved ones in your life
- As needed, preface your appreciations with words, "I'm going to tell you how much I appreciate you now," ensuring the recipient tunes into your wavelength and truly receives your gesture
- Persist every day with appreciations, regardless of whether others do the same
- Mentally find something positive about everyone you encounter

Power On

I loved that you helped me in the garden today.
I appreciate we worked this problem out together.
Thank you for picking up the groceries this afternoon.
You have a great laugh.

The Upside

- You spark feelings of love and moments of connection in yourself and others
- You feel better
- You naturally speak and act more kindly
- You feel more gratitude
- You look for the good and praise it and that feels good
- You're more attractive for others to be around
- You find life easier and have more fun getting things accomplished

5. Attitude: *Attitude: Judgmental (critical, disapproving, prejudiced)*

Suggestion: *See unity beyond differences.*

What You're Experiencing

- Make enemies and create social chasms because you believe your personal opinions are universal givens, feel entitled to voice and impose your views on others
- Attached to your own views, values, needs, wants
- Affix blanket judgments and labels to what you don't accept
- Lump differences into categories of extreme polarities: you vs. me, fair vs. unfair, good vs. bad, win vs. lose, wrong vs. right
- Think you know what's best for others, angry when they don't live up to expectations
- Channel your anger toward entire groups of people who are different from you
- Make jokes and put-downs at others' expense
- Commit crimes (small or large) against minorities (of race, sexual preference, body type, age, religion, or anything else)
- Believe and make others feel "lesser than" or wrong

The Price You Pay

- Thinking in black-and-white breeds a world of adversaries and disconnection
- Feeling alienated, antagonistic, intolerant
- Losing sight of the inspiration that differences can spark
- Failing to see that other people's needs, views, and values are as valid as your own

How to Change

- Accept diversity and differences as a reality
- Emphasize what you have in common with others, seek to make the "other" a friend

- When negative judgments dominate, acknowledge you feel angry, own it, and express it physically, then accept differences, look for the good
- Put duct tape over your mouth and listen more with an open mind, put yourself in the other person's shoes
- As appropriate, reach out with a loving tone, offer help, or at least say something kind
- Offer more appreciations and understanding
- If you're having trouble accepting divergent views and want to reject that person, recall an instance when your views were rejected by someone else
- Mentally find something positive about everyone you encounter

Power On

We're all on our own paths.

Your viewpoints and needs are as important as mine.

We see things differently, and we're still connected.

We are different, and we are the same.

We are the same.

The Upside

- You feel more connected and find it easier to listen to others' views with empathy, even when you don't agree
- You focus on similarities you share with others, finding common ground
- You recognize that we're all inextricably linked
- You feel more love
- You offer to be of service to others

6. Attitude: *Defensive (prideful, insistent, infallible)*

Suggestion: *Apologize.*

What You're Experiencing

- Refuse to apologize, you get defensive or make excuses when you make a mistake
- Suffer from unwillingness to take personal responsibility for your behavior
- Give apologies accompanied by justifications ("I'm sorry, but..."), negating the impact of the apology
- Struggle with pride, self-righteousness, need to maintain an air of infallibility

The Price You Pay

- Feeling terrified of being seen as weak, wrong, imperfect
- Downplaying or deflecting errors because they put a dent in your fragile self-esteem
- Feeling unsettled over unexpressed apologies
- Feeling separate

How to Change

- Remember it's never too late to apologize for a mistake
- Search for what's true for you about the specific event, apologize just for that. Try an approach like: "I'm sorry I didn't call yesterday to let you know that I couldn't keep our dinner plans. I wouldn't have liked it if you had done that to me," or "I apologize for the flippant comment I made about your outfit. I regret I said what I did."
- Admit your part, acknowledge your best guess about the effect it had on other person, and talk about what you learned
- Expressing regret verbally is only the first part; it's equally important to listen to how your actions affected the other person

- Don't justify, explain, defend, minimize, or repeatedly voice regret
- Listen with empathy and compassion to hear the other person's anger, hurt, and fear, with your only motive being to understand and reconnect
- How do you feel about what happened?
- I want to understand where you're coming from.
- I hear what you're saying, and I'm really sorry.

Power On

I did the best I could.

We all make mistakes.

Life is for learning.

If I knew then what I know now, I would have done it differently.

The Upside

- You join humanity as a fallible human being
- You don't have lingering guilt and unsettled feelings
- You take responsibility for what you did or said, knowing it's worth the effort
- Your apology shows your strength and desire to re-connect and clears the air so you don't have unfinished business

7. Attitude: *Betrayed (bitter, resentful, begrudging)*

    Solution: *Forgive others.*

What You're Experiencing

- Carry emotional wounds from the past, perceiving actions as violations or injustices

- Feel injured, betrayed, or crushed when trusted people don't live up to expectations

- Hold grudges and foster indignation, bitterness, and resentment

- Think really poorly about someone or something you previously cared about

The Price You Pay

- Constructing a wall between you and your own heart because of grudges

- Waiting for others to acknowledge their alleged wrongdoings, but likely you'll wait lifetime as it probably won't happen

- Suffering because you can't let go of the past and feel bitter

How to Change

- Forgiveness is the way to heal grievous injuries, whether from a parent, sibling, friend, stranger, business partner, institution, or God

- Understand resentment only prolongs your anguish

- Accept that the past can not be different, truly mourn, and say "good-bye" to what was Realize people's reasons for what they do is totally independent of you, reasons you may never know, so let go of taking it personally

- Identify a specific event considered a betrayal, state the perceived transgression, then add, "I forgive you." Marianne lied to me about using drugs, and I forgive her. Marianne did what she did, and I forgive her." Repeat the words "I forgive you," even if you don't believe them yet, because they bring up anger, sadness, and fear that keeps you stuck in resentment and bitterness. Rigorously interrupt "no way" or "you've got to be kidding," express your emotions while focusing on "I forgive you."

Power On

I forgive you.

I'm doing this so I feel better.

People are the way they are, not the way I want them to be.

Sometimes people act out of their own pain and fear.

She did the best she could at the time.

After processing your emotions, look within for the high road, then take whatever action feels appropriate, doable, and necessary

When communicating, use "I"s, specifics, and kindness, talk about the specific event

You can ask others to give you information about what motivated their behavior

Listen closely so you understand the other person's point of view

Make doable requests and define clear boundaries for the future, then follow through if crossed or agreements are broken

The Upside

- You've come back to yourself and healed your heart

- You hold on a larger reality, are able to think about what happened with love in your heart and no static in your mind

- You look within and discern what you need to do in order to feel fully resolved

- You understand forgiveness is the surefire way to always lighten your load

- You've learned something that will be of future use in dealing with them

- You feel more love

8. Attitude: *Ungrateful (entitled, unappreciative, inconsiderate)*
Solution: *Offer gratitudes.*

What You're Experiencing

- Don't appreciate what you already have
- Want more, want something different, never have enough
- Focus on what's lacking
- Create stingy atmosphere that doesn't inspire generosity in others
- Assume you're entitled to consume riches without gratitude

The Price You Pay

- Taking things for granted — health, friends, family, wealth, or life itself — shutting yourself and others off from love
- Robbing yourself from joy of achievement and negating the fullness of what life offers
- Assuming resources, people, places, things will always be at your disposal and being put off when denied what you want
- Having potential to over-consume, thoughtlessly use or to abuse privileges gifted to you

How to Change

- Pay attention to good fortune, and you'll realize you're fortunate in every moment
- Verbalize your gratitude, acknowledging the magnificence of what is presented
- Count your blessings whenever you're unhappy, flat, or dry — anytime
- In difficult or mundane situations, with friends or strangers, ask yourself, "What is the gift here? What are the benefits of having things turn out like this?"

- Reframe unplanned inconveniences by recognizing even situations like missing a train connection can offer gifts such as having a couple of hours to read your book

- As daily exercise, write, think of, or verbalize one to five things you're grateful for

- Remember your list throughout the day, witness the feeling that is created

- Say "thank you" often as giving thanks expresses recognition of life's bountiful offerings, from your good health to your children's well-being to every breath you take

Power On

Thank you!
I am fortunate.
I am blessed.
I am a lucky gal.
I am a lucky guy.

The Upside

- You feel more waves of love

- You're grateful for all things, great and small

- You recognize life is full of blessings in every moment, you feel blessed

- You give thanks continually widening your perception and warming your heart

- You give to others more without expecting anything in return

- You're more connected to others and your world

- You realize daily that it's a gift to be alive

- You smile more often, your heart is lighter

9. Attitude: *Opinionated (arrogant, bossy, nagging)*

Solution: *Empathize.*

What You're Experiencing

- Offer unsolicited advice or observations — "you"s, often jokingly
- Trespass frequently on others' emotional territory without permission
- Believe it's your duty to set others straight and enlighten them with your wisdom
- Treat others as if they need your superior guidance
- Think, speak, and act as if you are more important than others

The Price You Pay

- Producing defensiveness and distance with your words
- Coming across to others as bossy, abrasive, nagging, uncaring, conceited, judgmental
- Feeling closed off and disconnected from others
- Feeling less love and intimacy, lack of compassion

How to Change

- Stop and be silent when you catch yourself telling other people about themselves
- Listen with empathy, seek to genuinely understand
- Before opening your mouth to nag, boss, or offer opinions, distinguish whether it's appropriate. If your intuition confirms it's all right, lovingly make and receive permission before you plunge ahead: "I'd like to give you some feedback or make a request. Is that okay?" If you get a no, ask a couple more times to see if they reconsider — a consistent no, means no. If you get a yes, ask again to make sure they're not just being polite
- If people are open to what you have to say, go forward with kindness, offer your opinion with no strings attached, don't argue

with their reaction or try to convince them

- Let them know you'll elaborate if they want additional information

- Accept what is true for the other person

- Only if people are at risk of endangering themselves or others are you entitled to offer suggestions without permission

- Recognize your domain is yourself, spend energy on living your own life with love, respect, and personal integrity, and talk about yourself

- If someone is bossing, nagging, or offering opinions, don't get defensive, look beyond words and understand they're experiencing anger, fear, sadness

- Acknowledge unsolicited advice or commands, don't debate what was said, gently but firmly voice what's true for you

Power On

I want to understand where you're coming from.

We each get to live our own lives.

Your views and needs are as important as mine.

You may do some things I disagree with, but that doesn't alter the fact that I love you.

My territory is myself.

The Upside

- Your genuine understanding without judgment ensures love enters all communication

- You've increased trust in your relationships by respecting others' viewpoints

- Your practice of asking permission before giving feedback promotes receptivity, prevents animosity

- You have more opportunity to enjoy your own inner silence and full heart

10. Attitude: *Egotistic (selfish, narcissistic, possessive)*

Solution: *Give generously.*

What You're Experiencing

- Live in a scarcity economy instead of abundant universe
- Withhold yourself and your time, money, or information believing accumulation brings safety, security, and self-worth, act stingy, greedy, possessive
- Look for what's in it for you, feel like it is "you vs. me"
- Do what you want, regardless of how it affects others
- React overwhelmingly if people don't agree with you, and distance yourself

The Price You Pay

- Giving with strings attached, feelings of joy and love are lost, creating separation and distance, making emotional connection impossible
- Attacking or defending when people see, want, believe something different
- Losing genuine closeness because you're preoccupied with protecting what you have

How to Change

- Recognize that feeling superior or special is an illusion that covers deeper feelings of unworthiness and insecurity
- Implement actions of giving, repeat for weeks or longer so it becomes natural, "Fake it 'til you make it." It's okay to pretend until your old selfishness burns away
- Give material things, like gifts, flowers, money, cards, etc.
- Ask, "How can I help?" and carry through on promises you make
- Volunteer for a constructive cause
- Become a mentor, share your skills, experience, and knowledge with others

- Be affectionate. Genuinely use words of endearment, like honey, sweetie, dear
- Give loving looks, warm smiles, non-demanding hugs
- Give sexually without expecting anything in return
- Be generous with appreciations, praise, and applause
- Appreciate those who feel sad, understand those who feel angry, and reassure those who are fearful (the three communication bridges)
- Be welcoming and friendly. Take the initiative and express a heartfelt greeting ("I'm so glad to see you")
- Listen
- Think loving thoughts ("I wish you well," "I love you") throughout the day
- Speaking honestly about personal matters
- Give thanks, silently and out loud
- Cooperate and compromise. Teamwork is creative, productive, and connecting

Power On

Helping you is helping me.
Love first.
I wish you well.

The Upside

- You give without ulterior motives and feel full, no matter how the gesture is taken
- You feel generous, and that feels good
- You realize sharing, giving, and being kind brings immense rewards, like love
- You feel the oneness and unity that exists
- You feel more intimacy and create an atmosphere encouraging others to share

11. Attitude: *Meanspirited (aggressive, spiteful, cruel)*

Solution: *Deal with injustices and violations.*

What You're Experiencing

- Smolder over life's injustices and violations
- Perceive events and other people's actions as violations or injustices
- Believe it's your right to vent anger and displeasure on others
- Use mean, cruel, and damaging words, with rude and disrespectful behavior
- Think "You hurt me, so I'm going to hurt you back."
- Feel alienated, isolated, separate, different

The Price You Pay

- Harboring hostility and hatred towards others, turn specific events into ugly blowouts
- Shutting others out, becoming callous, passive-aggressive — anger but afraid to show it
- Inflicting abuse — if others fear for their emotional, mental, and physical safety — what you are doing is abusive. Your angry words and actions cause the victims of your vicious attacks to be devastated, insulted, or threatened, pushing them to lash back in anger, shrivel in sadness, or cower in fear and close their hearts in pain, withdraw
- All possibilities for genuine intimacy vanishes

How to Change

- Give up need to be 'in control'
- Revert to silence when impulse to strike out hits, walk away or respond when calmer
- When feel anger rising and desire to be mean, process real or perceived violations and injustices by expressing anger in a way that doesn't damage others or things of value, take a time-out to

pound some phonebooks, scream into pillow, or stomp around

- Accept that people, things, and situations are the way they are
- Apologize for unkind words and actions, then listen to hear about the effect they created
- Act in kind, compassionate, thoughtful ways that demonstrate a willingness to work together
- Take action to right the injustice or violation with clarity, directness, and respect
- Avoid hot foods, hot places, hot exercise, hot conversations

Power On

I feel so mad.

It's okay to feel angry.

I just need to move this energy out.

People and things are the way they are, not the way I want them to be.

Once you've dealt with anger and accepted what you don't like, look within to hear your intuition, and then obey, speak up about yourself about the specific event that triggered you, don't bring in other "transgressions" or hurl unkind labels

As needed make a specific request, or set a boundary and follow through if crossed

The Upside

- Your softness replaces harshness; humility replaces pride; optimism replaces negativity
- You feel love, respect, connection, and relish what you share in common
- You let go of the resentments you've been holding onto
- You operate from a loving space and people are drawn to you
- You sustain intimate relationships and feel more love than ever before

3

Moving from Fear to Peace

Knotted up, frozen, or agitated. Your mind catapults itself anywhere, backwards, forward, or out into the wild blue yonder, but never resides in the present. These are the repercussions of living in fear. Follow the steps in this chapter so you can live in each moment and stay specific, hold on to what you know is true for you, surrender to what is, and engage life fully. And here's the important part: no matter what attitude you want to change, remember to physically shiver the fear out of your body. It's the quickest way to quiet the mind and tap into your heart. Look for what attitude resonates and follow the quick chart steps. Prepare to relish life with faith, from a centered place of trust and serenity, freely expressing serenity, enthusiasm, and creativity in each moment.

Fear Attitudes	Solutions
1. Worried	Be here now
2. Rushed/Impatient	Slow down
3. Overwhelmed	Little steps
4. Moody	Shift your mood
5. Doubting	Reassure yourself
6. Irresponsible	Remember that actions have consequences
7. Dissatisfied	Find enough
8. Out of sync	Be mindful of the timing
9. Uncomfortable	Participate authentically
10. Controlling	Let go
11. Anxious	Deal with perceived threats to your survival

FEAR TO PEACE

1. Attitude: *Worried (nervous, preoccupied, scattered)*

Solution: *Be here now.*

What You're Experiencing

- Jump out of the present into the past or future
- "Futurize," or fixate on times yet to come or entertaining worst case "What ifs"
- "Pasturize," or drag in examples of what happened in the past to make a current case
- Overextend, making too many plans, endlessly fantasizing about unrealistic fairy-tale endings
- Replay good or bad about days gone, often giving more weight to the bad
- Go on tangents about unfinished business, blurring the specific topic at hand

The Price You Pay

- Spinning mind and body, agitated
- Distracting yourself from fully experiencing the now and feeling calm and relaxed
- Experiencing difficulty sleeping
- Obsessing about things out of your control or yet to come

How to Change

- Pause for a few seconds, take a couple of full deep breaths
- Shiver when body or mind is agitated
- Connect with physical surroundings and pay attention to your senses
- Sit with what you're experiencing and befriend the internal sensations
- If you must worry or daydream, designate ten minutes a day to indulge it, for the rest of day diligently interrupt thoughts that

take you out of the present, and shiver

- Make a list of what needs attention, prioritize items, breaking big jobs into small pieces, then do what's next
- Focus on one thing at a time

Power On

Be here now.
I am here.
Here I am.
I'll handle the future in the future.
That was then. This is now.
One thing at a time.
I'll do what I can, and the rest is out of my hands.
Worrying doesn't help.

The Upside

- You are more calm, content, and relaxed as peace takes over and fear loosens its grip
- You align with Ram Dass and are here now
- You live in the present moment of simplicity, order, and flow
- You're aware that this moment is a "perfect moment," take pleasure in it
- You know you can handle anything what happens
- You enjoy the grandeur of the ordinary and see the choices available to you right now
- You revel in the glory of what's happening right in front of you
- You feel more trust and have more faith

FEAR TO PEACE

2. Attitude: *Rushed/Impatient (restless, harried, exasperated)*

Solution: *Slow down.*

What You're Experiencing

- Live in warp speed
- Thrown off by unforeseen complications
- Speed up to catch up, rarely gaining time by moving fast
- Have accidents by rushing things
- Frantic to meet deadlines or goals, slave to the clock
- Hold your breath, or breath is shallow and irregular
- Obsessed and controlled by deadlines

The Price You Pay

- Lacking the ability to savor the moment, any moment
- Refusing to accept some things unfold in a time frame that can't be controlled
- Making more mistakes
- Pushing and becoming abrasive when people and events don't go at your speed
- Slowing things down further because others resist your tactics

How to Change

- Pause, step back
- Take a few measured breaths to slow down
- Shiver and quiver every part of your body intensely until you connect with the present and know everything will be all right
- Recognize if you're mimicking your parent's poor relationship with time, punctual or irresponsible, and make another choice that will increase peace

- Let go of your time expectation because it's rarely what you think
- Find something healthy to do while waiting, like power, hum a tune, or enjoy scenery

Power On

Everything is all right.
Everything will be okay.
Everything is unfolding in its own time.
Stop. Breathe. Relax.
This isn't life or death.

The Upside

- You feel more centered
- You're more relaxed and enjoy what's happening
- You're more aware of your environment, and able to smell the roses
- You're better able to peacefully handle whatever happens
- You enable others to feel more comfortable around you
- You hear your intuition better
- You maintain a healthier perspective about what is really important
- You realize things go at their own time, not yours

3. Attitude: *Overwhelmed (swamped, stressed, pressured)*

Solution: *Little steps.*

What You're Experiencing

- Lump topics together, distort significance of any single event
- Leap from specifics to global generalities and conclusions, losing sight of the issues at hand, launching into exaggerations and drama — limited only by your imagination
- Go on tangents, use one incident to pontificate about other issues, politics, ethics, or philosophy
- Use "stressed" as your favorite vocabulary word, stress = overwhelmed = fear
- Preoccupied with what needs to be done or should be done, becoming immobilized
- Take on too many responsibilities

The Price You Pay

- Losing perspective
- Missing the present because you're always in the future
- Living in a drama-filled world, small things become earth-shattering
- Other people feeling nervous, anxious, or rushed in your presence
- Accomplishing tasks consume you, you can't enjoy the journey
- Losing intimacy because with your mind racing, you rarely hear what people say

How to Change

- Calm your fear with good constructive shivering and powering
- Cut what's on your plate into chewable pieces
- Get concrete and "think small"
- Make a list of issues and projects needing your attention, being specific

- Consult your intuition to clarify priorities
- Develop detailed plan, breaking down the mountain of responsibilities into doable steps
- Focus on and do only one task at a time, shivering when you feel stuck
- Praise yourself lavishly as you take each little step
- Check in before accepting additional responsibility, saying no won't be end to the world
- Renegotiate what's not possible, delegate as necessary

Power On

Think small.
Stay specific.
One thing at a time.
Little steps.
Little by little.

The Upside

- Your life's tasks are easier to handle because you do them in small steps
- You take charge of your life and your interaction with others
- You deal with specifics in conversations and within yourself, to produce clarity, calm and centeredness
- You get more done
- You are present to your life
- You know if you remain specific, you can accomplish almost anything, little by little
- You surrender, knowing that if you let go, you can embrace what's happening right now

FEAR TO PEACE

4. Attitude: *Moody (unpredictable, changeable, brooding)*

Solution: *Shift your mood.*

What You're Experiencing

- Feel feelings and thoughts come out of nowhere, won't go away
- Believe moods are out of your control
- Pull back, become inaccessible, retreat into a brooding gloom
- Feel irritable, cranky, flat, powerless, moody, rocky, down

The Price You Pay

- Perceiving things negatively which influences your body, words, actions, tainting your life's experience for hours, days, weeks, or even longer and diminishing quality of life
- Exhibiting chronic 'mood' swings
- Feeling it's impossible to know how you'll feel or will see things at any given time
- Feeling like a victim to your moods
- Being perceived as erratic by others

How to Change

- Trace back and identify exactly when a mood started, because something upsetting happened, as simple as an edgy interaction or as big as a argument with your partner
- Pinpoint the event by asking yourself, "When did I start feeling like this?" or, "When was the last time I remember feeling okay?" Think back to various points in time to identify when your mood started. "How was I feeling three weeks ago when friends visited from out-of-town? How about last Saturday at the wedding? After I stepped on the scale yesterday morning?" The exact event will become crystal clear
- After identifying the trigger, deal with just that by constructively expressing your emotions physically about the event to defuse its impact

- Consult your intuition to determine if you need to say or do something to resolve the event, and if so, follow through
- It's never too late to initiate a conversation about the specific event if others are involved

Power On

This is just a mood.

This mood will pass.

This feeling is temporary. This situation will pass.

I'm just feeling some emotions.

If I express my emotions constructively I'll feel better.

Stick to the specific.

The Upside

- You are back to feeling more present, happy, content
- You feel and are more steady
- Your interactions with others will feel more meaningful
- You are in control of yourself, your experience, and your life
- You enjoy life more
- You are proud that others are able to count on you

5. Attitude: *Doubting (indecisive, confused, fickle)*

Solution: *Reassure yourself.*

What You're Experiencing

- Question yourself after a decision rather than sticking with what you previously knew so clearly

- Listen to fear based, doubting mental chatter such as "Yes, but…" because it's scary to step out and do something new

- Swirl in doubt, confusion, and indecisiveness, become immobilized

- Remain in a grip of fear, forgetting factors that led to initial decision

- Lose certainty about priorities, commitments, even facts

- Vacillate as your convictions and promises that previously felt ironclad become shaky

The Price You Pay

- Giving in to doubts leaves you fumbling around in confusion

- Living in limbo-land, reinforcing the status quo, missing new exciting opportunities

- Not trusting yourself or your decisions

- Supporting others' conclusions that you're unreliable, constantly changing your mind

- Avoiding risks

- Ignoring your intuition

How to Change

- Pause, calm your body and mind down, remind yourself of what you knew when you were clear

- Shiver to dispel the fear, get centered, and back in touch with what's true for you

- Reassure yourself that you and everything will be okay

- Write down what you know when you are clear
- Don't give energy to your fickle mind, know that doubts indicate unexpressed fear
- Interrupt sabotaging thoughts, tenaciously hold on to the reality you keep forgetting
- We had a huge fight last night, and I still love my wife.
- The doctor gave me a clean bill of health.
- My boss said my job is not in jeopardy.
- Ralph is dating other people.

Power On

Everything will be all right no matter what.
Hold onto what you know is true.
I can handle whatever happens.
My goal is more important than these doubts.
I'm doing better than I think I am.
Trust.

The Upside

- You reassure yourself so you are more in charge of your life
- You keep heading into new unfamiliar territory, despite the fear
- You honor and align with your intuition
- You feel more grounded and confident
- You open yourself to more creativity

6. Attitude: *Irresponsible (impulsive, forgetful, careless)*

   Solution: *Remember that actions have consequences.*

What You're Experiencing

- Live in denial, pretending what you do doesn't matter
- Succumb to impulses, don't honor commitments then act surprised by consequences
- Suffer a physical, mental, or emotional hangover from actions and inactions
- Need to make excuses and justify your behavior

The Price You Pay

- Resisting a natural law in the material world: all actions have consequences, "Whatever you do will come right back to you." The food you eat, the air you breathe, and the exercise you do (or don't do) have direct effects on you
- Making poor choices by not thinking things through
- Losing the trust of others by not following through, or ignoring agreements
- Causing negative consequences by your actions
- Making things more complicated than necessary
- Losing things, missing opportunities
- Causing more accidents to happen
- Coming off as unreliable, like you can't be counted on

How to Change

- Remember everything carries consequences: yell at your kids consistently, they'll pull away; abuse your privileges at work, deal with your bosses' wrath; spend more money than you have, end up in debt
- Be aware current reality is a product of the past; your future is the result of actions taken today

- Honor your agreements, and if you can't, notify the people involved in a timely manner beforehand
- Slow down, consult your intuition to confirm a given course of action, if you get a green light, confidently proceed; yellow, proceed with caution; red, reevaluate your options
- When you're about to do something impulsive, interrupt the urge, pause, shiver, slow down, remember the reality, then make a more conscious choice
- If I resist this cookie, I'll feel great.
- If I buy this today, it will be a struggle to pay rent on the first.
- If I stay out after my curfew, my parents will be angry, and we'll
- probably get in a fight

Power On

My actions determine my outcomes.
Actions have consequences.
I'm responsible for my choices.
I'm responsible for my life.

The Upside

- You make more conscious choices and are aware of the consequences
- You take more personal responsibility and feel better about yourself
- You feel more peace
- Your life runs more smoothly

7. Attitude: *Dissatisfied (unfulfilled, lacking, insufficient)*

Solution: *Find enough.*

What You're Experiencing

- Feel like there's never enough, have a scarcity mindset
- Believe more is better, rarely satisfied
- Measure everything against an invisible standard of what's lacking
- Believe if you had or did something else — got married, earned more money, looked more beautiful, had more time — you'd finally relax and feel worthy
- Complain about 'not enough' time, money, friends, opportunities

The Price You Pay

- Feeling deprived no matter how hard you try or what you do
- Engaging in never-ending struggle to obtain what you don't have, reaching for more to appease restlessness and affirm self-worth
- Thinking about yourself: "I'm not good enough," or "I'm not doing enough."
- Thinking about people/things: "What's coming my way isn't enough," or "You're not enough."
- Thinking about time: "There's not enough time."

How to Change

- Stop complaining and comparing yourself to others
- Shift focus to accepting who you are, what you have, what you've been given
- Accept and appreciate people, things, situations, and time the way they are
- Understand this moment and what is presented is perfect
- Focus on what enriches you, others, situations you possess right now

- Cancel thoughts of "not enough," when they surface
- Shake out fear of not having, doing, or being enough, express any sadness or anger

Power On

Choose statements from below, depending where your "enough" stuff is:

For a focus on yourself

My presence is enough.

I am good enough.

I've done enough.

I am fully satisfied with myself.

For a focus on other people and situations

This is enough.

I have enough.

My friends are enough.

For a focus on time

What's happening right now is perfect.

I have enough time.

There is enough time.

The Upside

- Your attention is on appreciating what is already here, who you already are
- You live in contentment
- You feel fully satisfied with yourself, with what you and what others do
- You accept yourself, others, things, and time exactly the way they are right now
- You enjoy life and marvel in your abundance

8. Attitude: *Out of Sync (procrastinating, impulsive, hasty)*

Solution: *Be mindful of the timing.*

What You're Experiencing

- Relax and start to have a good time only when a party is almost over
- Cram studying into last few hours before a test
- Out of sync with life's natural rhythm, sometimes frantic, sometimes lazy
- Disrespect time by acting impulsively or dawdling
- Sidetracked easily or leap into action without evaluating the implications
- Prove others correct that they can't count on you, losing their trust

The Price You Pay

- Thinking what you're doing right now is more important than paying attention to time and following through with your commitments
- Making convoluted attempts to control things, with negative repercussions
- Having a nagging, uneasy feeling when procrastinating
- Endlessly trying to beat the system
- Fighting against external "shoulds" and deadlines
- Dragging your feet, muddying original obligation, adding fear of failure
- Missing great opportunities
- Ending up rushing and not leaving enough time to do things well or completely

How to Change

- Realize living in harmony with time is not antithetical to spontaneity

- Remember you goal is to do what's required in a responsible way
- Ask and obey your intuition to determine what needs to be done and when to do it
- Keep track of what is required in the future
- If you're ahead of the clock (you wake up at 4:00 a.m. on the first day of school) or behind the clock (scrambling to the airport to catch a flight), calm yourself by shivering intensely so you can be present and bask in the moment
- If you consistently dawdle, try being early for every appointment for a week
- Ignore your self-sabotaging thoughts and do what's best, shivering if you start to stall

Power On

Be here now.
Timeliness brings peace of mind.
Honoring time makes things simpler.
I can do it.
I'll feel better if I do this now.
One step at a time.

The Upside

- You are more mindful
- You simplify your life
- You sleep better at night
- You enjoy life more and are more present
- You are more energetic
- You are in harmony with your true self and with others
- You've regained trust of others
- You stay steady, persevere, and are motivated to accomplish goals and attend to responsibilities

> **9. Attitude:** *Uncomfortable (ill-at-ease, dramatic, superficial)*
>
> **Solution:** *Participate authentically.*

What You're Experiencing

- Resort to being life of party or withdraw in indifference, afraid of being vulnerable
- Take center stage but remain superficial by reeling off stories, jokes, sexual innuendoes
- Act bored, become serious and dramatic, or hang out on periphery of social gatherings
- Leave little room for moments to unfold organically

The Price You Pay

- Masking discomfort and diverting others from paying attention to perceived shortcomings
- Avoiding authenticity or honesty
- Not enjoying opportunities present in the moment
- Feeling exhausted by all the pretense and lack of ease
- Feeling vigilantly on guard to fend off threats to vulnerability
- Feeling distance and as if people don't really know you

How to Change

- Let go of choreographing every scene
- Observe what's happening in front of you, and feel and express the fear even if you must take a moment to shake in bathroom
- Hang in, be a little vulnerable, you won't die
- Reassure yourself you're fine and that everything will be all right if you are yourself
- Prepare for events in advance, plan and practice little things you can say
- Say yes to invitations so you can try out acting in new ways, even if you just stay a little while

- When communicating with others, stick with sharing about yourself
- Fake it until you make it, act "as if" you were at ease
- Listen well

Power On

I'm fine. It's okay. I can handle this.
This feeling will pass.
Everything is all right.
Enjoy the ride.
I'm not the only person who feels uncomfortable.

The Upside

- You choose to participate wholeheartedly, enjoying being yourself
- You feel more open and relaxed
- You let moments unfold naturally
- You feel peace living in the moment
- You're more honest and authentic
- You make room for genuine playfulness, delight, and present moment simplicity

10. Attitude: *Controlling (domineering, phobic, obsessive-compulsive)*

Solution: *Let go.*

What You're Experiencing

- Try to control all situations to reduce fear
- Exert power over people and your world to reduce insecurity and anxiety
- Seize control, take the lead, plan obsessively, or organize the chaos
- Attempt to make the unpredictable world more certain, shape the future to your liking
- Develop elaborate rituals in order to feel safe

The Price You Pay

- Struggling with enjoying life
- Putting your wants first, and selfishly disregarding others' needs and desires
- Sacrificing your connection with others by feeling entitled to press own agenda
- Exerting power over others (money, a job, approval, etc.) as leverage to get your way
- Pushing others to resist, rebel, or distance themselves because of your actions
- Obsessing and practicing hyper-vigilance, such as feeling compelled to perform irrational action ("If I don't check on my girlfriend, something terrible will happen"), engaging in an ordinary acts over and over again ("I need to triple-check that I locked the door, or I'll drive myself nuts"), and avoiding certain "normal situations" with phobias ("If a spider crawled over my face while I'm sleeping, I'd have a heart attack")
- Feeding fears, making life more rigid, ultimately feel controlled by external

How to Change

- Realize relinquishing control won't kill you, make you weak or irresponsible
- Take a cue from the serenity prayer: "Grant me the serenity to accept the things I cannot change, the courage to change the things I can, and the wisdom to know the difference"
- Stop running away, face your fears head on
- Pause, shiver like crazy when you feel fear, pound or cry when anger or sadness arise
- Make list of what you're afraid of, from mildest to most intense, expose yourself to what you avoid in little doses, and deal with emotions, especially shiver, keep confronting different situations until emotional charge has dissipated
- Don't feed thoughts that perpetuate fears
- Congratulate yourself for each little step, no matter how small

Power On

Everything is/will be all right.
I'll do what I can, and the rest is out of my hands.
I let go. I surrender.
Everything is unfolding in its own time.
We'll see.

The Upside

- You feel liberated and rest in more abiding peace
- You realize that love is a sweeter reward than having things always go your way
- You understand love requires teamwork, cooperation, and personal sacrifice
- You surrender the need to be in charge
- Trust, faith, amusement grow
- You understand "the only thing we have to fear is fear itself"
- You gracefully participate in what's happening, feel more connected, creative, flexible
- You experience the freedom to be relatively normal again

11. Attitude: *Anxious (panicked, jittery, frantic)*

Solution: *Deal with perceived threats to your survival.*

What You're Experiencing

- Feel your survival is threatened when encountering unknown, uncertainty, uncontrollable, unpredictable phenomena or events
- Struggle with sleeplessness, a racing heartbeat, a knot in your gut, panic, paralysis
- Feel nervousness, anxiety or terror — whether the source of your fear is an upcoming surgery, a job interview, or being around somebody with a violent temper
- Believe your current condition won't end; random incidents set off an avalanche of anxiety: muscles tighten, you can't breathe, you feel like you'll die

The Price You Pay

- Losing the distinction between real threat or perceived threat
- Living in constant state of fight, flight, or freeze, frantic, numb
- Thinking less clearly, and confusion and indecision settle in

How to Change

- Shivering is most natural and efficient method to quickly release fear physiology
- Focus on bodily sensations, consciously relax tension in arms, legs, mouth
- Keep taking full, deep breaths, regulate your breathing
- Acknowledge what you're feeling, "I'm just feeling fear. It's okay."
- Don't feed fear by spooking yourself out with panicky thoughts, hold onto what's true
- Confront fear by repeatedly exposing yourself to what's scary in little steps
- Consult your inner wisdom about what to do, find what actions to take to feel resolved

- If fear is truly disabling and you need assistance to deal with panic and/or anxiety, seek the help of a qualified healthcare practitioner
- Don't miss meals and eat high-protein foods, such as nuts, meats, and grains
- Go light on caffeine, energy drinks, and sugars; they increase your fear physiology
- Get plenty of rest
- Reframe how you look at fear: highly creative people see fear as positive indicator they're moving into new frontiers
- Welcome fear as opportunity to expand horizons, ignite imaginations, spark invention
- Share your plight with safe people, get support

Power On

Everything is all right.
This feeling is temporary. This will pass.
Fear is normal. This won't kill me.
I still need to do or say this.

The Upside

- You feel more centered, more confident you can handle whatever is presented
- You can identify and handle any situation, by setting and taking doable steps
- You feel much more at peace and can witness life unfolding
- You feel safer
- You choose to see fear as a harbinger of something new
- You find it easier to let go and be entertained and inspired by the moment
- You can handle what's presented more flexibly

APPENDIX

Tables and Worksheets

Bodily Sensations Associated with Each Emotion

Sadness	Joy		Anger	Love		Fear	Peace
heavy heart	blissful		hot	warm		cold	relaxed
constricted chest	expansive		flushed	open		tense muscles	tranquil
weak	sparkling		tight muscles	full		shivering	content
low energy	carefree		aggressive	soft		trembling	quiet
tight throat	active		cold stare	smiling		stomach knots	perceptive
slow	exuberant		striking out	embracing		elevated pulse	alert
lethargic	light		explosive	connected		agitated	calm

Each Emotion's Physical Expression

Sadness	Joy		Anger	Love		Fear	Peace
crying	smiling		aggressive	open		agitated	relaxed
sobbing	bubbling		pushing	soft		shivering	silent
weeping	sparkling		pounding	smiling		shuddering	still
wailing	exuberant laughter		stomping	sweet laughter		trembling	alert
frowning	exhilarated yells		biting	embracing		nervous laughter	aware
	crying		yelling	undefended		quivering	smiling
			caustic laughter	reaching out		jiggly legs	

Some Feelings Associated with Each Emotion

Sadness	Joy		Anger	Love		Fear	Peace
unlovable	lovable		jealous	open		worried	relaxed
lonely	confident		dissatisfied	satisfied		nervous	calm
needy	secure		intolerant	tolerant		stressed	productive
guilty	self-accepting		resentful	kind		indecisive	stable
small	strong		disgusted	grateful		confused	committed
incapable	powerful		conceited	humble		impatient	patient
glum	delighted		stingy	generous		rigid	flexible

MORE

The Twelve Pairs of Core Attitudes

Focus: Yourself	
Sadness	**Joy**
Unworthy	Worthy
Dependent on others for approval	Self-reliant
Judge self negatively	Appreciate and respect self
Passive	Speak up and take action

Focus: People and Situations	
Anger	**Love**
Focus on the outside world	Open-hearted
Don't accept people and situations	Accept people and situations
Make negative judgments of what is	Appreciate and respect what is
Selfish	Selfless giving

Focus: Time	
Fear	**Peace**
Live in the future or past	Reside in the present
Overgeneralize	Stay specific
Lose sight of what is true or real	Keep sight of what is true or real
Attempt to control	Observe, enjoy, allow, and participate

Emotions, Doshas, and Illness

Doshas / Emotions	Physical Imbalances	Psychological Imbalances
Kapha Sadness	chest congestion sinus conditions asthma allergies coughs swollen glands tumors edema diabetes slow digestion sluggishness	depression lack of drive lack of motivation passivity slowness dependency preoccupied with what others feel and think low self-esteem complacency cautious
Pitta Anger	inflammation fever hot flashes infection liver / gallbladder disorders ulcers hyperacidity gastric pain skin rashes boils / acne / hives hemorrhoids	judgmental only see to own view frustrated critical lack of fulfillment aggressiveness irritability hate / hostility jealousy resentment defensive discontent
Vata Fear	insomnia panic attacks tremors paralysis dizziness low back pain arthritic pain exhaustion weight loss circulatory problems constipation	overactive mind agitations anxiety nervousness hypersensitivity dramatic thoughts living in thoughts ungrounded spaced out stressed out rapid mood shifts unpredictable

Destructive Thought versus Truth

Destructive Thoughts	Truths
This is killing me.	I'm in pain right now.
Do I have to do this?	This is an opportunity to learn something new.
I can't do it.	I can do this.
This sucks.	This is what is on my plate right now.
It's too hard.	I'll give this my best shot.
Me. Me. Me.	How can I help?
I can't believe this is happening.	Yes. This is happening. I better believe it.
He's weird.	We are all on our own paths.
I'm no good.	I am good enough.
I hate the way I look.	I am more than my body.
I shouldn't have said that.	It's human to make mistakes.
This is too much.	One thing at a time.
I want that.	I can't have it all.
I'll never get it right.	I did the best I could.
How could they do that to me?	People are the way they are.
What are they thinking about me?	What they think of me is not my business.
Why me?	Yes, me!

Pocketful of Truths Worksheet

Truths to Honor Myself (Sadness → Joy)

Truths to Accept People and Situations (Anger → Love)

Truths to Stay Present and Specific (Fear → Peace)

Other Helpful Truths

BIBLIOGRAPHY AND FURTHER READING

Aranya, Swami Hariharananda. *Yoga Philosophy of Patanjali.* Albany: State University of New York Press, 1983.

Chopra, Deepak. *Perfect Health: The Complete Mind/Body Guide.* New York: Harmony Books, 1990.

Frawley, David. *Ayurvedic Healing.* Salt Lake City: Passage Press, 1989.

Isherwood, Christopher and Swami Prabhavananda. *How to Know God: The Yoga Aphorism of Patanjali.* Hollywood: Vedanta Society of Southern California, 1953.

Lad, Vasant. *Ayurveda: The Science of Self-Healing.* Santa Fe: Lotus Press, 1984.

Latham, Glenn. *The Power of Positive Parenting.* Salt Lake City: Northwest Publishing Inc., 1994.

Rosenberg, Marshall. *Nonviolent Communication: A Language of Compassion.* Encinitas, CA: Puddle Dancer Press, 2003.

Reading Group Questions

1. Attitude Reconstruction proposes that unexpressed sadness, anger, and fear are at the root of most of our struggles and issues. Do you agree? Can you think of examples in your own life or the lives of others you've observed where the failure to deal with these emotions led to problems?

2. What were the messages you received from your parents about sadness? Anger? Fear? Joy? Love? Peace? What did you receive from friends? From church? From the media? What different messages would you have gotten if you were born the other gender? Born twenty years earlier?

3. Which emotion or emotions do you relate to the most? How does each emotion manifest in your body, thoughts, words, and actions? What is each one of your family members' most dominant emotion? How do you think the difference/similarity between your and their strongest emotions affects your relationship?

4. In what situations do you feel joy, love, or peace? Does the connection the author makes between joy and sadness, love and anger, and peace and fear ring true for you?

5. What did you like best about this book? What was your biggest "aha" learning? What concepts might you think about implementing?

6. Share a past experience that continues to bother you. Talk about how you might have behaved differently if you had followed the principles of Attitude Reconstruction.

7. What sort of a support system would help you make some changes in your life? Who could you approach and how, when, and what would you like your check-ins to entail? Consider initiating a plan to do this, perhaps by checking in with another member of your reading group.

For additional reading group questions, please visit.
www.AttitudeReconstruction.com.

MORE

WHY I WROTE THIS BOOK

Every life seems to be destined for magic in some way. You'd think that being the daughter of a pioneer in the field of behavioral child psychology and applied behavior analysis, I'd have been given all I needed to know. It's true his impact was powerful: he imparted the value of direct observation, being specific, and praising the positive. But something was still missing.

A yearning to be happy and a passion for understanding human behavior sent me on a journey to answer the question, why do we suffer so much when life can be so good?

After earning a master's degree in psychology, I taught introductory psychology at the university level and explored different approaches to understand myself and the world around me. I discovered pieces of the truth, little slices that resonated, but something was still missing. No system or philosophy seemed to illicit true happiness or fulfill my need to live in harmony with others.

In the early 1970s, I discovered Transcendental Meditation, an Eastern approach to living brought to the West by Maharishi Mahesh Yogi of India. In my heart, I sensed this was the key I'd been searching for. I plunged headfirst into years of study of meditation and philosophy. Thirteen years later, Gurumayi Chidvilasananda came into my life, and I devoted myself to practicing Siddha Yoga meditation. It was in this period that I learned about Patanjali's Yoga Sutras, and Ayurvedic medicine, the ancient science of health and self-healing.

Those Eastern schools of thought brought many profound experiences and insights about life, spirituality, and the mind. But my search continued. Underneath my highs and lows, I still felt flat, uninspired. I was trudging through my day-to-day life professionally, personally, and relationally. I was stuck, and nothing I did brought any sustained relief from my own unhappiness. With a strong desire to help others navigate their own inner maze, I was drawn to work with individuals, couples,

MORE

and groups as a licensed marriage and family therapist. It was like a secret door opened; something amazing began to happen. The more I led and participated in diverse classes, therapies, workshops, and trainings, the more I started to see patterns I hadn't seen before, all revolving around emotions.

There seemed to be an inner guide showing me previously hidden truths for the very first time. Attitude Reconstruction organically came into focus. I realized that while our situations and personalities were vastly different, everyone's difficulties lay in the three emotions of sadness, anger, and fear. They were either working overtime to completely suppress these emotions or expressing them in ways self-destructive or detrimental to others. They distracted themselves to numb out what they were feeling, rather than express them as pure physical energy.

This book is the culmination of my quest to reliably experience joy, love, and peace. These emotions are not merely holiday platitudes, but precious gifts available to each of us when we learn to deal with our sadness, anger, and fear. I thank you for allowing me to join you on the journey.

ACKNOWLEDGMENTS

Countless people have crossed my path offering information, insight, and experience, the moment I was ready to receive it. Without them, there would be no Attitude Reconstruction. I am eternally grateful.

I thank all my teachers, young and old, from east and west, who shared their sage wisdom. Foremost among them is my father, Sidney W. Bijou, diehard advocate of a positive and naturalistic approach to life, who willingly shared his perspective on whatever topic I was contemplating. I especially thank five teachers who are exponents and embodiments of ancient Indian philosophy: Maharishi Mahesh Yogi, founder of Transcendental Meditation, who first gave words and experience to my longing for something more; Gurumayi Chidvilasananda, head of the Siddha Yoga lineage, who opened my heart, satisfied my mind, and modeled a way of being; the revered Dr. Vasant Lad, who rendered Ayurvedic medicine understandable and useful; and Patanjali, whom I consider to be, among other things, India's greatest psychologist. I also thank George Harrison, who gave voice to my longing and set me on my spiritual path with his music.

Then there are those who patiently humored and supported me who deserve recognition, especially my ingenious and generous brother, Bob, who has been my biggest cheerleader and reality check, and my ever-loving mother, who never lost faith in me.

I also thank my psychology and self-help colleagues, both predecessors and contemporaries (only a small fraction of whom are noted in this book), who have assembled diverse pieces of the human mosaic. In particular, Dr. Annette Goodheart who introduced me to the transforming power of emotional expression, a concept that helped lay the groundwork of my work. Additionally, I'm grateful to the courageous clients in my private practice, eager students at the Santa Barbara City College Continuing Education Division, and workshop participants who continue to inspire me as they embrace and implement the principles of Attitude Reconstruction.

My heartfelt thanks also go to the long list of sincere editors for furthering the writing process over the last years, most notably Kimberley Snow, Ilene Segalove, Sabine Muehe, Peggy McInerny, and Deborah A. Lott. And finally I thank Mel Sellick, whose collaboration on this revised edition gave the book its dynamic flair.

I lovingly acknowledge the dear friends who patiently gave encouragement and input along the way. Without their unfailing support this book wouldn't be: Margaret Sweet, Page Latham, Jan Hill, Margaret Walker, Kathi Duval, Lynn Matis, Craig Penner, Bonnie Chowaniec, and Nina Wilding Rook. I am also indebted to Dr. Jianmin Zhang, who selflessly imparted the wisdom, teachings, and powerful benefits of traditional Chinese medicine.

Finally, I have taken inspiration from a wide variety of other sources. Two in particular are Don Henley, whose faded quotation on my bulletin board says, "We take care of the details so the worst we can be is great" and my Grandma B, who coined our family motto, "Go lucky. Come back happy."

MORE

CONTACT JUDE

Jude works with individuals, couples, and groups in a variety of settings.

Contact her if you are interested in:
- obtaining private sessions or coaching in person or via telephone or skype
- booking a speaking event for your business, organization, or school
- consulting for your business, organization, school, or group
- attending or scheduling a workshop
- receiving training in Attitude Reconstruction

On the website, www.AttitudeReconstruction.com, you can:
- sign up for her free newsletter
- read her blog and other informative articles
- purchase Attitude Reconstruction products
- find out about her upcoming speaking engagements
- download ebooks
- follow her on Twitter – http://twitter.com/AttitudeReconst
- connect with her – www.facebook.com/AttitudeReconstruction

Feel free to contact her with your Attitude Reconstruction questions, feedback, strategies, or stories. She'd love to hear from you.

jude@AttitudeReconstruction.com
or
Jude Bijou
133 East De la Guerra #25
Santa Barbara, CA 93101

INDEX